"How could a mother not know?" This is a question often asked about families where incest has occurred, and Eleanor Cowan's gripping memoir, *A History of a Pedophile's Wife*, steps up with answers that are courageous and heartbreaking. Cowan grew up in Quebec in the 1950s, in a large Roman Catholic family with a lethal mix of violence, addiction, and toxic pedagogy. Cowan details the dance of a survivor moving into adulthood: one step forward towards freedom, two steps back into conditioning, until a tipping point of consciousness is reached. As her memoir makes clear, that tipping point is not just a critical mass of abuse or even a touchstone of personal growth. It requires an enlarged and feminist context, permission to know the unknowable, and language to name the unspeakable.

Cowan's book is a primer in compassion, especially for those of us who were abused as children and left to struggle with legacies of distrust and rage towards our mothers. It's a vivid indictment of a mother-blaming culture that protects the very institutions that perpetuate child abuse.

— Carolyn Gage, playwright, performer, director, and activist

*August 11, 2017*

*Thank you dear Aunan for showing all of us in Free Fall how bright a star's light can be! You're wonderful! ♡ Eleanor*

# A History of a Pedophile's Wife

*Memoir of a Canadian Teacher and Writer*

## Eleanor Cowan

Eleanor Cowan, a retired Canadian teacher, writes in Quebec.

*I dedicate this memoir to all those who have been traumatized by ridiculous religious dogma, frightened families who never knew the meaning of the word 'natural.' May this book encourage righteous revolt so that autonomy in a real world can be experienced at last.*

\* \* \*

*We make our own criminals and their crimes are congruent with the national culture we all share. It has been said that a people get the kind of political leadership they deserve. I also think they get the kinds of crime and criminals they themselves bring into being.*—Margaret Mead

# ACKNOWLEDGEMENTS

I thank my children for their permission to write about our small family, and my siblings, for their encouragement.

I would also like to thank, most sincerely:

All educators – the activists, writers, radio show hosts, film makers, social workers and law makers whose artistic energy turns the wheel of human evolution; Canadian writer Elaine Kalman Naves for her strong advice to write my true story as a memoir rather than fiction, and to stand behind my opinions; playwright Carolyn Gage, columnist Barbara Kay, film maker Virginia Hastings and teacher Steve Canty for reading and commenting upon my work with such thoughtfulness.

Vancouver editors, Lara Kordic and Irene Kavanagh, Montreal editor Kathe Lieber, Ontario editors Erin Stropes and Wendy Carroll and Florida editor, Marlene at Firstediting.com for invaluable skills and sensitivity while working with my manuscript.

The Yellow Door (YD Generations in Montreal ) who introduced me to two volunteer readers and thoughtful commenters, social worker Neeti Sasi and doctoral candidate, Hannah Wood.

# INTRODUCTION

## Open Heart Surgery

I was forty years old when I was invited to a group I'd never expected to join – for parents of sexually abused children, the stark name uncompromising. Even at our first meeting, I was to learn about revising my vocabulary, about calling a spade a spade.

Because more women than men were present, the women were ushered to a larger space at the social services center. Worse than our numbers was the fact that I recognized many of the women finding places in the rows of rickety, collapsible chairs. As I looked around, for a jarring instant I thought I was at Mass. Restraining a bizarre impulse to genuflect, kneel, bow my head, and cross myself in the name of the Father, Son, and Holy Ghost, I managed to sit down, tuck my purse under flimsy chair legs, smooth my skirt, pick up my purse again, and shuffle through it for my planner and a pen. When a hand touched my bare arm, I looked down to see a familiar scratched gold bracelet and chipped pink nail polish. Mabel? Could it be? A head of red hair faltered behind Mabel's shoulder. Marta too? My co-volunteers at the church? We stared at each other, our faces flushing. We oriented ourselves. Marta's eyes filled and Mabel's streamed. I'm afraid I couldn't cry at that moment. It would have been nice but I couldn't get past my fear. When the meeting was called to order, Marta's right hand automatically sailed to her forehead to make the sign of the cross before she noticed and slid her fingers through her hair instead.

Mabel and Marta were mothers too. The moms of Teddy's and Nell's friends. I knew them from the two Catholic churches in the community where we'd cleaned or fundraised or held bazaars to pay the enormous heating bills for the high ceilings of God's house, where the priest presides.

The sensation that I was at Mass dissipated instantly when we rearranged our chairs on that first day. It took only a minute or two. We no longer faced the front. Instead, in a circle, we encountered each other. One of the things about Mass is that people don't have to interact. In rows of pews, you can view the backs of your fellow churchgoers for years and years and never do more to engage with them than shift slightly to wish them peace as part of the liturgy. In our painful O, we had to get to it on the first day. We were to say our names; and when I heard myself say, "Hi, I'm Eleanor" and acknowledge where I was, I felt sudden anguish. I was in fact here, on this seat, in this room. I was introducing myself to this particular group.

After we'd completed the enormous task of identifying ourselves to each other, the head social worker introduced herself. Her name was Georgia. She spoke in sometimes gentle, other times insistent tones about the benefits we might expect if we all worked together to share our experiences related to sexual abuse, not only the crime committed in our present family lives but the corruption in our past. "There is no unimportant detail," she said. "Everything matters."

Slowly, over those first meetings, one group member after another awakened from a long sleep. On one occasion, a tiny kernel of information resonated so emphatically that my eyes snapped open. I understood. I recognized. I knew what the speaker was saying. Even though there were differences among us, there were also recurring religious, cultural, and social motifs that we'd all inherited and that bound us together, good and tight. During those early meetings, I noticed that despite Georgia's challenging us to become risk-takers, each of us stuck to polite traditional vocabulary as we recalled our own histories of "being tampered with" or "touched inappropriately" by "troubled individuals." Our soft blanketing language minimized the effect of molestation and thus offered protection to our abusers. After all, the molesters were often people we knew and perhaps had loved. It gets complicated.

Indeed, at the end of the first meeting I was grateful for one rather grisly fact: that the molester in my family was not my son. With Mabel's brief testimony about her eldest son's molestation of his younger sister and brother, I felt the one emotion I'd never expected to feel in this room. I had it easier. Imagine the pain of having given birth to the victimizer of your other children.

Back in the safe confines of my kitchen that first night, I sautéed floured drumsticks in olive oil and, while they were browning, finished a lesson prep for the next morning's class. I'd have my work done before Teddy and Nell arrived home. The children would be glad to eat chicken and rice tonight. Teddy's gym teacher had asked my teenager to tell me that I should serve more meat at home, that red kidney beans and oat bran were used in the old days to stuff pillows and mattresses, not to nourish growing young men. It had hurt to hear what I perceived to be an accusation rather than a suggestion. I was sensitive to criticism about my care of my children. Very sensitive. Funny how all along I'd believed there was nothing this mother did not know about her two favorite people.

At one of our meetings, our social worker wanted each of us to speak for two to three minutes. "Tell us what changes in your lives, however small, you're thinking about making or what your worries are," Georgia said.

"I had a dream," said Mabel, staying on safe ground. "I dreamed I was in charge of a whole orphanage."

"Ah, of course, abject service," Georgia interrupted. "That's how passive women siphon power into their lives. Enablers always look after needy others. They love to rescue losers. They consider it heroic. Of course, there's a pay-off for that kind of heroism. Rescuers don't have to take any risks to develop their own autonomy. They don't have to chance rejection either. After all, what loser is going to reject the sucker who pays his rent? And few co-dependent women have hobbies or interests other than inflating themselves through another adult's dependency upon them. Sadly, enablers like you often hook up with narcissists who can never, ever love you in return. It's all unconscious of course. Both of you are in an elaborate game of using each other, hand in glove. Why? Because neither of you can tolerate the intimacy love demands."

"I thought we were supposed to do the talking here," Mabel whispered.

"Yeah, and orphanages are filled with needy children, not adults," Marta whispered back.

I felt sick to my stomach. I wanted to leave. I wanted a good smoke at break time. I wanted to feel better fast. I was trapped in a place of no escape, unless I killed myself, and that was not going to happen. I was different from my mother.

# PART I:

## *Feeding a Hungry God*

Even now, in my sixties, I recall Mother's stories, because she told so few. Ann didn't speak a lot about herself, probably because she lived first by rules, later by desires, and never by introspection.

Mother had once thrived in her job as personnel manager at the Joseph Robb factory in Montreal. It was a senior position of which she was proud: she had her own secretary. Life was good in post-war Quebec when she was in her early twenties, a single woman living with her parents. Mornings, while her French-Canadian mother Odette was scurrying to six o'clock Mass to anchor her stability in the invisible male deity she needed to believe loved her, my mother was applying mascara and dabbing on red lipstick before hopping the trolley to her fabulous job. At twenty-three, she was earning her own money. On paydays she bought smart business skirts and sheer silk stockings at Eaton's on Sainte-Catherine Street. What was left over was deposited into a private savings account. She carefully calculated what the interest rates would yield.

And yet, despite this level of independence, when she brought a handsome Polish boyfriend home and my grandpa kicked him out, Ann obeyed. Even though she was in love, even though she suffered, she ended their relationship. When my father Neil showed up, Grandpa approved of the self-supporting 35-year-old Irish businessman at once—and my mother convinced herself she was in love.

"I was 24," she said, weeping, years later, the day she drove me to the convent school seamstress who had me kneel to make sure my uniform skirt touched the wood floor. "In 1945 I was an 'older' bride."

The year I was born, 1948, my mother cast her first ballot in a provincial election, a right my grandmother, who gave birth to six males, never had. Quebec had just given women the vote, and my mother's opinions now mattered to the men in charge.

In all areas of business, my mother was sure of herself and competent. Yet, as her children were to learn, intimacy was a skill she never mastered.

By the time my mother was married, her home life had deeply traumatized her. On her wedding day, she left her parents' home in a dark dress splashed with yellow daisies, and for the ceremony itself she wore an off-white gown. In her photo, there is a subdued smile on her lovely face. She may not have known much about trauma but she knew she wanted something different than what her pious, passive mother endured and allowed her children to undergo.

My mother was frightened in her childhood home. Her father was a covert drinker, a shameless bully, and a sex addict. For my mother, the main thing was to get out, get married, and get on with her life.

My father had a heart condition that had exempted him from service in World War Two. Perhaps it had its roots in unresolved distress that began with the sudden death from ectopic distress, her fifth pregnancy in five years, of his warm-hearted mother, Nellie, at the Queen Elizabeth Homeopathic Hospital on Northcliffe Avenue in Montreal. Within a week of her death, my six-year-old father was sent to St. Patrick's Orphanage in another part of the city. In those days, a well-paid businessman like my paternal grandfather couldn't possibly be expected to look after his two motherless sons. While he could have afforded a housekeeper, he didn't hire one for himself, his sons, and his adolescent daughter. Thus, despite their desperate protests, my father and his brother endured the loss of both parents in one week, their agony worsened by the fact that their father did keep their young sister at home with him. At St. Patrick's, when little Neil wet his dorm bed in the middle of the night, the exhausted night-duty nun, a teenager saddled with the charge of a dozen orphans, hauled him into a chilly bathroom, pulled off his pajama bottoms, and plunged him into a bathtub of cold water. It didn't matter that his cries disturbed other sleeping children, nor did it matter that the punishment did nothing to solve the problem.

I never really got to know my father, a travelling salesman who was home only on and off, on and off, in and out of limbo.

Dad had been married before, to a lively young Nova Scotia woman named Fiona. They'd had a little boy and named him Gordie. Fiona died suddenly the day she was to return to Dad after a summer with her family on the east coast. Hours before she was to board the train to Montreal, the 24-year-old suffered an asthma attack. She died overnight. Did my young father feel as abandoned as he had when his mother died? Did he wonder if his wife's fear of his bad temper had triggered her asthma attack? If she was afraid, she had reason. At the beginning of his second marriage, that bad temper was in evidence. My father beat Gordie regularly, for infractions no two-year-old could possibly understand or correct.

Like many post-war couples, my parents migrated to wide open fields, country air, and sunshine. Hoping to turn a bright new page in their lives, they saved up and bought a farm in Strathmore, close to Montreal. There was lots of land, wide open sky, and a barn with chicken coops for Dad's special hobby, an egg business he said would guarantee that, however the economy fared, we'd never go hungry.

I was born in 1948, ten months after Maureen, my artistic sister whose unique pronunciation of Eleanor created my family nickname, Norda. A year later, my little sister Mary Irene was born, making us, by 1949, a family of six.

When I was a toddler and Gordie a five-year-old on my parents' farm, my half-brother would scrunch down in front of the wheels of the new family car parked in the driveway, perhaps acting out a death wish. At the same age that my father had shivered in a bathtub in an orphanage, my half-brother now shuddered in our chicken coop. Unconscious of his own history, my father repeated it. He beat the only child of his first marriage, sometimes naked, up in the barn loft.

If little Gordie failed his new mother in any slight way, she threatened to tell on him, to make it go worse for him. My mother knew about the spankings in the barn. She blamed Gordie. She said it was his fault. She had no qualms about assigning improbable blame to her children. In later years, she once told me that somehow, at two years old, I managed to fall off the roof of the chicken coop onto a pile of field rocks next to the barn door. It was my fault I broke my own leg. As she spoke, I could almost taste the delicious vegetable soup fed to me in the arms of the warm, smiling nurse who loved me during my three-month hospital stay. Mother said I cried more on the drive home than I did on the way there.

Over time, I reacted to my parents' abuse of Gordie as any helpless child would have done. I was vigilant. I cried. I accommodated. I worked hard for my mother's affection and stayed on my father's good side. I became Dad's smiling little friend. When I began to talk, I said "please" and "thank you" too much, my politeness annoying my mother. "Say it once! Not fifteen times!" Mother shouted.

When I was three, Dad found better-paying sales work and we moved from near Montreal to Leaside, Ontario, where baby Brigit was born. Up to this point, my mother had continued to work despite her pregnancies. She had kept busy, her own ghosts well at bay. Even though the move meant she'd have to leave her job behind, she was glad to leave the Strathmore farmhouse, where the menacing headlights of transport planes at the nearby international airport beamed right into her bedroom window, night after night.

Within a year we moved again, this time to Galt, Ontario, my third home at four years of age. Mother said it seemed that pregnancy and moving house came together. On our first visit, I discovered that one of the bedrooms in our new house was perfect for parents with a newborn. There was an alcove for a baby's crib connected to a tiny kitchenette where Mother could heat night-time baby bottles. Had my parents chosen that space instead of a small bedroom down the hall, a second baby's life might not have been lost. Instead, it was decided that my sisters and I would occupy the larger room, dormitory-style, and our brand new baby, Eric, would sleep downstairs in the living room at night, behind closed doors. Possibly this choice was made to strictly clock baby feedings, as Dr. Spock advised; or perhaps undisturbed sleep was the only consideration given to Dad's chronic heart disease. Then again, maybe my parents' choice of a smaller, private room represented unconscious retaliation for being forced into having unwanted children.

My parents were strict Catholics. They knew the drill: kids and more kids for a God whose addiction to glory was insatiable. They obeyed their invisible dominators, aged men in Rome who'd never changed a diaper in their lives but felt free to dictate women's maternal role. After her marriage, my mother's Roman Catholic job description became as ancient as Grandma's.

Still, while my mother obeyed church doctrine and had as many children as possible, she could, and did, delegate their care from the get-go. After all, while the Catholic Church insisted my foremothers bear a multitude of souls for God, details about their care were fuzzy.

Not long after our move and just weeks after Eric's birth, my parents welcomed into our home two Italian brothers, Carlo and Nick, war orphans in their early teens, brought from Europe by the Canadian Children's Aid Society. A feature article in the local newspaper detailed Mother's account of the transaction:

"Neil, away most of the time on business trips, gave me a choice of either hiring a maid or adopting the war orphans. I figured the two brothers could help out with my ever-growing brood just as easily as one maid, maybe even more so. The amazing thing is that now we're saving more money than we were before they arrived. I buy food in bulk now, which, as it turns out, is cheaper than buying smaller amounts. So, all in all, I save money, have the extra help I need, and the boys have a home."

Mother assigned endless tasks to Nick and Carlo, including the daily entertainment of their new sisters, who, in effect, became their only friends. In wintertime, Gordie and our two new brothers sculpted snowmen or slippery ice slides for us in the back yard while our ever-pregnant mother napped until it was time to cook supper. When Mother called them inside to peel vegetables and set the table for supper, our brothers would trundle us in, remove our snowsuits, and lock us in the basement until we were summoned to eat. If we all hollered and kicked on the cellar door in unison, my sisters and I could be heard through a second door at the top of the stairs. Often, though, Mother shut that door too, a second layer of muffling while she and her helpers worked. I knew the sound of that click.

The smooth cement of the cellar walls became, for me, a porous skin upon which I drew the face of a green-eyed imaginary friend with rosy cheeks and upturned lips that smiled back at me all the time, without fail, solidly in place.

My inclination to seek the company of others grew stronger as I approached school age. My own siblings weren't enough for me. When Dad found me at a Salvation Army summer camp one day, he pointed to his car in silence. I'd been told twice before that I could not be part of this children's group at Lincoln Park. For this repeated disobedience, Mother was up and awake, poised for my arrival. My brothers and sisters were eating ice cream cones on the front lawn when I stepped out of Dad's car.

"Go upstairs," Mother said when I arrived, her eyes like chilly half-grapes.

"Pull down your underpants, Norda," Dad instructed me before delivering a series of stinging slaps to my bare skin. "Are you going to run away again?" he asked.

"No, Dad," I wept, my bum burning.

"Are you going to ask for permission?"

"Yes, Dad," I answered.

"We have swings in our own back yard. We have a sandbox. You have friends to play with right here."

"Yes, Dad."

"So sit here on your bed till suppertime, till one of the boys comes to get you."

We were routinely referred to as "one of the girls" or "one of the boys." Mother would stumble over our names, "Mo, Ro, Ir, Car," and finally, in flushed exasperation over sounding like her youngest child, point and scream, "You!"

Usually Mother napped while the older boys looked after us and did the chores that were constantly assigned to them.

~

I recall things from as far back as the early '50s that revealed something was terribly wrong. I had struggled to tell my mother a painful secret. How, in her response, could she have called her stuttering five-year-old daughter a "tart" for revealing that someone in the family had touched her "down there"? How could she have ordered her child to wash her hands with soap and hot water before apologizing for being such a liar? How could she dismiss her child without first asking who or how or when? The discussion slammed shut before it began. Trapped as she was in her own dark basement, in a concrete crawl space where her own early history had been muted, my mother silenced me. Listening to me was impossible for her.

"Now get out of my sight, you silly tart!" she screamed. I ran upstairs to my room, crying in confusion, and locked myself in.

Mother referred to me as "the liar" after that. When she did catch me lying, she used it as evidence to underscore her assessment of my faulty character. I began to doubt myself. I wove in and out of clear memory, wondering if I was, in fact, a little liar. I prayed to Jesus to make me a good girl. And somewhere along the way, I forgot the face of my molester, erasing it forever. It might have been my father or one of the older boys; I simply don't know. Still, I recall being awakened countless times in the middle of the night and led to the bathroom, where my legs were pried apart to extend over each side of the hairy lap I sat on and my vagina was stroked until I felt as tense as the strings of a violin and fingers dug deep inside me, causing a burning heat.

"Okay, Norda," my molester would say when he was done. "You can pee now. Go ahead. I helped you let it out."

A burning trickle of hot urine would dribble out. I would beg to go back to my bed but was only permitted after I'd said "Thank you for helping me pee." While Maureen slept beside me, I'd squeeze my legs together to ease the tension between them. My body felt large and heavy and dense, yet at the same time I was afraid I'd float away. Once I could feel the solid mattress beneath me, I'd concentrate hard until I'd shrunk back to my regular size.

Perhaps I was too young to grasp distinctions like "last night" and "the night before last," but my body knew for sure and certain how good it would be to get away from our house. As far as I consciously knew back then, I only wanted to have fun in the park.

∼

"Mummy," I asked the day after my spanking, "May I go to Lincoln Park?"

"No, you may not go to Lincoln Park." Mother mimicked my little-girl voice and delivered her usual refusal.

The gate latch opened easily and I scampered through neighbors' back yards, avoiding the main road. My camp counselor welcomed me, her smile a kiss, and within moments I was lost in a colorful art activity on the soft grass. At lunch, solicitous mothers gathered their kids around them.

"My Marina won't eat her crusts," said one mother, taking strange pride in her child's fussiness. "I'll eat them!" I volunteered.

Every day that summer, without any ado, I inherited a half-sandwich here, celery sticks there, hunks of cheese, and my favorite treat, homemade peanut butter cookies. Sometimes I sank my teeth into quadruple layers of mustard-coated salami so strong my eyes watered. My first taste of chopped liver on cream cheese was heaven. I learned about generosity. I learned that acts of kindness were performed quietly, casually, without making a big deal. It was well worth the slap on the back of the head when I got home.

"I'm not going to chain you to the back fence," said Mother. "If you don't like your own family, then go. Leave. Who cares anyway?"

I was too young to suggest we all go, that my pregnant mother pile four toddlers into the car, toss in a lawn chair, and loll with other moms while we abandoned ourselves to play under her loving gaze. Instead, at the park, I watched other boys and girls run back and forth to their mothers in a constant conversation of reassurance and love. When moms anchored their children's hips between their own bare knees to change damp shirts, when they boasted about their children's accomplishments right in front of them, I stood in awe of such natural affection.

On the last day of summer fun, our counselor lifted me to the rough plank seats of the baseball stand to sing "Jesus Loves Me," accompanied by the Salvation Army's full brass band. Afterwards, pressed against her warm body, snuggling under the fleshy arm she threw around me, nibbling a second vanilla ice cream bar, I knew happiness. It was an evening of childhood suffused with pleasure.

$\sim$

In September, Mother phoned Saint Mary's School about Maureen's Grade One registration. I begged her to ask for me too. When the school phoned to say I was registered in the brand new kindergarten class and Mother said I could go, I was beside myself.

"Thank you, thank you, Mummy! I'm so, so happy!"

"Stop announcing how happy you are, Norda. No one cares," Mother said with a laugh. "No one cares if you're happy or not."

When Mother made statements like these, she cracked up. She laughed. She looked at me with interest too, a quizzical regard. So I continued to foghorn my sentiments, to challenge her, to earn her smile. Mother was, after all, beautiful. Of French and Irish heritage, she had dark brown hair that seemed black in contrast to her flashing gray eyes. A magnetic confidence emanated from her. With all the power of a child's love, I adored her and basked in pleasure under her intense gaze. I tried crawling onto her lap to snuggle against her softness. She didn't like it.

"Stop pressing yourself against me," she scolded as sudden heat flashed through my body. "Don't paw people. Keep your hands to yourself." My chest and fingers began to throb, and I stumbled backwards, my face red with shame.

"Okay, Mummy," I said. "Okay." I didn't cry about it. I recognized her moods.

Little understanding the invisible forces that stifled my mother's life from afar, I ran out to meet a beautiful world while she stayed home.

There was Johnny, our crossing guard, whose tall figure I sought out daily as I walked the ten blocks to St. Mary's.

"I see you. Even when you're a tiny speck down the road, I see you," he reassured me, gray hair escaping in wild tufts from his toque as he raised his stop sign for me. He asked me my name on the first day of school and called me Norda every day after that. When Sister St. Paul taught us about Jesus, I pictured this loving man, whom I saw far more frequently than my own father.

Then our smiling teacher, Miss Rose, welcomed us to her enchanting room of color and light. Thoughts of the basement far away, I finger-painted bright wet designs onto blank paper. I pulled wool through small holes in picture cards with a blunt wooden needle. I learned my letters. Every Friday morning, my new friends and I would line up single file, slip on our magic "quiet boots," zip up our mouths by compressing our thumbs and index fingers to tug an imaginary zipper-pull across them, and tiptoe to the senior cooking class, where teenage girls served us oven-warm cookies. One day an eighth grader named Alice, assigned to the little table of four where I sat, offered me a second cookie. When I said "Yes, please," she also poured more milk.

"Thank you for coming," she said at the door. I looked around to see who she was talking to. "I mean you!" She laughed, so grown up in her plaid pleated skirt and matching sweater set. "Did you enjoy your treats?"

"Oh, yes, thank you!" I exclaimed. I can still see her brown eyes half closing as she grinned at me.

"In the future," she said, "you'll bake cookies in this class too." Then she scooped me in her arms for a big hug. I fairly twirled back out into the hallway, marveling that there was such a thing as a future and that I could have one too.

～

Strict routines were observed during this period in our family life. I came home from kindergarten at noon. After Mother or Maria, her part-time maid, served a good lunch, I napped along with the younger ones until the three older boys came home from school. The boys woke us, dressed us, and took care of us until Mother opened her bedroom door to prepare our dinner.

I don't remember ever being hungry back then yet we'd devour Mother's tasty meals in minutes. She shopped smart and fed us well in a sparkling clean kitchen. Generous plates of roasted meat, fish, and poultry, along with mashed, baked, or scalloped potatoes, covered our fifteen-foot table. "All that work and gone in five minutes," Mother would say, closing *The Joy of Cooking* for another day.

Every Sunday, holiday, and birthday, we ate in the dining room. I would marvel at the dozen perfect squares Maria had ironed into our stiff linen tablecloth as I centered my plate on one. There was plenty of food, seconds of the main course, and as many milk refills as we wanted.

The living room was a space set apart, used by the children only on Christmas Day, when we had guests, or when one of us was charged with rocking Eric in his tiny crib, which was kept there instead of upstairs. Yet I remember every detail of that room in our graystone house in Galt. A red oriental carpet bordered the pale olive couch and loveseat. I loved to run my hand back and forth over the tweed upholstery, its texture giving me an unhurried sense of peacefulness. Crystal ashtrays atop rosewood tables caught the sunlight just so, and the framed photographs of pink trees over a garden path promised me a flowery future. I imagined my life just beyond the apple blossoms.

On a good day, Mother would read to us from *Good Housekeeping* magazine while we ate lunch at the kitchen table on unbreakable plates obtained with our grocery store's "Pinky Stamps" that we'd licked into dozens of redeemable booklets.

"'A squirt of fresh lemon juice on your carrots, a dollop of real butter, a handful of brown sugar turns a grumpy boiled carrot into a glamorous Beauty Queen, a glazed delight,'" she read aloud. "Grumpy carrots, indeed," Mother scoffed, and we giggled.

Other times, while we ate our meal, Mother consumed only TUMS and Canada Dry ginger ale to quell the constant discomfort of pregnancy.

∾

In 1950s Galt, Mother ran a small home business. Without disobeying the Church-endorsed post-war turnabout that had returned professional women to the kitchen, Mother made money—enough money to pay for periodic getaways to Florida, trips she took by herself. A successful Beauty Counselor of Canada, Mother saw her customers at the house, where she demonstrated de-clogging facials, thick moisturizing creams, and heady perfumes while her three older sons peeled vegetables and muffled any disturbances from below stairs.

One day, Mother was preparing to show a customer how to apply rouge. For some reason, her customer was reluctant to have Mother touch her face.

"You can show her on me, Mum!" I offered, hopping up onto the stool in front of her. What a wonderful moment, Mother's warm fingers working in creamy color, touching me, my face upturned to hers as she focused on me.

"In this way," Mother continued, unperturbed by her client's hesitation, "your eye color is highlighted, bird-bright, alive and awake. You never, ever want to change your face." Though addressing her client, Mother was looking into my eyes. "You want only to enhance the beauty you clearly do have."

While I was never called upon to be Mother's makeup doll again, that moment of affirmation did the trick for me. I've always loved my face.

No visitors ever came to our house without a purpose though. There were no girlfriends dropping by unannounced, no casual chatter over the back fence, no close friends at all. Mother's satisfied customers left with cosmetics packaged in brown paper lunch bags that had little bills stapled on them, each woman reassured of her innate attractiveness. While she always treated her customers with courtesy, Mother socialized only with selected individuals. And these were mostly educated men she called "Father."

Mother developed strong links with the Society of Jesus. Perhaps she first met one of Dad's cousins, Father Stu, at her wedding in 1945 and subsequently invited him to family dinners. He in turn may have brought one of his fellow priests to our house, and the connections grew from there. I do know that Mother admired these priests for their erudition and I suspect she was reassured by their unavailability. They, in turn, found her to be a fine example of Catholic womanhood.

Their approval—praise she'd never received from her own father—meant a lot to her.

Perhaps my mother's attraction to the Jesuits was an attempt to offset her own inherited sense of female unimportance through an association with prestigious males, uniformly named 'Father.'

"Jesuits sit on their behinds for fifteen long years, studying every minute," Mother explained to us, laying out her finest dinnerware in preparation for their visit.

"They read Latin and Greek. They improve their minds," she said, snipping her home-grown gladiolas in the garage sink. "These guys are brilliant, and I mean Brillo bright. Education is a very big deal for them." Yet I could feel a tension in

Mother when she was around these highly educated men, who wouldn't be caught dead reading carrot recipes or collecting Pinky Stamps.

~

Memory of a time of calamity: I was sitting on the hall stairs, tracing a purple flower in the textured carpet with my finger. Something had happened early in the morning, I still didn't know what. Now I could hear muffled voices behind Mother's closed bedroom door. Maureen was in there, and Dad too. I had no idea what was going on but I knew it wasn't good. Then Maureen emerged. I saw her shoes first then her thin legs with a thick bandage on one knee and the navy blue hem of her school skirt. When she spoke, I looked up.

"Mother's pillow has little raindrops all over it. She can't stop crying. Eric's dead."

"Shhhhh…" My father hurried into the hallway, closing Mother's door behind him. "Your mother's going to sleep now. The doctor gave her some pills."

"Dad, I want to see Mummy too. Maureen saw her!" I pleaded with my father, who quickly ushered my sister and me downstairs.

"You'll see her tomorrow, not now. In the meantime, you can say three Our Fathers for baby Eric's soul and then go help with the kids in the basement." My father disappeared into his office and I slumped on the bottom steps, running my hands back and forth over the carpet's weave. Images of Eric's soft baby head crowded into my mind, along with a black, inky fearfulness. A week earlier, as I was feeding Eric his bottle in the living room, I had held him in my awkward five-year-old embrace. When I shifted on the couch and tried to get up with my brother in my arms, I couldn't manage it and plunked back down. I heard a soft thump as Eric's forehead hit the radiator behind us. My brother yelped in pain. His toothless infant mouth formed a silent round of pink before he began to cry. Afraid to tell Mother, I soothed him with kisses and comforted him as best I could. He stopped crying and, still struggling to balance his weight and mine, I managed to get up and put him back into his crib, but not without hitting his shoulder against the crib railing. As he flopped onto the mattress, his little legs flew up high, but he didn't cry this time. I rolled his tiny crib on wheels up and down the living room until Mother called me for supper. Eric had fallen asleep and I went to supper and forgot all about the episode.

Now, crouched on the stairs, I wondered if that bump to his head could have killed him.

As I learned later on, Eric's body was autopsied and the finding was that he'd suffocated, what today we would call crib death. It was hard to be sure about what happened because of Mother's practice of having her infants sleep by themselves on a different floor. While it's possible this had begun as a way of making sure Dad's sleep was undisturbed by midnight feedings, the lightweight mini-crib on wheels remained downstairs even when Dad travelled for weeks. It had been just the same for baby Madeleine, who'd also suffocated.

But that afternoon, after being shooed downstairs, as I sat in the stairwell, I heard Dad speaking on the phone to his sister, a nun in Montreal. He told her that when Mother had come into the living room that morning, she'd found her son cold and blue. She'd rushed to the phone and within minutes a fire truck had screamed into our driveway, orange lights flashing and siren blaring. The fire chief himself had rushed to Mother's side, Dad said. When the chief had begged her, over and over again, to hand him the baby, Mother had refused. She'd held on to Eric, burying her head in the blue bundle. I wept as I listened to Dad recounting the gruesome events.

"No, no, no, not my son, not my only son," Mother was crying to our parish priest in the living room later that afternoon. I sat quietly on the rosewood sewing bench as Mother wept, unaware that her other sons—three teenagers who called her "Mother," cooked with her and obeyed her every order—were watching from the kitchen door.

Dad made arrangements to bury Eric in Montreal while Mother stayed in her room for four days. This was Mother's introduction to what a pill could do for her. Yet another male authority, this one equipped with a prescription pad, had dictated the best course of action for her life – exemption from grief. Why grieve when you can sleep? And then, why stop sleeping?

After her complete isolation with her prescribed medication, Mother emerged to make supper with her older boys. She ordered Gordie and Carlo to get our winter boots out of storage before winter. "Check who fits what," she said, waving us downstairs.

There was no mention of Eric after that, no church or family service. Only once did I see Mother break down during an evening rosary, and I knew she was weeping for her laughing baby boy. As she cried and brushed away my attempts to press against her, I wondered what would happen if I died. Would Mother lie on her bed pining for me, swallowing pills to deaden the grief for her beautiful little daughter named Norda? I imagined her massaging pink Beauty Counselor lipstick into my stiff flesh and praying to God that I would wake up. I dreamed of her gazing at my picture, the way she did at Eric's.

Three babies came in quick succession after Eric's death: Danny, Paddy, and Joey. The infant crib remained downstairs when Danny was born, although Mother did take a new precaution and followed it for all three babies: she sewed flannelette sacks for the newborns. She'd pop the new baby's entire body except for its head into the cloth bag, and the bag in turn was secured to the crib by strings.

"Why did Eric die, Mummy?" I asked one day.

"A bubble got trapped in his air passage," said Mother. "He couldn't breathe."

"Why did you sew bags then?"

"For extra protection," said Mother. "Now scram, I'm busy."

The new sleeper bag resembled a white bat, wings stretched tight so no loose material could come in contact with tiny baby nostrils. There was something eerie about seeing Danny's head poking out of a large cloth triangle secured to the rails of the crib. It bothered me that he couldn't touch his face, scratch an itch, or wave away a fly as he waited, unattended, far from his parents at night.

My kindergarten teacher Miss Rosemary had asked me if I would like to make a goodbye card after my baby brother's death. "Good," she said, when I finished. "You did a beautiful job!"

Miss Rosemary was kind and open. I wished I could ask her if my inability to carry my younger brother properly had caused his death, but to ask that question was simply impossible. There were other things I would have liked to share with her but I could not articulate them: the dark resentments of our home, the older boys' smoldering anger that had brewed for months before the death of the only son our mother acknowledged. I could only tell Miss Rosemary that sometimes, at my house, people got awfully mad.

Once during that year of kindergarten, Miss Rosemary invited a colleague into our classroom and together they whispered over my pink-and-red finger painting. I was worried they didn't like it. My heart began to thump when my teacher called me over.

"What's your painting about, Norda?" she asked.

"Fingers," I answered.

My stomach ached. My hands felt hot. I asked Miss Rose if I could please do a new painting for her. I wanted her to be happy with me.

"Sure you can, my darling," she said, and her kindness comforted me.

I pulled the stiff paper off the easel and crushed it into the garbage pail, stamping it down hard. The new painting showed yellow sunshine, red flowers, and a little bird far out at the tip of a long, thin branch.

～

A rift grew between my mother and me. That year, Dad had to comb the neighborhood to bring me home to celebrate her birthday. He found me at a friend's house.

"Come back after, all right?" offered my friend's father.

"Yes, go to your mother's party!" her mother said, fairly pushing me out the door.

Holding my hand, Dad tugged me along the street. "What's wrong with you, Norda? It's your mother's birthday! I'd have given my eye teeth to have attended my mother's birthday when I was your age." I knew Dad's mother had died when he was six, the same age I was now.

"What about your sister?" I asked.

"My father kept her with him."

"Why?" I asked. "Why did your father send you away but not your sister?"

"I don't know." Dad extracted his pipe from his smoking jacket pocket. His teeth clamped the hard stem and I heard the dry inhalation as he pulled smoke into his mouth. "But look how lucky you are. Here you have a mother whose birthday it is today and you're both alive to enjoy it.

"When we get home," he continued, "I want you to go to your mother, smile, and wish her a happy birthday. Then sit down, eat your meal and be grateful for it."

"Happy birthday, Mother," I blubbered as we walked through the door, my face streaked with tears. I took my seat at the dining room table and began to sob.

Dad escorted me upstairs, sighing deeply. "Look what you've done," he said. "Your mother, who works for you day and night, who gives up her life for you, is now crying in the kitchen on her birthday. You hurt her feelings. I don't understand you, Norda. What kind of little girl doesn't love her mother? When you're ready, come downstairs and tell her you're sorry for your behavior today. Otherwise, stay here for the evening."

Feeling heavy and dull, I fell onto my bed and curled up. My throat ached from so much crying—crying because I didn't want to be with my mother on her birthday, because she didn't want to be around me the rest of the time, and because no matter how hard we tried, I knew instinctively that something was definitely not right with our family. Somewhat later, Carlo stealthily brought me a hamburger, a piece of birthday cake, and some vanilla ice cream. I downed the lot and fell asleep in my party dress.

The next morning Dad left for a lengthy business trip across Western Canada. Before he left, he asked me to pray for myself while he was gone and I promised I would.

With Dad out of town, Mother screamed at Gordie almost daily. My half-brother's skin eruptions, angry pimples that demanded care and extra expense, were a frustration to Mother. My stomach tightened as I watched the hateful scenes from the kitchen doorway, bracing myself as Gordie's face flushed a violent red. If he'd once returned the slaps and shoves that Mother routinely inflicted on him that might have been the end of it, but he'd learned from our parents that you attack only those who are weaker than you are. So while he stood there taking it, I'd run to the upstairs bathroom and lock the door behind me, knowing what might follow if I didn't protect myself. I'd hoist myself onto the sink and blast the cold water tap. Soon the roar of water would become the sound of crowds hailing me, their beloved six-year-old princess, and I waved back, smiling and nodding to the cheering masses. Once I fell off the sink edge when Gordie pounded on the door, ordering me out of there. When I opened it, he thrust me down the stairs pell-mell, as roughly as Mother had treated him.

As Mother's rages became increasingly frequent in the mid-1950s, Dad found a way to bolt. He escaped her explosiveness by withdrawing more and more, ultimately revising his title from "salesman" who occasionally travelled to "travelling salesman." His escape just added weight to Mother's unacknowledged burden.

We feared our Mother. Dad, by comparison, was the good guy, made calm and reasonable by frequent absences, the parent who seemed more and more like Ward Cleaver as time went by. Whenever Dad came home from his weeks away, I sought comfort from him. I'd run to the door to greet him the way kids in sitcoms did. Dad must have felt that as long as he gave Mother all the money he earned, as long as he maintained his role as responsible provider, he was doing all that was required of him. So nothing was done about Mother's moods and they became the most important factor in my life.

My parents didn't talk about the source of Mother's crushing anger. They didn't question a church doctrine that was obsessed with uncontrolled procreation or a social structure that was equally obsessed with preserving traditional gender roles. If my mother had complained about her lot in life, she would have been seen as a whining, scolding nag. No similar words were ever, of course, used for a man. The war had made shaming a woman as easy as preparing a Betty Crocker pie crust. Had she lost any arms or legs? Had her flesh been marred by shrapnel? Did she lack a roof over her head? Attitudes like these functioned like censorship: Free expression was banned both inside the confessional box and out, and so Mother adopted her father's "bottle and blast" template – bottle your anger up and then explode.

When she was toeing the line, when she was trying to accommodate and fit into the social constructs of her time, Mother watched National Film Board presentations of dinner etiquette and closely followed actress Grace Kelly's new life as a member of royalty in Monaco. Her crystal candlesticks, her starched linen tablecloths, her vases with sponges pierced by stems of her own dried flowers, testified to the way Mother coped: by working desperately to conform. She bought her husband a tweed house jacket to wear to the dinner table. She insisted the boys call him Sir instead of Dad. While my older brothers were instructed to nod their heads once and shake hands with Dad, we girls were taught to sink to the floor in a full curtsey before we sat down for dinner.

"Your curtsey signifies humility and respect to the head of this house, so just do it," said Mother, caught up in another adopted version of what living was supposed to look like.

Giggling, I dropped to my knees in front of Dad's chair. "Curtsey, curtsey!" corrected Mom. "Not genuflect, you nitwit!"

For my frightened parents, considered responses, careful discussions, talking things over, and reasoning things out would have meant voicing stored-up feelings; awkward, denied, and illegal sentiments they'd never before acknowledged. In order to be happy, they'd have had to make each other and their children a priority above all else; but Catholic marriage wasn't about relationships, it was about roles. My mother, who had balked at her mother's domestic life, found herself sitting at home stitching halter tops for her little girls that required no skill or imagination to assemble. Nor had she time or opportunity to investigate a past that gnawed at her day and night.

I decided early on that I wouldn't scream like my mother. I'd modulate my voice. I'd speak softly and calmly. I'd be unnaturally repressed.

∼

When Dad was in town, he'd position a straight-back chair in the girls' bedroom so we could see him as he read aloud to us at night. While Irene tended to fall asleep within minutes, Maureen and I would remain alert, two little sponges absorbing toxicity we had no way to filter out. Dad selected stories of the saints and of mutilated martyrs who stuck to their faith even on pain of death. The tales described in minute detail what the faithful were willing to suffer for God. Some of the tormented were hung upside down or immersed face first in boiling oil. Others were released into the Roman Colosseum, where thousands of Christian-haters cheered while courageous Christians were torn limb from limb by crazed lions that had been starved so there'd be no chance of them befriending their lunch.

As I lay in the bed I shared with Maureen and listened, my hands pressed to my face, I'd review the menu of atrocities and consider the ones I might one day have to endure. Starvation was among them, along with dangling from a cross (either nailed or tied to the wood), being roasted alive strapped to sizzling iron chairs, having my eyes gouged out with hot pokers, and a quick death by beheading. Perhaps these stories were Dad's way of showing us that no matter how much we suffered at home, at least we weren't being tied to a torture device. When he finished, Dad would lead us in our simple night-time prayer: "Dear God, I love you. Please teach me to love you more and more every day, Amen."

I'd scrunch up and pray to be brave, to endure any persecution for dear God. One night I made my decision. I opted to get it over with, to die quickly when my time came rather than squeal for hours in unspeakable terror. I'd begun to dislike my cowering, shivering, comfort-seeking self. "You'll jump in to be tortured when it's time," I reassured myself. "You'll die fast, and God will be pleased."

One day I watched Dad take a capon from the chicken coop and slaughter it for dinner. Its headless body ran around the dirt floor for several seconds before it fell, its face still on the chopping block. If I opted for a martyr's death by beheading, would I also reel about with blood pouring from between my shoulders?

Recoiling from that scenario, I moved on to abandonment in a lizard-infested desert or being cast from a boat, my pockets filled with heavy stones to make sure I wouldn't bob up somewhere downstream. I also began to practice splashing scalding water from the tap onto my face to evaluate my tolerance of heat. It didn't go well. Also, I could not deal with the idea of being deprived of my vision, so just the thought of being blindfolded in a dark box or buried alive caused my skin to crawl. Nevertheless, I told myself over and over I could and would do it—if I had to.

Still, I bargained for survival.

"Daddy, how long would I boil in hot oil before I'd die?" I asked during one of those bedtime sessions about the agonies of the saints and martyrs.

"About three minutes, I'd guess, Norda."

"And drown?"

"A good two minutes of struggle."

"Buried alive?" I asked, my hands sweating.

"A day at most." I weighed the options, considering the duration of each torture. Even sticking my toe in too-hot bath water scared me but, still, could lingering in a dark box for a day be worse than three minutes of being cooked?

"Daddy," I said as he turned out the lights, "I could be a secret Catholic. That way I could live. I could run around serving God in other ways." I waited in silence.

"But which offering do you think would please God more?" Dad replied.

Desperate, shivering in my bed, I imagined my heroism. "I love God!" I'd scream to the jeering crowd that would hush when I appeared on the Colosseum grounds, a girl bride in a pure white robe, red roses woven into my hair.

"The saints willingly sacrificed themselves for God," said Dad. "They suffered horribly. So let's not complain about our small irritations and minor tribulations around here. Let's honor God's magnificent love for us."

After Dad said goodnight, Maureen and I would grapple with what we'd heard. "Let's practice," she'd say, grasping first my right arm then my left with sweaty hands. "A little bit of salt, a little bit of pepper," she'd say, as she seasoned my flesh before biting into it. "See how long you can take it, for God."

At other times, as I contemplated how much God would love me, Maureen explored a strange mouth torture—unnatural sounds, odd sticky utterances she'd make with her tongue. "Daddy!" I'd call out. "Maureen's doing it with her mouth again. She won't stop!"

"She'll stop pretty darn quick if I have to come in there!" threatened Mother from her bed.

Soon enough, perhaps in reaction to Dad's stories of the saints, my sister began to have problems with food. Salmon, cooked macaroni, porridge, boiled eggs—she could no longer eat fleshy food textures without threatening to vomit. Even if Dad peeled the skin off an apple and sliced it into little white bites, she gagged. Mother began to call her Your Royal Highness.

"Do you think you're a queen, Maureen?" Mother quipped. "You better start eating what's put before you or I promise you'll be eating nothing at all!"

Meanwhile, my constant worry over my ability to endure torture took its toll on my digestive system. My clenched spirit manifested in a clenched body.

"You think Castoria's cheap?" Mother asked, annoyed by my chronic constipation, my straining over the toilet, sculpted round bullets pinging against the enamel bowl. "Open your mouth wide," she said, shaking the bottle of liquid laxative before unscrewing the cap and inhaling its liquorice scent. "I'm doubling your dose."

As our family got bigger and Mother's temper hotter, Dad left us more frequently. One day, when I was eight and Gordie about fourteen, with Dad on a sales trip, Mother stood in the bathroom scraping acne sores from Gordie's face with a steaming hot facecloth. She demanded he stand still. "Obey your mother," she screamed, citing the Fourth Commandment, which effectively permits parents to abuse their children. I stood at the door, unable to move. Gordie's strong arms hung powerless at his side but I knew his rage would ricochet later. I watched the steaming cloth as the scene hot-pressed into my memory. When I learned in school that God the Father hadn't been around for his son's crucifixion, I wasn't at all surprised.

My father's absence from his children meant he spent thousands of hours alone in his car, his living hearse, travelling from one prairie farm to the next, visiting each of his clients briefly, for an hour at most. His life crowded with customers, I think Dad was as lonely out there with all of them as Mum was at home with all of us. Dad took his meals alone and sorted out his thoughts at a restaurant table. He regrouped. A few years later, at his funeral, sweet French-Canadian waitresses told us how kind he'd been to them, how he'd remember all their children's names—children he'd never met. On lonely Saturday afternoons, Mother would select a record from her cherry wood stereo set and slip off its jacket. She'd drop it onto the turntable and place the needle on the groove. Then, from a safe distance, a deep male voice, perhaps Robert Goulet, would croon to her. Sitting on the window bench, she stared not out the window but into a mirror that hung on the wall across from the seat, like the Lady of Shallot, alone, aching, sad, not really longing for any Lancelot at all, but for herself.

Every few months, though, her ennui would evaporate and be replaced with a flurry of excitement and tension as she welcomed the Jesuits to our house for dinner. During those grand meals, my eyes travelled back and forth between my parents seated at opposite ends of the table. Dad's polite cheerfulness would give way to quiet bewilderment as his slight frame was overshadowed by these intense scholars in black. Aside from obtaining a post-secondary certificate in business technology, my father was a self-educated man. Instead of St. Thomas Aquinas in Latin, Dad read Dale Carnegie in plain old English. He showed me his dog-eared copy of *How to Win Friends and Influence People* and his trusty Norman Vincent Peale tract, *The Power of Positive Thinking*—both of which he kept in the glove compartment of his car. Though he sought "afterlife insurance" from the Catholic Church, perhaps he was best nourished by the empowering ideas of these two Protestant men, who simply encouraged people to be nice.

At his own dinner table, my father's face would soften as he shared stories about the results of being kind to his customers, tales that were a stark contrast to his bedtime stories about the grisly tortures of Catholic saints and far removed from the beatings Gordie suffered until he was ten years old. Dad passed on Dr. Peale's theory about problem-solving:

"No matter what the trouble, give it over to God for a while and then go about your daily lives as though everything's already taken care of. Trust that a solution is sailing down the pike for you. And it does come," he insisted. "Out of the blue, I'm jolted with a new sales pitch. It works! My sales record is through the roof!"

The priests smiled tolerantly as Dad shared his excitement. I intuited that they found his stories lacked depth. Meanwhile, with each glass of red wine, Mother transformed from an army sergeant into a rosy-faced hostess who couldn't stop laughing at the brilliant word choices and dazzling repartee of her Jesuit guests.

∾

Even when she was in her last months of a pregnancy, Mother would kneel down on the linoleum floor of the dining room for evening prayer. All of us would look up at the statue of Mary, the Mother of God, atop our carved oak buffet. One afternoon, alone in the room, I sensed the Virgin's brown eyes upon me and clambered onto a dining room chair for a closer look. I placed my hands behind her plaster head and pressed my face to hers, gazing into the shining eyes of a powerful woman who I believed loved me. We stood there for long minutes, brown eyeball to brown eyeball. In a whisper, I hazarded a request. I asked Mary for the India rubber ball on sale for twenty-five cents at the store where I regularly cashed in Mother's ginger ale empties, bottles I took without her knowledge. "Please, Mary," I begged, "make Mother give me a quarter."

A minute later, to my astonishment, Mother pressed the very coin into my hot hand and even threw open the front door for me to skedaddle. My faith in the Virgin Mother surged as I raced to the five-and-dime to make my purchase.

"Happy moment!" the store owner laughed. I didn't care that my India rubber ball bounced up and smacked me hard in the nose. The proprietor coiled pieces of Kleenex in my bleeding nostrils and tucked a Tootsie Roll into each of my pockets. Off I tore with my little tusks, a bit of candy melting in my mouth as I bounced my new ball in ecstasy. At night, I tucked my gift behind Mary's alabaster robe after we'd pressed heads and eye-gazed for a long time. Mary was my friend.

Yet our family's truly spectacular and most sacred moments did not occur as we knelt before household shrines or sat below the altar on Sunday mornings, but rather when we were gathered round the TV on Saturday nights. Our best preachers were two comedians, Art Carney and Jackie Gleason, who played an uneducated sewer worker and a confused bus driver. Mother couldn't stop laughing at the emphatic truths belted out by their wives, Alice and Trixie, on episode after episode of *The Honeymooners*. Oh it was holy joy to watch tears of laughter anoint Mother's face. Both my parents shook with hilarity at the bold retorts of four spunky characters who gave themselves permission to spit it out, lay it on the line, and say whatever they pleased. This unheard-of license to speak up brought my mother more cheer than she ever drew from the authoritarian Roman Catholic middlemen who ruled her life.

What a bleak contrast were Sundays. We marched to Mass in two somber shifts. Mother went to the early service with the older boys and then hurried back to cook the noon meal. Dad attended the later liturgy with the rest of us. All through a repetitive and lengthy Mass filled with requests for mercy and pardon for sins, I'd dream of the succulent roast and steaming mashed potatoes and gravy that would be served piping hot the minute we got home.

"We're a lucky family and what a blessing this hearty meal is," Dad would say while we tucked in. Then he'd launch into a tale of riding the night freight trains with other raw youths during the Depression.

Dad's slim 1930s diaries detail the labor he exchanged for meals on prairie farms or the fish he and some new pals would catch and fry riverside. Dad went from one boarding house to another, even after his father re-married. Even though he was invited home, he declined. He was jumpy by then, with a temper that flashed on and off. Dad tolerated his older brother's criticisms about not taking the steady job that was offered to him in town, instead living the uncertain life of a travelling salesman. To his credit, Dad maintained a polite connection with his elder brother but developed a closer friendship with his younger sister. Reading Dad's journals, I can almost pick up the clean scent of the penny soap he never lost in the creeks where he washed. The year he spent sleeping in barns and tents, working, fishing, playing cards, and sharing stories with other men was the happiest time of my father's life.

During our walks home from church, but only until we arrived at the front door, Dad would talk about his sister, a young woman who abruptly cancelled her wedding plans weeks before the ceremony and dashed into the convent with a speed that astonished her family and broke her fiancé's heart. My mother maintained a polite, cool distance from her sister-in-law all of her married life. Still and all, it seems Dad had enjoyed a fun-filled bachelor life of horseback riding, swimming, golfing, and hiking in the summer and skiing and skating in the winter, carefree activities he dropped after he got married and his sister became a nun. Perhaps in both his marriages, Dad felt jolted and even threatened by the demands of marital intimacy. Perhaps he was surprised he had to give so much, giving that jostled baggage he didn't want to inspect.

"Let's be grateful for all we have," Dad would say as Sunday dinner came to an end, holding his empty spoon aloft while we downed dessert.

As soon as we'd eaten, the older boys would wash up and Mother would return to her bed for a three-hour nap. The end of dinner signaled the completion of her obligations to us kids.

While Mother and the babies slept, Dad and I would attend an hour of prayer at church, where our priest freely dispensed the plenary indulgences of all the angels and saints in heaven. Attending benediction with Dad exempted me from nap time and allowed us some rare time together, even if I had to endure more church to earn those exclusive moments. I'd slip my hand into my father's on the way into the somber place of worship and briefly again on the way out. While my father never hugged me, he tolerated brief gestures of affection.

During the benediction service, side by side in our pew, we responded as the priest went through the Litany of the Saints.

"Saint Clare of Assisi, pray for us!" he would begin from his elevated altar.

"Pray for us!" we replied.

"Saint Philomena, who preferred torments of the flesh to the splendors of a throne, pray for us!"

"Mother Inviolate, pray for us."

The enumeration of suffering saints went on and on.

"Saint Mary of Nazareth, pure and most chaste, Mother undefiled, pray for us!"

The regular rhythms and soothing cadences of the chanting mesmerized me, even as the subtle implications of having one's body violated over and over again wormed its way into my psyche. We prayed together.

"Oh my Jesus, forgive us our sins. Save us from the fires of hell. Lead all souls to heaven, especially those who have most need of your mercy."

The words "Saint Mary of Nazareth, pure and chaste" echoed in my mind on one occasion as we walked home. "Who chased Saint Mary, Dad?" I asked, vaguely aware that it was the body being alluded to in the haunting benediction that featured, for the most part, women anxious about the safety of their physical person.

"No one chased her. She was pure. She was never touched by man," said Dad, confusing me further.

I told Dad I was worried I'd die with sin on my soul. "What if I have an accident and don't get to confess to Father?"

"Don't worry about that," Dad assured me. "At the instant of your death, Jesus provides a moment of clarity for you. Only if you still stubbornly refuse to acknowledge your sins do you go to hell." I thought about the Canada Dry bottles I regularly stole and cashed in for ice cream at the dairy on South Street. I asked Dad about the gravity of my theft.

"That's a venial sin, a lesser infraction. Those sins burn off fast."

"Oh," I said, alarmed.

"We're always *this* close to committing sin, Norda, this close to acting upon the evil lurking within. We walk a thin line. Sin is always right there, ready to trick us into wrongdoing. That's why Jesus had to give up his own life in order to save ours. He knew our natural inclinations. Jesus knew our violent natures," he said, projecting his own terrible fragility onto me. "That's why he established the Catholic Church, so there will always be an ordained priest to purify us. Without the sacrament of confession, we're in trouble."

Since my father's deeper reconnection with the Catholic Church, perhaps under the influence of his sister who became a nun, Dad's behavior had changed. Perhaps it was the fear of hellfire that restrained his hand and kept him from beating the rest of us as he had Gordie. As for me, though, the lure of chocolate ice cream, purchased with the refund money from the ginger ale bottles I stole, melted my resolve to sin no more, time and time again. The alternation between sugary indulgences and Catholic confession became a habit—Father Frank got to know me well.

∽

Five years before his early death at the age of fifty, Dad had approached Mother with his fear. He felt his heart weakening. He said he needed to rest. He suggested they stop having children. What was it that made Mother so angry at Dad and so insistent on bearing more kids after that, even when she was supposed to be the one obeying him? Were Mother's moods improved during pregnancy? Or was it a matter of avoidance? Pregnant Catholic women were not to be "bothered or touched" while gestating new souls for God. So while uninformed neighbor kids asked me if my parents "did it day and night," in fact, those bulky bumps may well have been Mother's annual defense system, a wall warding off unwanted intimacy.

"Don't think I'm going to be your prostitute, Neil!" screamed Mother one night, slamming the bathroom door. What would Mother do without constant pregnancy, that fetal defense against her unresolved past? Catholic Church dogma not only constructed the wall behind which Mother hid but honored her for barricading herself behind it even as her mental health deteriorated. The religious men trained to oversee her spiritual development did not encourage Mother to articulate her childhood pain or her adult dissatisfaction. They preferred to hear about her sins, not her history.

∾

During the winter months, I read story books to the hum of Mother's sewing machine pedal coming from one floor up. Later, when she bought a modern electric Singer that made zigzags and loops, I read to its more distant whirring sound. One summer Mother bought a bolt of cloth on sale, one pattern for the lot of us. She sewed turquoise, gold, and white striped pants with cute matching tops for the girls. To our neighbors, this must have further underlined what they saw as our military theme.

I progressed from easy to slightly more difficult books, most first read by my older sister. The only situation that would make me kick the basement door and scream in frustration was being stuck without my book. My brothers took to checking, on the way downstairs, if I had one with me. Mother had Gordie and Carlo carry the encyclopedia down to the basement too, so there'd be no shortage of reading material for us.

As soon as he could, the eldest foster brother, Nicky, left our house. He was seventeen and he didn't want to help out any more. Mother thought this was because Nicky was selfish and ungrateful. I overheard her say that an "interfering" school counselor had encouraged him to move into a Toronto group home. It seemed that while living there, he participated in sports, sang in a choir, went to movies, and played guitar. Carlo stayed on with us despite Nicky's pleas for him to come along. Carlo believed he owed it to my parents to work hard at our house.

∾

As I look back on growing up with our strange and unloving home life, it seems to me that my siblings and I milled about together without getting to know each other very well or forming close friendships. I think we all knew we'd betray each other at the drop of a hat for a moment of attention.

For example, when Mother criticized Maureen for her slumped shoulders or for eating with her mouth open, I'd zero in for an instant of short-lived glory.

"Not me, eh, Mother?" I'd pipe up. "I stand up straight and I eat with my mouth closed too. I eat like a lady."

"Yes, and you lie like a rug too," was a typical retort from Mother.

Although such betrayals were common between my sisters and me, we worked well together, most often under Maureen's direction. She developed imaginative little codes to telegraph our tasks to us. The word "snow" meant we'd soon be folding baskets of white diapers warm from the dryer, and "fruit" identified colored clothing.

A year younger than me, Irene, my skinny, green-eyed, pale-skinned sister, suffered from asthma and got scarlet fever and hepatitis. I recall her folding clothes slowly, each movement whisper-delicate. Mother often assigned her to rock the babies. That way she could sit down and still be useful. Brigit, an apple-cheeked beauty three years younger than I, stuck close to Mother, soothing and attending her all the time, as though her job was to keep her mother happy every waking moment. When I drew pictures of Brigit at school, her eyebrows were always way up high.

At school, I ached at being left out of yard games and had no idea what it was about me that repelled my classmates. I pretended I didn't care and quite often, for the fifteen long minutes of recess, I slunk away to a wet grain field behind the school into which I could slip away undetected. Once, when I'd gone a few steps into this vast acreage, I saw a shimmering spider pick her way over strands of barley and carry on without a care in the world. I stood there, watching her.

"I'll remember you," I promised the fragile being, spinning my own magical moment around the eight-legged creature with purpose.

Another day, after school, I followed the sound of a strange voice to a local barn sale and came upon an auctioneer who spit out words even faster than our parish priest saying Mass.

"What'll you give, I say, what'll you bid for this fine solid sow, look at 'er, a solid female breeder three litters in and a lot more to give! Starting fifty dollars, what'll ya gimme, okay, gentleman over there thirty dollars, yes, sir, over here, thirty-three…" Farmers on wooden benches leaned close to bid, straw clinging to their scuffed boots, their sunburned faces intent. The scent of sizzling pork sausages drew me in another direction, and close to a small grill I saw a basket of puppies. Out of the hamper, two gleaming brown eyes fixed upon me. This was no mere passing glance. Our gazes held steady. I gasped with sudden love.

"Twenty-five cents," his owner said.

Without a word, I paid.

"Keep him warm," said the farmer, handing me a potato sack, my new baby wrapped up so well only his panting pink tongue waggled out. "And don't worry about his little nips, they're his kisses."

I carried my short-haired, pulsating black-and-tan puppy home, stopping to cuddle him on the curb outside our house. Even with my cheek pressed against his pink panting belly, he still managed to lick my face with a passion I'd never known. In that instant, we bonded. I'd never felt such a powerful presence nor known such physical affection before. I'd never heard my own heart beat so loudly. At first I thought it was his, but no, it was my own heart pounding.

"Your name is Nipper, and I adore you," I said, before a thought dawned. What would Mother say?

I hurried into the house, Nipper in my arms. Mother looked first at Nipper, then at me.

"We'll see how it goes," she said.

For the next few days, my pregnant mother cleaned up Nipper's unruly deposits of poop on her carpets while I was at school, and nearly slid in his puddles of pee while holding a new baby in her arms. One day, she managed to grab a kitchen chair just in time as Nipper skidded between her legs, sliding across the linoleum in his own wet mess before hitting the stove and whimpering in pain.

Maureen delivered the news. "Nipper's gone. Mother said he bit our neighbor. The SPCA took him."

I couldn't get into the house fast enough. "I hate you, Mother!" I screamed at her for the first time in my life, earning my first slap across the face. I said it again, sobbing with rage. "Now I'll never ever see Nipper again! He was mine! He was my baby! Oh, I hate you, Mother!" To her credit, my mother did not strike me again.

"Did you ask my permission first before buying an untrained dog?" she yelled. "No! No, you never do! You do whatever you darn well please. Well, this may come as a very novel surprise to you, Miss Missy, but that's not the kind of world we live in! You can't just up and do what you want! You can't just up and make your own decisions!"

At supper that night, one last serving of apple crisp remained in Mother's restaurant-sized glass casserole dish.

"Pass your plate, Norda." Her lips compressed, her tone official, as if this wasn't the apology she hoped to convey, Mother chose me from among my siblings to be the recipient of a second helping of dessert, including a generous dollop of vanilla ice cream on top.

"Anyway," she added, once I'd downed the lot, "we're moving to Fergus. And there's no room for a dog in the car."

~

My fourth home, as listed by the Historical Society of Scottish Presbyterians, Fergus, was a fourteen-room red brick mansion. In June of 1957, with yet another better job for my father, we moved to a street of elegant stone houses set far back, some completely hidden by tall fir and maple trees. Stable professional people, our Fergus neighbors sent their children to a modern, beautifully equipped Protestant school. They treated them to skating and music lessons and tutors if necessary. I sensed how valued the neighbors' children were. Our well-to-do neighbors were uniformly shocked when dozens of fluffy white chickens came tumbling in and out of our garage, now a veritable chicken coop. Parking his car under cover of the heavy spruce trees in the circular driveway, Dad gave no thought to how his mini-farm might pique our elegant neighborhood. Daily eggs and weekly roasts saved money and fed the family, end of story. Our invasion of Fergus must have been quite a shock.

As Catholics in this rural town, our educational lives came to an abrupt halt. Our two-room school, taught by two teenage nuns who hadn't completed high school, contrasted with the Protestant school across the street, which sprawled over an entire city block and contained a music room, library, gym, and science lab. Be they Jewish, United Church, Presbyterian, or Anglican, the other residents of the tree-lined avenue would have up and moved before sending their children to a two-room shanty like ours. Our Catholic school, Saint Joseph's, couldn't even afford a magnifying glass through which the flaws of our impoverished curriculum might have been amplified. For my parents, though, Catholic obedience super-seded such considerations, just as it did in their burdened marriage. Enrolling their children in this school entailed shooting their family in the foot (includ-ing the ten little toes extending from it), an expected act of fidelity to those who controlled their eternal life. Just as our family had reached the apex of our material advancement, we children were hurled into a stifling backwoods of brainless religious indoctrination. Several years later, in my first year at the non-denominational Fergus Public High School, my math teacher was not at all shocked that a kid from Saint Joseph's found long division problematic.

Soon identifying us as an unusually strict fundamentalist Roman Catholic family, our adult neighbors pretended not to notice the blood-curdling screams emanating from our house every day. Their offspring had no trouble asking questions though.

"Who yells at your house all the time?"

"It's my mother calling us for supper," I'd say, downplaying the daily occurrence.

"How can you stand it? It sounds like a murder!"

While polite parents raised their eyebrows as Sheilagh's birth added to our numbers, their children readily repeated what they'd overheard at home.

"My mom said she'd be a screaming banshee too if any pope made her have a baby every year," said Jill.

"My Dad wonders how the heck your Dad plans to pay for so many university educations," said Manny. "Unless you get scholarships, Dad says your boat is sunk."

"We'll be okay," I replied. "We can read."

When the screamer emerged, however, and started joining committees and demonstrating her organizational prowess, the town took notice. Mother hit the ground running. By the fall of 1957, she'd joined the Catholic Women's League and the Parent-Teacher Association. Both my parents joined the Library Board in 1958. My mother joined the Cancer Society in late 1959 and eventually became the first president of its new Fergus branch. In the fall-winter of 1959-1960, Mother earned a diploma in public speaking, the Christopher Leadership Certificate. It was awarded in March and Dad proudly pasted it into a brand new album labelled "Fergus."

A month later, he glued in a newspaper photo of Mother presiding over the Cancer Society's Daffodil Tea. Yet another article in the scrapbook praises her presidency of the Library Board and even quotes her: "Today, it's standard practice to use the Dewey System. So let's hop to it." Mother had prevailed over the long-time librarian, who'd begged the committee to keep the old cataloguing system in place.

"The widow, Mrs. George, won the 24-inch bride doll at the Valentine Tea today," laughed Mother, home from a Catholic Women's League meeting one winter afternoon in early 1960. "Some prize. Her own mother drew the winning ticket."

"Did you bring home treats for us, Mum?" I stood as close to her as I could, breathing in her Lanvin perfume.

"Yes, I did," she said, unveiling a grand tray of sharply cut squares, sugar-dusted shortbread cookies, stacks of brownies, and flaky butter tarts. As we ate the goodies, I admired her blue silk dress, her matching satin shoes, and her white kid gloves with tiny pearl buttons at the wrist. When Mother was out and about, her screaming and napping stopped. Mrs. Clarence, Mother's hired helper, did the laundry and ironed Dad's shirts the exact and precise way he insisted they be done while we girls pitched in to clean and look after the younger kids.

"What's your next accomplishment, Ann?" Dad said with a smile as he pasted her published photo and an accompanying article praising Mother's successful fundraising efforts for our church into his treasured album.

~

In May 1961, Ira Needles, a founder of the University of Waterloo, addressed a gathering of the Fergus branch of the Cancer Society. After praising our town's community fundraising and volunteer work, he honored Mother personally: "If you, the mother of so many children, can devote countless hours to helping others struck down by this terrible disease," he said, "then would someone kindly tell me, who cannot?"

As president of the Fergus branch of the Cancer Society, a standing she achieved in early 1961, Mother made long lists of her project objectives with a blue pen and checked each item off in red as it was accomplished.

At eleven years old and in Grade Six, I entered a community-wide public-speaking contest, one that included both Fergus schools, Protestant and Roman Catholic. I was chosen to represent my class by default—no one else would do it.

"This is our chance to shine. Imagine winning over our competition," said Sister Brébeuf, our classroom teacher, gesturing towards the Protestant school across the street. "Imagine winning against the bigger, better school," she said, before Sister Pius, our principal, gave her a sharp look.

Every day, I practiced my speech about the founding fathers of Fergus to rounds of applause, both at school and at home.

"Gesture when you speak," said Sister Brébeuf. "You're not made of wood."

"Smile often," said Dad. "Enunciate carefully, speak slowly."

"Wear makeup," said Mother. "People have to see you from the back of the room."

"Will you be able to see me, Mum?" I asked. "Will you be there?"

"I'll see," she said. "I'll see how I'm feeling."

~

"Come see me speak, Mummy. Come with Dad," I pleaded the day before the event. "You hire Mrs. Clarence to babysit when you go to the Cancer Society meetings. Ask her to come tomorrow too!"

"I'm exhausted beyond human belief," said Mother.

"But you drove to Kitchener for your public-speaking course last night," I complained. "You managed that! And you slept all afternoon."

"I have a new baby!" Mother snapped. "My work hours go well beyond your daytime spying, Miss Nancy Drew."

All too soon, the day came and I found myself mounting the school stage. As instructed by Sister, I sought out one particular person, Loretta Rooney, in the crowd of friendly townspeople who came to hear Fergus youth speak. My classmate smiled and nodded at me, as we'd practiced in class. Midway through, my gaze travelled to Dad and to the empty chair beside him. My speech froze in my mouth.

"I'm sorry," I squeaked. "I'm sorry."

Moments later, in a small room off to the side of the stage, Dad encouraged me to ask the judge to try again.

"I'm proud of you, Norda," he said.

With permission, I sailed through my speech the second time.

"Well, isn't she a chip off the old block?" Dad's boss clapped my father's shoulder out in the lobby.

"Thank you, George," smiled Dad. "Your boy looked pretty fine on that stage himself."

"Don't get a fat head about it," said Mother when we got home, oblivious to my brain's steady shrinkage at school. Still, I could tell she was pleased. I fell asleep that night to the sound of my parents' quiet conversation.

Dad left for Montreal a few days later but not before pasting the newspaper article about my little victory into his Fergus album, right next to Mother's Christopher Leadership Certificate in public speaking and his own latest published book review. He tucked the family album into his briefcase to share with his sister at the Sacred Heart Convent in Montreal.

~

Sister Pius filled our school days with lectures of an archaic kind, sermons that soon had me suffering stomach aches and keen anxiety.

"Children, you have tremendous power," she told us during one such talk. "Did you know that you can usher a soul to heaven? Think of it, children!" Sister's skin flushed rosy as she warmed to her topic. "You can usher a soul to God! Do you have any idea how much the dead, those who are utterly helpless, depend on your prayers?"

Patrolling the aisles during her colleague's sermon, Sister Brébeuf assured Sister Pius of a rapt audience.

"As you skip along the streets at play," said Sister Pius, introducing our religious role as rescuers of hurtful people, "as you tuck into the contents of your lunch pails, the pleading eyes of the dying turn to you, begging your help. Your sacrifice, children, makes the difference between prolonged physical suffering in Purgatory and a fast flight to God. Your personal penance can save, say, a vicious murderer who is now deeply sorry for what he has done, a man who wails in constant unheard grief. If you help him, you can shorten his time of penance. You can reduce his fiery torment."

Sister Brébeuf explained her exotic name. She said it had once belonged to a Jesuit missionary priest who sailed to Canada from France and had his beating heart sliced out of his body and eaten warm by Natives from the province of Quebec. I raced home at lunch to ask Mother if she knew about this Catholic martyr from our birthplace. When she confirmed the truth of the story, my heart drummed. I couldn't do math to save my own life; I couldn't locate Ireland on a map, or Fergus for that matter, but I did have the power to rescue a world of unsavory characters whose sins had landed them in Purgatory. I never once questioned why an omnipotent God would require a little girl's help.

"Through your daily sacrifices," Sister Pius said, reviewing her lesson after lunch, "you erase sin. The instant you release a troubled sinner, Our Blessed Lady's mantle covers his burnt nakedness, and he is with God."

Sister cast aside her own veil and turned to Patrick, whose bright blue eyes and freckled face I'd loved to observe ever since we'd shared a laughter-filled moment months before. On that occasion, Sister had swept down the narrow aisles for art class, distributing small portions of floury white glue onto a small square of paper on each desk. When Patrick observed his portion, the tiniest single dot, the incredulity in his face unleashed a torrent of laughter, first in me and then, like wildfire, in him. Hands over our mouths, heads bobbing on our desks, we bonded instantly over a speck of glue.

On this day, Sister Pius began to enunciate the last consonant of every word, a cue Sister Brébeuf recognized, as did I. Astute at monitoring the fine nuances of exchange between the two nuns, I watched Sister Brébeuf catch the unspoken orders and locate the miscreant at the end of Sister Pius's pointed gaze. I watched as she delivered a tiny but exceedingly painful-looking pinch to Patrick's neck. Without missing a beat, Sister Pius nodded brief approval to Sister Brébeuf as Patrick re-employed fingers so abruptly released from his nose to rub his searing skin.

"The desperate eyes of killers watch you, beseeching the sacrifices that lift them from flames purchased by their own willfulness," Sister Pius finished up, inspecting our faces for long seconds. Then, skirts swishing, she set sail for her office, bowing slightly to Sister Brébeuf, giving our young teacher pleasure. On her own, though, Sister Brébeuf was frosty, especially towards the teenaged nun assigned to teach grades one to four in the only other room in our school. Seventeen years old and an affectionate teacher, Sister St. James often wept in the principal's office. I'd see her pass, puffy-eyed and blotchy-skinned , collecting herself on her way back to her crowded class. Time and again, Sister Brébeuf ignored the tremulous smiles her oppressed colleague sent her way. At the end of each school day, I saw three square-shaped head dresses in Mr. West's taxi, the principal and the two teachers returning to their convent in Elora, their slumped backs shoulder to shoulder, all three squeezed into the back seat, leaving the front seat vacant. Two teachers to seventy kids was a typical ratio for small-town Catholic schools in those days, unlike the one-to-one ratio between the priest and his personal housekeeper at the rectory.

After school, I would feel frantic eyes tracking me, unbidden, all along my paper route. Perhaps it was because I had already been molested by a man, someone I knew was doing wrong, somehow I knew the eyes following me were those of a man. I saw him roasting in hellfire, screaming and begging for my help, and I prayed hard for the strength to sacrifice the sugar I loved, a small penance to relieve his suffering and bring him closer to God — but time and time again, I failed to set him free.

~

"How are you, my dear?" Dr. Craig welcomed me whenever I came to collect her newspaper money, her brown eyes crinkling with pleasure. I knew she liked me.

A member of the local United Church of Canada, Dr. Craig wrote articles about family planning, openly stating that couples should bring into the world only the number of offspring they could afford to feed, clothe, and educate.

"Steer clear of her," Mother warned me, adding that one fine day, and that would be the day she died, she'd be a very sorry lady indeed for tampering with the work of God. Standing on Dr. Craig's doorstep, I caught the scent of the bright yellow flowers I could see on her writing desk and spotted a book in butterfly position on her couch.

"How 'bout I wrap up some warmed muffins for you to eat along your route?" she offered, handing me some change.

"No, thank you, Doctor." I punched her card and handed it back to her.

"Goodbye now, my intelligent one." She smiled while doing up my coat buttons for me. My throat ached whenever I left her because I found her kindness so moving. At Trahey's Hotel, the gummy purple gelatin of a Turkish Delight soothed the strange distress I felt at Dr. Craig's affection. I tucked a stowaway, a creamy Three Musketeers bar, under my newspapers in the wire basket screwed to the front of my bike. My mouth full of flavor, I pedaled on, comforted until I heard the distinct voice of my criminal, his body covered in sweat and cinders.

"No! Don't eat it! Please! Sacrifice the candy and shoot me miles closer to heaven!" he pleaded with me. I sincerely wanted to save him but despite my best intentions I ate both bars, chocolate swilling down my throat with every delicious swallow. The criminal's eyes widened as he watched me eat what he couldn't have.

Next, I pedaled towards the quarry at the end of Union Street but stopped at Lilly's Booth, a lonely snack bar. I used Dr. Craig's change and sank my teeth into a double-thick Dairy Milk bar. The next day I did the same.

"Dear God," I would pray, "today, no candy for me. I want to get this poor killer into heaven, and many more. Please help me to sacrifice myself."

Despite my sugar addiction, I found a way to set sinners free. I can't recall the first time I used my body in this way but my bizarre behavior became a habit. I decided to offer up my urine. It wasn't blood, as Christ had given, but it was nevertheless liquid from inside my body, and it hurt to hold it in. That pain would be my sacrifice to save evildoers from the consequence of their sins. As often as I could, thighs compressed tightly, sensations of bursting pressure notwithstanding, I crossed my legs to hold my pee in, each additional minute of burning physical restraint shooting one criminal closer to God. I learned to wait until I could no longer hold it, and even as I pulled down my tights and underwear, even as I hoisted myself onto the toilet seat, I accomplished a magnificent release for my cruel sinner, now so regretful of his sins. I'd hold off another full painful minute by counting to sixty, slowly, and at last the urine bubbled frantically from the prison of my body.

More miles on the path out of Purgatory were accrued for sinners in other ways. I restrained my responses to events around me, my patience a gift to the invisible sinners who now relied upon me. I knew they needed me. I knew my sacrifice of silence could earn their faster flight to heaven. I found plenty of opportunity to help sinners out. When I inhaled the diaper-soaked scents of the youngest children who cried at 5 a.m. as I dressed them, I held my tongue. In the morning chill of our poorly heated house, I herded our half-asleep, whimpering kids to the long green breakfast bench Dad had built and snapped a chain seat belt around each tiny waist so there'd be no slipping onto the floor during meals at the table. If we were not all present when the porridge was ready, Mother would scream at the stragglers through the intercom system she had installed. It was modeled on similar devices she'd admired in homes in the wealthy Montreal municipality of Westmount, back when she was growing up in the neighboring working-class district of Saint-Henri. Saving time was essential for Mother, as tight morning routines guaranteed long afternoon naps, welcome stretches of oblivion that had begun when Eric died and she'd learned what pills could do.

"Why don't you get the kids up after we leave for school, Ma?" I ventured, hauling my vacuum into the kitchen after breakfast. "They cry. They cry when I wake them up so early."

"Because, when I'm exhausted beyond human description after the meal I spend all morning cooking for you, not to mention washing the never-ending mountains of dirty laundry you heap upon me, I can put the kids to bed until you girls come home from school! The older boys did it for you. It's your turn now. Or is a little rest around here too much to ask?" Mother's face flushed as she finished her unhappy tirade. For all her complaining at home, however, never once did I see my mother protest to a priest about her burden. God's love was earned by suffering our problems well, not in solving them.

∾

Once, Mother confided to me that she'd wanted to be a nun like her older sister.

"I could've worked in Africa, saving orphan pickaninnies, starving victims of war and hatred. Those kids live in pure hell," said Mother. She was entirely unaware that the same Church that threatened her with eternal damnation should she interfere with "God's Plan" of having as many children as possible also menaced African believers who dared use birth control. "I could have had supper every night with a community of intelligent, well-read nuns."

"But Mother," I suggested. "You can pretend we're your mission children! Imagine we're your orphans!"

"Oh, get out of my hair," she replied, ascending the stairs for her nap. "And take the phone off the hook downstairs while I rest." The final click of her bedroom door lock effectively repelled annoying visitors.

∾

One morning, shortly after Sister's Pius's talk at school, I sent a sinner directly into heaven in one fell swoop. I made the beds up exactly the way Mother required: top sheet stretched tight to the top of the bed, all wrinkles smoothed, corners tucked or "mitered." Mother said top Canadian professional nurses made up hospital beds this way. She had once praised the way my blankets flowed evenly on both sides of the bed. As I smoothed the soft covers of my sun-warmed bed, I admired my finished work. Mother would be happy. Maybe she'd even smile in recognition of my effort to please her.

"Get a move on up there!" Mother's scream from the intercom sparked an idea.

My heart thumped wildly as I lunged at my bed, clawed off the bedspread, leapt onto the center of the bed and sent pillows flying. I ripped out the bottom sheet, whose edges had been tucked under the mattress, and hurled the mad mess of twisted bedclothes to the floor.

"Are you completely crazy? What in the name of God are you doing?" Mother appeared in my doorway to see what was delaying me. Blue eyes flashing at the mess I'd made, she moved her bulky force forward and slapped my face, hard. "Stop wasting time. You have thirty seconds to make that bed exactly the way I taught you and get downstairs to help out!" She slammed the bedroom door.

My face stinging, I remade my bed. Before I left the room, though, I looked in the mirror over the dresser and made the sign of the cross. "You're in heaven now, my friend!" I sobbed, throwing my hands up as though releasing a dove to the sky.

When Sister started up about "Our Mission on Earth" that day in class, I floated, victorious. I'd done my part. No one knew about it either, so the gift wouldn't be erased in the eyes of God. At noon I stopped at the Scotch Bakery to pick up Mother's order of hot cross buns and downed three of the soft, sugary treats. As I walked home, I concocted a lie that would explain why so few buns remained in the bag.

∼

One Saturday morning, Mother told me that as a reward for the excellent cleaning work I had been doing at home, she was taking me to a party for Grandpa in Montreal. Astonished, I packed my small suitcase with party clothes and shiny shoes. When we found our seats on the train, I watched her bend her head to read her *Chatelaine* magazine and later her library book, *To Kill a Mockingbird*, for which she'd soon write a review. I observed the slight rise of her left eyebrow, her top lip slipping over her bottom one, her brow furrowing as she flipped the pages, eager for more. I edged my hand closer to hers on the armrest.

"Stop staring at me," she said, withdrawing her arm. "Look out the window. Look at the nice view." The train travelled past snow-covered farms, frozen fields, and small towns, their names bellowed out loud by the conductor. Belleville, Kingston, Cornwall, Brockville, Dorval, and finally, the city of my birth, punctuated by spire after church spire piercing the air.

"Will we go to Mass on Sunday, Ma?"

"If there's time, we'll go to St. Gabe's," Mother replied. She was much less rigid about Mass than Dad was. Her Irish clan had been Catholic forever and were less observant than Dad, the son of a first-generation Catholic convert from an anti-papist Protestant history.

Grandpa's triplex sat on Marguerite Bourgeoys Street in the working-class district of Pointe-Saint-Charles, next door to his grocery store. Two of Mother's handsome brothers worked in the store. Ed, the manager, and Ted, the butcher, greeted me warmly. I knew they liked me.

"Choose two chocolate bars," said Grandpa, close to the cash register. Without hesitation, I tucked a Macintosh taffy, a buttery treat that could be counted on to last, and a Turkish Delight into my pants pocket.

"Good selections," laughed Grandpa, patting me on the head, lightly, as my father did. My Uncle Ed's blue eyes, so like Mother's, highlighted the influences of heredity. Grandpa's eyelids drooped with age, but the resemblance was there. When Mother and Grandpa smiled, the world smiled with them, but when they stopped, look out. After some Campbell's soup back in Grandpa's cramped kitchen, Mother suggested I nap before the party.

"If you want to stay up late, you better rest now."

I didn't feel like it but I wanted to show Grandpa how well I obeyed. It would make Mother proud. She showed me Grandpa's twin bed without warning me that next to it, in a steel-sided hospital crib, my grandmother lay in a deep sleep. I'd never known her. She'd visited only once. Her blue-veined, translucent white skin frightened me.

"What if Grandma wakes up?" I asked, looking nervously at her sunken eyes and fine white threads of moist hair.

"She won't," said Mom, handing me a pill and a glass of water. "Take this vitamin and I'll wake you in time for the party."

"I'm so excited, Mummy," I said. "I'm so excited my stomach hurts."

My scheme to lie back on the pillows, enjoy my taffy for a while, and then get up claiming I couldn't sleep, wasn't successful. Instead, I awakened stiff and aching. "Time for the party, Mother?" I asked, stumbling into the kitchen to a breakfast scene of toast and eggs.

"It's over," she said. "You slept through it."

I stood there listening to back bacon sizzle in an iron skillet. I gripped the wooden chair in front of me. "I missed the party?" I began to cry, standing there dressed in the same pants and shirt I'd worn the day before.

"Maybe you were tired from the trip," said Mother, trashing one liquor bottle after another into garbage bags. Grandpa's face remained hidden behind the *Montreal Star.*

"Come," said Grandpa. "Maybe those handsome uncles of yours have a treat for you."

"What about Mass?" I asked.

"No time," said Mother. "We're on the three o'clock train."

We drove back to Windsor Station in the delivery truck. I toted a large silver imitation champagne bottle called a Cookie Magnum, a gift from Grandpa. Mother slept until Guelph, while I munched my way through the whole jug of sugary biscuits. That evening, I hung up my party dress in the cupboard again, angry at myself for not waking up on time. Looking back now, I can see that the pill Mother gave me was no vitamin, but one of the pellets of oblivion she herself swallowed for years to guarantee habitual afternoon sleep.

Weeks after the episode at Grandpa's, Mother, Dad, Maureen, Irene, and Brigit left for a two-week vacation in Myrtle Beach, South Carolina. As Mother packed bathing suits and sun tan lotion into the trailer, she reminded me that I'd had a solo weekend in Montreal and now it was my sisters' turn to have some fun.

"Help Mrs. Pratt with the kids," said Mother. "I need to leave one reliable person behind, and that's you."

Soothed by Mother's approval, I tamped my upstart anxiety right back down where it came from. My daily doses of chocolate, two bars a day purchased at Trahey's Hotel, also helped me to feel better about a holiday I knew my sisters would be wide awake to enjoy.

Home from the ocean the following Saturday, everyone tanned and happy, Dad joked that the car would hardly cool down before he had to head back out on the road.

"Would you like to trade places, Neil?" snapped Mother, not appreciating the humor. "How does that sound to you?"

It was around this time that Dad began scratching secret pencil lines on Mother's wine bottles to determine how much she drank, his jaw taut, regular pulsations visible under his sallow skin.

The Sunday after my twelfth birthday, Dad tried to coax Mother to come out with him.

"The Simpsons invited us for a visit this afternoon," he said hopefully.

"No," said Mother. "I need my sleep."

"Not even for an hour? I'm leaving tonight."

"You go ahead, Neil. Take Norda. I need my sleep."

Mother did not suggest that Dad invite Maureen, because she knew my sister would refuse. Maureen was always deep into her drawing, painstakingly sketching detailed pictures, layouts of Florence Nightingale's hospital dormitories overseas. An arched pencil stroke on each bed indicated the bulky form of a patient who lay under blankets that skirted the floor. Only the peanut-shaped heads and feet of the sick poked out. I marveled at the number of bricks in her cobbled streets of London and the elaborate addresses of the Tudor-style houses she drew, like Number 1 Cobble Muse, Upper Mold, Brighton-by-the-Sea. I understood, without knowing the word, that Maureen was frightened. If she had a single blemish on her face, even the tiniest red spot, she'd stay home, anxious and upset, checking the imperfection often. If my sister declined an invitation, there was no changing her mind. Dad knew that. So it was I who accompanied him that day in my new cream-colored Princess Anne dress pumps. We walked side by side under Union Street's grand canopy of trees, each click of my heels tapping out the miracle of my adolescence. We were the same height now and Dad told me I was a beauty, like his mother and his sister, the nun he so admired. I got the sense that Dad would have been pleased if Mother was a little more like his sister.

Mrs. Simpson answered the door on the first ring. When she saw me instead of my mother, her face fell and she shot her husband a quick look.

"One of the children had a fever last night," Dad explained. "Ann is exhausted today."

"Yes, yes, of course," said Mrs. Simpson, unable to disguise the hurt of the snub. Mother definitely knew better. She knew how to use a phone. She knew how to politely signal her absence or suggest a rain-check. Mrs. Simpson served us fresh crab on crackers and a delicious Bavarian cream that must have taken her hours to prepare—perhaps an effort to impress Mother, to earn her friendship. I felt bad for her. I knew the feeling.

Mother's active involvement in the community had definitely raised her status in the eyes of Fergus's elite, the Protestants and Jews who had initially dismissed her as an endlessly fertile Catholic woman. I wonder if it somehow appeased Mother to win over her neighbors, convince them she was indeed a contributing member of society, and then drop them for ever daring to doubt her. She didn't appreciate that it was only normal for them to wonder about her when our enormous family came barreling into town. But ultimately, the arms-length distance she insisted on keeping was not spiteful. Even with a husband, children, brothers and sisters, her Jesuit visitors, and a community interested in her, Mother socialized reluctantly with her peers.

Dad said nothing to Mother about the hurt we saw in Mrs. Simpson's face and she remained ignorant of the effect of her snub. Mother rose to cook supper when we got home and Dad lay down on his twin bed for a nap before the long night's drive to Montreal.

Dad took not a pill, but something larger; not round, but square — a suitcase, his prescriptive six-week trips his way out, his equivalent to Mother's pills, his solution to unhappiness. I stretched close alongside him and felt my toes touch his. We recited the rosary together, a mesmerizing repetition that knocked me out until Mother called us to eat.

# PART 2

# A Thousand Milky Shards

The news that one of our neighbors, Mrs. Roy, had up and left her husband simply because she was "unhappy" spread like wildfire. She rented an apartment in Guelph, got a job as a dental assistant, and picked up her daughters after school every day. We soon heard she was taking acting lessons with a local theatre group. Finally, she filed for divorce.

"Happy or unhappy has nothing to do with it," Mother pontificated, her wine glass filled with Bright's Sherry beside the chopping board. "On a certain sunny day in the past, Mrs. Roy made a sacred vow and now she's tossing it, eh? She was all smiles then, eh? Now, because the grin's worn a little thin, she's flying the coop? What if we all did that? What if we all jumped ship when we're 'unhappy'? Good God. What a ninny." It was around this time, in the kitchen one day, that Mother gave Maureen, Irene, Brigit, and me "the talk." She explained that the "sex act" meant planting a new seed for the glory of God, period. She added that thanks to devoted Catholic women, the world would, one day, be entirely Roman Catholic.

"Sex outside that mandate is nothing more than cheap prostitution, a disgrace in the eyes of God," Mother said. She set a bowl filled with a dozen speckled eggs on the counter and began cracking one after the other against the ceramic rim.

"Our lives are not for enjoyment," she concluded, enunciating the final "t" with contempt. "Our lives are for God."

At school, I asked Sister why our neighbors claimed that Catholics have too many children.

"What the Protestants and the Jews of this town fail to believe," Sister began, "is that God looks after all His children. There's nothing to fear for those with real faith. Protestants and Jews believe more in themselves than they do in God. That's their problem."

"But what if parents die?" I asked.

"Think of the miracle of the loaves and the fishes, Norda," Sister said. "There were so many leftovers Catholics had to lug them away on camels. God provides in all cases."

～

While I recall little about Danny's or Paddy's or Joey's arrival home from the hospital, Sheilagh's had been memorable, perhaps because I was nearly twelve years old when she was born, and I knew that in my own body a chalice-shaped nest of woven blood vessels could also hold a new soul for God. If I got married to a Catholic man, I too would give birth to a child, a power of creation greater than any other.

"Well, that annual holiday is clearly over," said Mother, handing me her worn hospital suitcase to store in the utility closet. "A whole week in bed, a private bathroom, and three meals a day cooked by trained male chefs. Who could ask for more?"

Months after baby Sheilagh's birth, Dad mailed a card to me from Calgary. The top left-hand corner read, "From Romeo."

"Who's Romeo?" I asked.

"A character in a play," Mother said, a sharp edge to her voice. "Both he and his girlfriend end up dead."

I didn't know why Mother was upset about Dad's adolescent card. But if my father, like his God, had to rely on a little girl for adoration, there was indeed a problem. It also occurs to me that Mother may well have engineered my trip to Montreal to keep me back from the two-week beach holiday in South Carolina. Perhaps she had her reasons.

That afternoon, Irene dropped Sheilagh's milk bottle on the kitchen floor, where it smashed into a thousand milky shards.

"Maybe I'll follow Mrs. Roy!" Mother screamed. "Maybe I'll bloody well take the hell off too!"

Late that night I heard music downstairs, romantic yet plaintive. I found Mother curled up on the couch, drenched in tears. From the gramophone a powerful woman's voice poured out "Bali Hai," from her album of the musical *South Pacific*.

'Your own special hopes, your own special dreams,

If you try you will find me, where the sigh meets the sea,

You'll hear me call you, Swinging through the sunshine,

Here I am your Special Island, Come to me, Come to me.'

Mother gazed past the hall mirror, weeping, her eyes puffed closed.

"Are you thinking about Dad?"

"No."

"Who are you thinking about?"

"There's no name," said my mother, lost and dispossessed. "I just cry when I listen to that song."

Sad as I felt, I knew better than to approach Mother with any unwanted hugs.

At school, Sister Pius lectured about the laws of the afterlife.

"Only Roman Catholics achieve heaven," she told us on many occasions. "Everyone else dies in hellfire, their skin curling like onion paper."

Non-Catholics, Sister told us, had all the days of their lives to listen to God's invitation, and yet, year after year after stubborn year, they turned a deaf ear. When Sister Brébeuf confirmed the terrifying news, my body froze. At last I understood the implications that somehow I'd missed before. I had only one thought: to publish the news. As soon as school let out, I ran. I could barely land one foot in front of the other as I stumbled to the newspaper office, dread seizing my limbs. Mr. Wood, the editor of the *Guelph Mercury*, the man who had given me my first job, would help me, this I knew. Unlike my teachers, who kept to themselves, I knew the townspeople who would be consigned to hell. I knew my paper route customers were good people, always happy to see my face at their doors. I had to save them.

"Holy smokes, Norda," was all Mr. Wood could say when I delivered the terrible news.

"Maggie, get this kid some water," he called to his secretary, who did better than that and handed me a chilled Coke.

Mr. Wood reasoned with me. "Norda, you're twelve years old now and you need to know this: it's not true! People can be any religion they want. They can even have no religion. They can be kind, helpful neighbors to each other without ever setting foot in a church. There's no punishment for not being Catholic, Norda. It's not true!"

"Yes, there is, Mr. Wood! Sister said so. Please," I begged, crumpling to my knees beside his desk. "Please write the flyer. Tell this town what will happen if they don't become Catholics today! I'll insert it. I'll pay for it." I grabbed his hand and, to his round-eyed horror, pressed it to my sticky face. "I beg you, Mr. Wood. I don't want Fergus to burn."

"Jesus Christ," he said, withdrawing his hand to reach for his Rolodex. "Norda, you're the best paperboy I have. What the hell's gotten into you?"

He located my home phone number and called Mother right in front of me. Maggie reappeared in the doorway, looking quizzical as he hung up. "Her mother says she can be dramatic," he reported.

"But you didn't ask her the question!" I cried. "Call her again! You only talked about me!"

"I'll drive you around your paper route today," said Mr. Wood. "We'll talk this over."

The sugary Coke provided delicious relief while Mr. Wood considered our plan of action.

"Look, Norda, in journalism, information must be correct." He lit a cigarette and sweat beaded on his forehead. "Look, I promise you that, as a responsible writer for the *Guelph Mercury,* I will personally interview your sources tomorrow. And I will take careful note of what is said. And I tell you now that if your Dad and the Sisters stand by what you say they teach you, I'll quote them for all of Fergus, Elora, Guelph, Mount Forest, and Acton to read. In fact, I'll headline it."

"Thank you, Mr. Wood." I clambered to my feet again. "And will you interview Father Conner too?"

"Oh yes, my sweet. The good padre will not be forgotten by this Dick Tracy. Point to your customers' houses," Mr. Wood said as we drove along my route. He pulled a Hershey bar out of his pocket. "Eat this and point."

"Hell can burn without our town in it, eh, Mr. Wood?" I said, tasting my first bite. With chocolate in my mouth and the caring Mr. Wood beside me, I was already in a kind of heaven.

"You can be sure I'll be visiting Father Conner as soon as the cock crows tomorrow," Mr. Wood assured me as we came to a halt at Mr. Singer's driveway. He was the big tipper with a number tattooed on his arm. I didn't want anything to happen to him.

~

"Mr. Wood is visiting us tonight," Mother said, giving me a cool look as I finished up my dinner. "He'll be here in ten minutes."

I smiled up at him at the door. A big man, Mr. Wood tramped into Dad's office, where the two men shook hands and lit their smokes, social behavior that sent little chills up my spine. I wished girls could shake hands too. I ran down the hall to make instant coffee for them, with lots of sugar. I waited in the living room until I heard my name spoken and the library door swung open. Mr. Wood said a formal goodbye to my father, nodded to me, and left. Dad spoke to me from his desk.

"Let Father Conner take care of this, Norda. It's his job."

"But Dad, Sister said non-Catholics will burn forever when they die. We have to hop to it right away, Dad! The martyrs boiled in oil for God, remember?"

"We're all martyrs enough in this cold and unbending town," said Mother, entering the room.

"Leave it alone now, Norda," said Dad. "And anyway, at the last moment of life, at their final breath, God gives everyone a last chance. At that point, most people jump to take it."

"And why put Dad's job in more jeopardy?" added Mother. I knew there'd been some recent talk about my father's company being in trouble.

"Lead by example," concluded Dad, "not by wild newspaper articles that upset people. If this side of town sees you being a good girl, that's all they need to see. Then they're free to go to Father Conner or your mother or me, or even you for that matter, and we'd gladly help them into the Church. God knows what God's doing."

~

Tensions gathered as the future of Dad's job grew more uncertain. My parents found ways to save every penny. One Sunday, Dad appeared in the kitchen, waving a roll of toilet paper.

"All right, everyone," he said, "I saw over a foot of this costly wipe in the toilet, an unnecessary waste. Two squares are plenty ample."

No one answered.

"Okay, Dad," I volunteered. "We'll be more careful."

"Easy for him," laughed Mom after Dad retreated. "He's been constipated for years, like you have. He's never required more than one tiny square himself and has no idea others might!"

"Why am I always constipated, Mom?"

"Maybe you don't chew your food well enough. You gulp as though someone's going to take your plate away, as though it's your last supper. And while we're at it, your handwriting is cramped too. It's way too tight and small. If you want to look good in the world, you have to present yourself with attractive script," said Mother. A moment later she brought me four white plastic strips, lower case letters of the alphabet hollowed into each tile.

"Try this," she said, handing me an inkless pen and pointing to a kitchen chair.

She started reading from the package. "'Fit your pen into each groove and copy the letters for an hour a day. In thirty days, your handwriting will be attractive, elegant and readable. It's guaranteed successful.'"

"Thanks, Mum!" I replied and set to work. Over and over I traced the invisible letters. A month later, Mother slipped a postcard and a real pen under my nose.

"Write to Aunt Eleanor," she said. With the phone tucked in the groove of her shoulder and held in place with her chin, Mother stirred the soup and extolled the virtues of her new Presto pressure cooker to her youngest sister, the brave one who'd thrown caution to the winds and married the Italian man of her dreams, even against the wishes of her father. Mother sometimes told me the story of my aunt, my namesake, the young woman who fell in love, as my mother once had, and who, unlike my mother, defied her father's racism and married a man she adored.

"You'll be thanking me," Mother told my aunt. "This cooker saves time. I no longer stand at attention in front of a hot stove. I can turn cheap cuts of budget meat into tender, delicious meals. Butt end tastes like filet mignon! It's a real treasure and personally, I'm thrilled with it." Mother peered over my shoulder to examine my script. "Good," she said. I was ecstatic. Though I failed my social studies test the next day, the letters of my failure were beautifully shaped.

~

"God chose Mary to be the Handmaid of the Lord." Sister referred our class to the statue of Our Lady of Virtue on the windowsill. "She was created to serve God. Can you imagine a better calling for a young woman?"

"I want to be a chorus girl on the *Ed Sullivan Show*," I said. "That's my dream."

"Humility is the mother of many virtues." Sister ignored my comment and read on and on from her book of St. Jane Frances de Chantal, her daily alternative to complex math lessons. I could recite phrases from that book, along with the Baltimore Catechism, in my sleep. "'From obedience springs holy fear, reverence, patience, modesty, and mildness. For whoever is humble easily obeys all, fears to offend any, is submissive to all, does neither offend nor displease any and does not feel the insults which may be inflicted upon her.' St. Jane de Chantal conceived so much affection for humility that she watched over herself with the greatest attention, in order that she might not allow even the smallest occasion for practicing humility to escape. She once said to St. Francis de Sales, 'My dearest Father, I beg you, for the love of God, help me to humble myself!'" Listening to Sister read about this woman's silent submission and her gratitude stirred up strange feelings in me. Tension crept high up between my legs, a sensation both pleasant and irksome. I wondered if St. Jane said "thank you" to the priest who helped her to humble herself.

~

Upon a child's desk at the front of our classroom lay a homemade crown of thorns studded with real nails from the hardware store and wired with sharp shards of glass from a smashed-up Coke bottle. Attendance at First Friday Mass entitled us to pull one spike—a single shard of glass or a nail—from Christ's headdress, reducing, by our sacrifice, the pain in His battered head. Morning chores at home usually prevented me from participating in this monthly rescue mission, except for the one time I begged Mother to let me go. She agreed and even packed a sandwich, a fine blend of Millionaire Sardines and Worcestershire sauce refined to a smooth paste by her latest kitchen aid, an Oster blender. Walking in the snow to Mass that winter morning, it occurred to me I could become a nun, a thought quickly banished as I recalled Sister St. James sobbing on her way back to her cramped classroom. After attending First Friday Mass in the chilly church, my classmates and I prayed around the torture device. "Oh my Jesus, forgive us our sins. Save us from the fires of hell. Lead all souls to heaven, especially those who have most need of your mercy." I considered which embedded spike hurt Jesus most and drew it out with great care. The next First Friday, when I asked Mother if I could go to Mass again, she said no.

"Pull a nail out here! Help at home and give up the big, fat, public show. That's what will please God most, not pulling slivers out of something Sister rewires once a month anyway!"

~

As much as I wanted to qualify as a saint, pure and undefiled, there were energies brewing within, dark anger that confused me. One day, my little brothers were playing a game in the living room, jumping from sofa to chair to the carpet below. I watched how well they balanced themselves, their arms strong airplane wings, their feet solid gliders. I challenged Paddy to fall over onto the floor without putting his arms out to protect himself.

"Imagine your arms are cut off," I suggested, promising to pay him a quarter if he could accomplish that. "Pretend you're a girl with no arms." After several tries, time enough for me to know this game was bad, Paddy's face hit the floor. I heard the crack and felt my shame.

"I'll pay you tonight," I said when he wept for his quarter. "I have to get the money."

Leaving the tearful scene behind me, I realized two sickening things. I'd been cruel to my sweet little brother and I'd caused him to hurt himself. I'd removed his only means of defense, his arms. Another hot summer afternoon, while Mother napped and I led all the younger kids home from the community pool, sinful swear words kept bubbling up in my head, words like *damnation, ass, big fat ass, stupid ass, dumb ass, hell, stupid fart,* and even *goddamn.* Behind me,

Paddy and Danny lagged, their little legs pumping as fast as they could. They were far too slow. I yanked Paddy and shoved him forward, giving him a hard slap on his sunburned back. When he cried out in pain, Mr. Scott flew out of his garage.

"I know it's been a long day, Norda, but one day you will regret what you just did. You can decide the kind of person you're going to become, you know. It's your decision whether you're a good person or a bad person. Would you like to apologize to your brother?"

"I'm sorry, Paddy," I said to the little tyke, whose red skin now featured a large white imprint of my hand.

Mr. Scott told us to wait, and soon reappeared with popsicles, including a lemon-lime one for me. That night Paddy hugged me and kissed me goodnight, all by himself and unbidden. I promised I'd never hit anyone again.

∾

Mother treasured her attractive home, her bulbous-legged oak table and her matching carved buffet. "Beauty and order are as important as reading good books," Mother said, placing vases of fresh flowers on each side of the statue of Our Lady. With the publication of each of Mother's book reviews in the local paper, Dad added more pages to our family scrapbook. When Irene won a figure-skating prize and Gordie took first class honors at school, Dad pasted the newspaper reports into our family album. That summer of the year I was twelve, my friend Linda and I won a prize in our town's annual parade. My little brothers shrieked with joy when we appeared in a horse-drawn wagon behind the marching band on St. Andrew Street, Linda the groom and I the bride in our replication of an 1800's wedding day. With Joey on her hip, Mother swung first Paddy and then Danny into the back of the cart I'd hired for the day with my paper route money. As I turned to wave goodbye, Mother gave me her quizzical smile. Throwing her head back, she laughed out loud as our horse and crowded cart trotted up the driveway and onto the street.

"Ya can tell they're Cat-lickers," joked a parade onlooker. "Kids in the caboose from day one!"

"Smart Catholics pay no mind to dumb Protty-dogs," said our driver, smiling back at me. Still basking in Mother's admiration, I couldn't have cared less about who said what.

From time to time my father would test Mother, little tricks that didn't fool her one bit. One evening he returned from six weeks in Saskatchewan and instead of using his key, he rang the front door bell. Even as the chimes resonated, a quick glance down the hallway told Mother exactly who stood there. At the stove, she continued flipping thick slices of fried Prem dusted in white flour, sugar, and cinnamon. I knew she wouldn't budge and so, before another tone sounded, I found myself running pell-mell down the long corridor towards my father. Like Betty in *Father Knows Best*, I squealed, "Daddy, Daddy, Daddy's home!"

"What a phony!" I heard Mother snort as I skidded to the front door. In that instant, a huge smile on my face, I observed myself pretending for the first time in my life. I consciously decided that Dad must be joyfully welcomed. It could not be otherwise. I couldn't leave him to stand outside, unanswered, all alone. I couldn't bear it. And so I greeted him, expressing a noisy delight I didn't feel. Once I'd hung up his coat, I escorted him by the hand to the kitchen, skipping, making noise to redeem the unbearable silence.

"Daddy's home, everyone!"

"Oh, hi," said Mother, serving up canned meat.

"Hello, Ann."

"How was your trip?"

"Good. It was good, Ann."

I monitored their conversation. If they entered into a deeper one, I would leave them to it.

When it didn't progress beyond a superficial discussion of bills and phone messages, Dad asked who'd like to prepare a cup of instant coffee for him just the way he liked it. No one else offered; even if I waited for one of my siblings to take care of Dad, no one would offer. I pretended after the awkward lapse that perhaps I'd not heard well.

"I'll take a look at my mail before supper, Ann."

"You go right ahead," said Mother, a hair this side of a brush-off. And soon, I'd be hurrying down the hall with a steaming mug of coffee for Dad, all smiles and light.

When had it happened? When did I first step up to buffer reality like that, to insinuate myself into my parents' marriage problems?

Too bad I didn't mind my own business and leave them to investigate their own unhappiness. But it was too late. I was already indentured. I'd already internalized the rescue script. Sometimes I'd deliver to Dad, along with hot coffee, a sizzling report on Mother.

"She screams, Dad," I said during one such conversation. "My friends hear her all the way down Union Street. It's embarrassing! And she's drinking every day, Dad. Every day after her nap."

"Try and get along with your mother, Norda," Dad would sigh. "I depend on you while I'm away."

That afternoon I found him penciling a line on her Bright's Sherry bottle.

~

On Saturday mornings, my sisters and I raced to finish chores by lunchtime, when we'd gather in front of Mother's kitchen blackboard to watch her check off each completed task, chalk dust falling from her swollen hands. As soon as we finished our work, we were free to go and spend the afternoon at the library while she and the other children napped.

I recall blissful hours of Cherry Ames, who said "Yes, Doctor, Oh! Yes, Doctor," but secretly thought her own thoughts; and that smart Nancy Drew, whose ability to connect the dots always saved the day. I recognized Johnny, my grade school cross-walk guard, in *The Secret Garden*. At first he hid himself as a grumpy gardener but eventually his reserve melted, warmed by the steadfast love of a powerful girl, a child I assumed must be Catholic because she could heal the sick. Our librarian recommended *The Five Little Peppers,* which made me feel grateful for all I had. Supper was two 28-ounce tins of concentrated Campbell's tomato soup with skim milk powder and Velveeta cheese sandwiches that only Mother could grill to perfection. Never once did I see a stray dot of waxy fluorescent cheese hit the cookie sheet when she did the job. In time, Mother cut our milk bill by seventy-five percent. She loved to share her secret: forty-pound sacks of powdered skim milk from the Fergus Co-op. Cautious at first, Mother mixed small portions of the grainy white powder with water and added this to our jugs of whole milk, and no one noticed. Too soon, though, she started adding more. Then we noticed.

"Yuck, baby powder!" I complained.

The milkman got his walking papers and Mother ploughed the dreaded grit into her baking. Pancakes, oatmeal cookies, and puddings lost their thrill. No one wanted Red River cereal with the tiny surface explosions of dry milk particles.

"Stop whining!" snapped Mother. "Milk is milk is milk. Some children have none at all!"

I stopped drinking it entirely. Unlike the younger ones, I had experienced the pleasures of whole milk for the first decade of my life. After Mass on Sundays, Dad sat at the head of the kitchen table with a cup of Nescafé instant coffee, smoking his pipe, and staring blankly out the window, oblivious to the spruce trees outside. His jaws ground back and forth, back and forth, like a dresser drawer pulled in and out, in and out. He gazed far into another world, one his children couldn't enter. Even when he was at home, Dad was absent.

"Daddy, Daddy," I'd say, tugging at his tweed jacket. He didn't hear me. Only when his coffee cup was empty or his pipe went cold would he be motivated to bring his attention back to us. Then he'd head into his private library and close the door. He'd work until suppertime.

One Sunday, though, Dad didn't disappear into his paperwork.

"Ann," he said to Mother at the end of our meal, "I informed Carlo that we won't be attending his wedding this summer."

I felt a thump inside me, then silence. My heart beat faster as I stood at the kitchen door and listened to Dad talk about my foster brother and his wonderful Scottish fiancée, Barbara. During their recent visit, Carlo's bride-to-be had sat beside me in the living room, her eyes sparkling like the diamond on the hand her man held so tenderly. Barb and Carlo looked away from each other only after a long pull, a tug of conscious effort. Barb's curly brown hair softly framed her face, and every time her glistening blue eyes sought Carlo's, he smiled back, his face aglow. Perched on my footstool, I watched this radiant young woman in her baby pink sweater set and matching pleated skirt. I felt her joy.

"You'll dance at our wedding!" she promised. "You'll eat a big piece of our wedding cake!"

"I told Carlo we are Roman Catholics," Dad continued, "not only in good times but in bad. I told him point blank that as long as he and Barb plan on using contraceptives to prevent giving life to a new soul for God, then no matter what their faulty reasoning for doing so, we cannot, as good Catholics, witness that union."

"Did you ask him if he'd change his mind?" asked Mother.

"Yes, I did," said Dad, knocking ashes from his pipe. "But he insists that the medical advice from Barb's doctor is to be careful about having babies with her delicate health. I told him the Church says it's up to God to decide who is to be born, when, and how. Carlo and Barb don't trust that. They're taking matters of life and death into their own hands. They're disobeying Church law."

"Why were you silent so long on the phone, Neil?" Mother asked. She stood still.

"Carlo was sobbing," said Dad. "I waited for him to get hold of himself, but he couldn't seem to stop."

Crumpling inside, I remembered Barb and Carlo holding hands so sweetly on the couch. My throat ached. There didn't seem to be anything more to say. I wished Carlo and Barb would obey God's law so that I could dance at their wedding, so I could see them again.

"Well, time for my nap," Mother sighed. "Neil, can you look after Danny, Paddy, Joey, and Sheilagh if they wake up early, or grab one of the girls to help? The baby's bottle is in the fridge somewhere."

"Certainly," replied Dad absently, his jaws working hard. "You go to sleep, Ann. Get some rest."

"Mummy, may I come with you?" I asked. "I feel sick."

"When are you going to stop calling me 'Mummy'? I've told you a hundred and fifty times already, call me 'Mother.' I'm not a dead Egyptian! Now may I please get some rest without kids constantly underfoot?"

"Leave your poor mother alone, Norda," said Dad. "Let her rest."

Slowly, I left the room to search for my newspaper delivery bag. Hidden in its tarpaulin folds was the chocolate that consoled.

The next day, Dad left for a sales trip across Western Canada. "Obey your mother," he told me as he stowed his suitcase on the back seat of the car. "Keep the peace."

"Okay, Dad," I replied, sniffing the Amphora tobacco scent of his brown wool coat.

~

Wonderful brown-paper-wrapped parcels would regularly arrive at our house containing new volumes from the *Time-Life* illustrated series or exciting novels. Mother ordered them and encouraged us to read them.

"Money spent on books is as important as dollars spent on food. Feed your own minds or one fine day someone else will be doing the thinking for you, of that I can assure you," Mother said, oblivious of those who'd planned her life. She shared her *Reader's Digest* condensed books, often accompanying them with a brief book review.

"Here, try this one. A rich Irish girl falls in love with a Mountie and goes off to live in a remote village in the North. She soon trades her flimsy pearls for a dog sled! Maybe one day you'll adventure to the North like Mrs. Mike too. And read this one, about Madame Curie, a woman with smarts—maybe even more so than her husband, Pierre."

I devoured those stories by Pearl Buck, Daphne du Maurier, Taylor Caldwell. Mother claimed the Jesuits were the smartest human beings on earth but I treasured the stories of brilliant women investigating the world.

"And here's a Prairie writer who knows the score about Quebec," said Mother, handing me Gabrielle Roy's *The Tin Flute,* a book that would inspire me for decades to come. "When you see the hell Rose-Anna lived through, you'll stop complaining about your own lot in life."

~

The night of Dad's return from the West, I sat alone at my desk in the roomy bedroom I shared with Maureen. In our larger Fergus house, Irene and Brigit shared a room, Gordie had one to himself, and the youngest children shared a dormitory. I abandoned my homework and began to draw a picture of Meg, the eldest sister in Louisa May Alcott's *Little Women.* Two half circles formed the downcast eyes on her angelic face. By erasing little patches on the tremulous line that formed her mouth, I made her appear to be wearing white lipstick. Her wispy hair was pulled into a bun, with a single wave floating across her high, brainy forehead. Mother said you could measure intelligence by forehead size—the larger the brow, the greater the smarts—so I too kept my hair swept back. A cameo brooch rested on the ruffles of Meg's floor-length empire-waist dress. In tiny letters, I penned *The*

*Lives of the Saints* on the cover of the book she was reading, and I imagined that she looked up only when spoken to. She'd reply to questions with humility, her pale fingers limp on her lap. Dozens of sea pearls, teary ovals, fell from the throat of her dress to the floor. Her feet were invisible under her gown.

Suddenly inspired with another vision, I started on "Bad Girl." Drawn with strong strokes, her curly, sassy, short haircut showed off brassy earrings, a wink away from the plunging neckline exposing plump breasts squished into a lacy black see-through blouse. One dense line made instant cleavage. "Hi, Betty," I whispered. I drew two eyes heavily outlined in black, staring brazenly at me from the page. I darkened the mole above her lip and crisscrossed net stockings up shapely thighs that disappeared under a tight skirt. Stiletto heels on her big, strong feet, she click-clicked along in my mind's ear, her ample behind swaying this way and that. I sat her on a barstool, where she tapped a ditty with crimson nails on the side of her frothing beer mug. She told everyone what she thought. She said "stupid ass" and "fat ass" whenever she damn well pleased. With her big red lipsticked mouth wide open, she shrieked, "Go to hell!" from the generous word bubble I provided for her. As I drew, powerful sensations swelled and pulsated in my body. My hand slipped between my legs to touch the source of inexplicable excitement.

"What have we here, Norda?" I heard Dad's voice behind me. Stunned, I slapped my hand up and over Bad Girl. How had he crept up behind me like that? I had no idea he was home.

"I'll take this," he said, slipping my drawing out from under my hand. He studied it for a moment while I burned like onion paper. "This kind of drawing is sinful. I don't want you doing it again."

"Okay, Dad." I couldn't cry. A match snuffed out, even my toes felt hot with shame. Dad, my one ally, looked disappointed. He showed the drawing to Mother.

"Mother glanced at it," Irene reported. "She didn't say a word. She started complaining about the heating bill, how high it is this month."

"She did?" I was surprised. I took this as an expression of Mother's love for me.

At school that week, all desire to doodle and draw full-body pictures evaporated. I did sketch heads, though, facial profiles secured by collared shirts. A strange power began to possess me: I believed that the faces I drew were actually born into the world. They became real people. I tried to make them as attractive as possible. If I made a slight mistake on the nose, for example, or the lips or ears,

I went to great pains to correct the maligned feature so that the girl wouldn't suffer all her life. Once in a while, though, no matter how hard I tried, I'd botch up a face so badly, I couldn't fix it. I'd stand over the garbage pail and apologize, with a prayer for her immortal soul, as the torn-up face fluttered to the bottom of the bucket.

∾

On Mothers' Day of my last year in grade school, Father Conner praised the incomparable excellence of the Blessed Virgin Mary, Our Heavenly Mother. With her sweet, giving nature, uttering never a harsh word, she embodied perfection beyond human comprehension—a model for all women: mothers, nuns, nurses, clerks, teachers. My mother's face flushed during that sermon. One pew ahead of us, the longest feather in Mrs. Rooney's felt hat began to tremble slightly and then shook ever more violently as Father's homily gathered momentum. I watched Mother watch the feather, her jaw set in grim solidarity with the wearer of the palsied plume. After Mass we were treated to one sorry mood. Father Conner, Mother fumed, had not a single word of praise for women like Delores, a mother of nine, who hand-washed and ironed the very gown he wore at his elevated lectern. A month later, on Fathers' Day, Father Conner spoke plainly about the hardworking Catholic men of Fergus, who slogged to support their families, and about the honor they deserved.

∾

On my last day of grade school, in June of 1960, Father Conner gathered our class around the statue of the Virgin Mary, not to the right but to the left of the altar, the less important side, and gave us a farewell talk.

"The Virgin Mary so loves God that she is never, ever angry, and that's what I want you to be like as you go out into the wider world now. Mary forgives, all the time, endlessly. Nothing you could do or say to her would go unpardoned. When soldiers pounded nails into her Son's hands and feet, she forgave. When a sword slashed His side and His blessed blood poured out, she forgave that too." Father let that sink in. "So what am I saying, boys and girls? What do you think the Virgin Mother felt?"

"Hatred?" asked Patrick.

"No, Patrick." Father Conner sighed. "Didn't I already say the Virgin was incapable of it?"

"Scared?" asked Barbara, tearing the edge of her song sheet.

"Be careful with your music sheet," said Father, removing it from her grasp. "What the Mother of God felt," he went on, "was pure love. You see, her unspeakable compassion soared well beyond that immediate gruesome moment of the crucifixion of her Son to a future time when those very same soldiers would be on their knees in front of her, begging her forgiveness. Her immensely loving heart flew into the new world her Son was creating by his death. She knew if she got all hysterical, she'd spoil God's plan."

"She knew her Son had to die so we could live," added Sister Brébeuf.

"Nuns get married too, you know," said Father, to our surprise. "They marry Christ. Nuns stand a little closer to Our Redeemer than women who marry ordinary men."

"How many wives does Christ have?" Patrick asked, interested.

"All the nuns in the world," said Father, grinning at Sister and making her blush. "Yes, and nuns are higher in God's estimation too. Our Lady remained a virgin. Nuns are virgins too even though they marry Christ in their hearts. Married women, though, are not virgins. They've been carnal. Therefore, they're less pure in the eyes of God."

"What about priests?" asked Pat.

"For nuns, Christ is a husband, a loving man to guide and direct. For priests, though, Christ is a brother. So in effect, while nuns marry Christ, priests never do. After all, you can't marry your brother, can you?"

"What about married men?" asked Patrick, his brow wrinkling. "Are they less pure than priests?"

"It's quite simple, Patrick," said Father. "Ordinary married men and ordinary women engage in carnal sex. Nuns and priests don't. Nuns and priests give up that behavior in order to serve the wider world. God acknowledges their costly sacrifice."

"But Mary married Joseph," I said.

"Ah yes, but she never *lay* with him. Not once. They never shared a bed. They didn't perform the ordinary crude physical act in order to impregnate Mary either.

They never touched each other, even though Mary loved Joseph in her mind and in her heart. She loved him as you would your brother, Norda." A quiet descended there at the altar. My stomach ached with a dark, confused fear I couldn't name.

"So the question you must ask yourselves, boys and girls, is: What is your calling? Is God calling you to matrimony or is He inviting you to a religious vocation, to Holy Orders?"

"So even though my mother had all of us kids to please God, she's less in God's eyes than Sister?" I asked, worried sick about how I would break the news to Mother. Sister lowered her eyes, fingering her rosary while Father had the last word.

"Well, yes, strictly speaking, religious who give up the raptures of physical love for God are seen by Him as, well, yes, more laudable."

"What raptures?" scoffed Mother an hour later, ladling macaroni and tomato sauce onto our lunch plates. "Tell that snuffling blockhead he can go pee up a rope. And tell him to use Kleenex. His constant sniffling and swallowing, right in front of people, is revolting."

"Father said Mary and Joseph never touched each other, not once. They were brother and sister, pretending to be married." I collapsed onto the dark green storage bench in the kitchen and began to cry.

"What's there to cry about?" asked Mother.

"Father said God loves priests more. They give up everything so they are higher in God's books."

"They give up precious little," snorted Mum. "Priests give up worrying about where their next meal is coming from. They give up worrying about who's going to cook it for them. They give up paying rent and electricity bills. They give up making their own bed. And all during the Depression, they gave up being hungry just fine."

"Do you think Sister Pius is closer to God than you are, Mum?"

"No! Each woman earns her own reputation in heaven. Don't listen to that snuffling priest. He's not a Jesuit. He never studied a day in his life. He doesn't know his arse from his elbow. What a sorry, uneducated excuse for a man he is!"

I mulled over these conflicting world views on my way back to school after lunch and finally agreed with my mother. Each woman was in charge of her own report card.

After Mass that Sunday, Mother approached Father Conner with a special request. He ignored the Kleenex I proffered and fixed his gaze slightly above my mother, as though she wasn't there, standing in front of him.

"Father," Mother began with a smile, "friends of mine, a well-to-do family, have given me some colored silk dresses, previously worn by their daughters." Father's face remained immobile. He waited in silence.

"We're struggling financially right now, Father," Mother continued. "I'd like to save a few dollars and have my daughters wear these dresses on their confirmation day."

"Girls wear white," said Father, compressing his lips and turning away.

"But Father, new clothes are an impossible expense for us right now."

"Pure white for girls, Madam," Father called back, sweeping down the center aisle in his long black frock. There'd be no goodbye. No wishing us a good day.

"To the Parents' Committee I go," Mother fumed. "We'll take a vote is what we'll take, a community decision." After dozens of telephone discussions so heated that Mother forgot to take her afternoon naps, Parents' Committee meeting night arrived.

"*Vox populi*," she declared as she swept out the front door. "We'll hear the voice of the people tonight."

At the meeting, Mother told me later, she suggested a secret ballot.

"No!" protested Father Conner. "No secret anything! If you disagree with my position, you raise your hands right in front of my face. If you agree, you raise your hands right in front of my face too."

"Father, it's not a secret vote," explained Mother. "It's a private one, like what happens at the public election polls."

"Fine," said Father. "Those who wish to have an underground vote, raise your hands."

"Private," said Mother, raising her arm. "Not secret, not covert. Private." Then she looked around and noticed that hers was the sole arm sailing in the air.

"Thank you," said Father, scanning the room filled with parishioners squeezed into child-sized seats. "Now, who among you, which self-respecting parent, would agree to have your daughter confirm her Roman Catholic faith in anything but pure, unsullied white? Who among you wants your girl to approach God in brown or black or even polka dots and stripes?"

"What did you say then, Ma?" I asked, riveted, as she sat at our kitchen table with a cup of Red Rose tea.

"I said nothing," said Mother, her feather fascinator still clipped to her hair. "I stayed to finish up the meeting. I wished everyone a nice evening. When Mrs. Grady whispered to me in the parking lot that she was sorry, that she's too afraid of Father's anger to say anything, I smiled. I left like a lady." A tear coursed down her cheek. She raised her tea mug, her delicate upper lip trembling the tiniest bit as it hit the heat. Suddenly, her moist blue eyes flashed a combination of unshed tears and steel force. "I have an idea," she declared. "You'll wear those silk dresses for your confirmation day and that's bloody well that." I found my mother beautiful that night.

At breakfast the next morning, Mother announced we'd make our Catholic confirmation with our former classmates in Galt instead of in Fergus. She made no call to Father Conner to inform him of our planned absence nor did she take any calls from nervous parents wanting to explain their reluctance to stand up to our parish priest.

At our confirmation in Galt, it was fun to see my former classmates, now so much taller. The Blair brothers, dressed in their family tartans, smiled warmly at me, the Singh girls wore patterned saris, the Italian kids flashed white dresses sprinkled with glass diamonds, and we, Ann's daughters, proceeded up the aisle, each in a different color: green, purple, and blue.

"Sometimes, girls," said Mother as we stopped for gas and ice cream on the way home, "you vote with your feet."

~

In late June of 1960, two dreams came true for Dad and one for me, an unforeseen gift. Dad got a wished-for motor home, making it possible to fulfill his other dream: the family trip of a lifetime, a tour of Canada from Atlantic to Pacific. And I got to see everything. Weeks before our family holiday, Sister had led us one by one into the coat rack hall, where an optometrist examined our eyes. As it turned out, I was in dire need of glasses. Even though Mother laughed and asked if the doctor had examined my head while he was at it, she did take me to get glasses immediately. She also said it was nice that the government had legislated this new benefit for all Ontario school children. When I picked up my new specs, I thanked the optometrist, who gave me so much more than those who blurred my mind with images of chaos. I could now read endlessly, all I wanted to, without headaches. I could distinguish the sharp indentations of maple leaves and make out the spiky fringes of our green and blue spruce trees, clear as a coastline. I could lie on the grass and see the clouds transform into faces and animal shapes high above. I could notice a classmate's wave from a car window and smile back. My world opened up.

~

Mother stocked the trailer for our summer trip. Sacks of Red River cereal, oatmeal, onions, rice, prunes, peanuts, and popcorn kernels flopped over cases of red kidney beans, Chef Boyardee spaghetti, and Campbell's soup. Mother bought an extra can opener in case one got lost, which, she said, it most definitely would. An ice box full of Dad's frozen capons was tucked under the camper table that collapsed to a bed at night. A dozen loaves of Mother's homemade bread and as many jars of her strawberry jam started us off to Nova Scotia, where Mother's sister and her own enormous brood awaited. Mother relinquished her afternoon naps and enjoyed the opportunity to live a full day. On our trip, we visited two of Dad's distant relatives, religious men he referred to as "remarkable individuals." We met Stewart first, a Jesuit who lectured at a Catholic university in Halifax. He'd often dined with our family in Galt.

"What a brilliant man," Mother whispered after our visit with him. "What a mind!"

"What does he know about?" I asked.

"He knows plenty," said Mother with conviction, though not answering my question. "Did you see his eyes? You can see the brain power in those eyes."

We visited Dad's cousin, Aunt Irene, in her Halifax convent. At the oak refectory table on Spring Garden Road, she passed me a sheet of paper with the word *sacred* printed across the top.

"It's the *Sacred* Heart," she instructed, producing three envelopes I'd sent to her, each one bearing the shameful address, *Scared*. I dutifully corrected the word in my elegant new script, and my aunt said she'd check my next letter to her, but I was too embarrassed to write one. What if there were more mistakes?

Farther north, we pulled up in front of the rambling house of Dad's childhood friend Stan, now known as Stan Senior. He was an important engineer, unafraid of big ideas, and the proud father of ten children. "I was best man at his wedding," Dad said.

Before she stepped out of the car, Mother asked Dad for the name of Stan's wife. Dad had no idea. He'd forgotten her name. While the two men chatted outside, I strolled inside, where Peter, a little handicapped boy, sat in his high chair eating Cheerios from his high chair tray.

"Picking up small items enhances his fine motor skills," his mother explained, offering me a plate of date-filled cookies.

"What shall I call you?" I asked, taking one. Stan's wife, the mother of ten children, said I could call her Auntie Edna.

"What a lovely home you keep, Edna," Mother said, nodding her thanks to me.

As we wandered through their four-story house, my sisters and I couldn't help but notice how exceptionally good-looking all of Auntie Edna and Stan Senior's kids were.

"This is my son, Stan Junior," Edna introduced us to her eldest son in the kitchen. He nodded to us, his hands immersed in the sink, busy washing baby new potatoes.

"With my husband working so hard, Stan Junior's my right-hand man," Edna said proudly. "Why, he's spent this entire summer on his back under the cottage, re-insulating it for us. He cooks and cleans alongside me. He diapers Larry, Gerry, and Catherine. He devotes hours and hours and hours to them. What with little Pete and the older kids, I have my hands full."

Stan flushed, hitched his glasses up over his nose, and turned aside. A little later, I noticed Edna's fine helper reading a story to his little sister, a rosy blond child with a sweet Irish face. He held her warm and snug on his lap, while two little brothers waited their turn. The night before we continued on our journey to the beautiful West Coast of Canada, Dad snapped a photo of all eighteen children at our farewell barbecue.

"That son of theirs is not only a godsend to his mother but apparently a bit of a scholar too. Shy as he is, he's a serious honor student, as bright as you are,

Gordie, and as helpful to his family." Dad nodded to his eldest son as he backed the car out the driveway.

Mother sighed, probably thinking of the Jesuit scholar we'd visited on our trip.

～

Sheilagh sobbed convulsively when she was returned to us after our six-week trip. This had been our new baby's second separation from her family in her first year of life, the first having occurred when my parents had vacationed at Myrtle Beach with Maureen, Irene, and Brigit. I watched my baby sister's terror as she struggled to get out of Dad's arms and into the warm embrace of our Spanish-speaking neighbor, who'd been hired to care for her. Mrs. Ricardo wept at the helpless sobs of a child she'd grown to love.

"Don't worry, she'll adjust," said Mother. "Somebody take her out for a walk."

～

In August, Mother asked me to escort Brigit to her test to earn her swimming certificate. From the bleachers, I saw my little sister's toothpick arms flutter nervously at her sides, her brave smile so at odds with the dread in her eyes as she took her first step down the watery cement stairs. With one breath she threw herself in and dog-paddled with an intensity that moved me to tears. My heart pounded as I watched her baby hair flying, lips gallantly compressed and eyebrows higher than usual as she paddled and gasped for air all the way across the pool without touching bottom. Standing up, she turned to her examiner, as did I. "Well done, Miss B!" he said. When we got home, Mother propped her certificate against the statue of the Virgin Mary and Brigit beamed her joy all day.

Soon after that, Gordie won an award for his speech, "Our Greatest Modern Need, Religion."

"Our family is looking good," said Dad, packing for his next trip. "Our family is progressing well."

Whenever Dad got into his Chevrolet to leave for a trip, he took a moment to fill his pipe, light it, pull out the ashtray, turn on the car heater, and lower the window slightly. Then out the driveway he'd roll, without a farewell glance back at the house, oblivious to me waving on the front steps inches away. Dad slipped into his other world the minute his car door closed.

~

In September, Mother dispensed with her naps. She said Sheilagh was her last baby and she'd decided to make some changes in her life, to move forward, to shake things up. She concentrated on her strengths and threw herself into two mammoth fundraising drives, one for the Jesuits and the other for the Catholic Carmelites. She set new financial goals, not for herself or her children, but for the religious communities she served. If she wasn't going to make any new souls for God, at least she could serve the Church in other ways. She committed to excellence and fundraised until she'd met her objectives for both religious recipients.

"When your capable mother sets her mind to a goal, it's only a matter of time before it is achieved," said a Jesuit one suppertime, raising his wine glass high. "To a woman of drive and determination!"

"If I hold that phone against my ear one more hour, it may fall off!" Mother laughed one afternoon after a marathon solicitation of possible donors.

"When will you finish helping, Mother?" I asked, placing a supper plate next to her brand new electric typewriter.

"The hour I draw my last breath," she replied. "That's the precise hour you stop helping your fellow man."

~

When Dad's company downsized in the winter of 1960-61, he lost his managerial job. Mother was blindsided. Her nerves frayed. She got scared. In a single week, vague rumors of the company closing became stark reality.

"We're living hand to mouth, Neil!" she cried. "This can't go on."

Dad chipped the ice off his motor home, hitched it up to the station wagon, drove to Toronto, and rented a small plot in a snowy campground. That week, he landed a sales job with a hair products company that paid half his former salary. Mother put away Robert Goulet and *Camelot* and tuned in to CBC radio news. She froze meals for Dad to heat up in the trailer.

"We're in big, fat trouble," Mother said. "Trouble with a capital T."

With only a kerosene heater to warm his tin house on wheels, Dad weakened. He shivered in the cold, night after night. He reassured Mother. He lost weight. His cough worsened.

"Let's ask the Jesuits to help us," I suggested brightly. "They can fundraise for us now!"

"Mind your own business!" snapped Mother at my ridiculous proposal.

$\sim$

When school ended in the summer of 1961, Mother informed her older daughters of a good job opportunity, saying that, lucky for us, she'd signed us on. She explained that a family friend who ran a nursing home for handicapped children in Montreal needed our help.

"You'll be needing money for school in September, funds you are quite capable of earning for yourselves." Mother said we'd learn French and that we were going, period.

Predictably, Maureen balked. She begged to stay home and help Mother with the younger children. When Maureen said no, she meant no. If she didn't want to eat soft-boiled eggs or gooey porridge, she didn't. If she wanted to turn a tiny linen closet into a private room, away from me, then that's precisely what happened. Although she called Maureen "Madame Queen," Mother did pay attention to Maureen's gagging threats to vomit over certain foods, and her emotional fragility over unnamed stressors that caused her hands to sweat so much that she took to wearing white cotton gloves all the time. For my part, I had no idea that what I'd suffered as a child was sexual abuse and had no inkling that my sisters may have been subject to similar predation and were showing the effects of that trauma. At all events, with the helpful Canada-wide connections of Dad's sister, the nun in Montreal, it was decided that Maureen might be happier at a convent school in British Columbia and so late that summer, off she went, dispatched and dispensed with.

So it was Irene and I who unpacked in a humid basement bedroom at Hôpital Notre Dame des Anges in Montreal North. Rita, the French-Canadian head nurse, handed each of us a flat cellophane package containing the white nursing uniform we were to wear while on duty. We were introduced to Martin, a gray-haired, wiry chef, who rolled his deck of Du Maurier cigarettes in his white T-shirt sleeve and sometimes mysteriously disappeared for a day or two. When he smiled, his face folded into a well-oiled grin, exposing gaps between missing teeth. The greasy cowlick flopping over his wrinkled forehead made him look boyish, like a sailor-boy or Johnny, my long-ago cross-walk guard. I could tell he had a good heart. At a Monday morning staff meeting in Martin's steamy kitchen, we met his eighteen-year-old niece, Suzanne, a nurse's aide four years my senior. I was assigned to her tutelage, and I noted her pride at being publicly honored.

"Suzanne is now your teacher, Norda," announced Rita. "She will make a good nurse out of you." Suzanne blushed again and I smiled at her. I knew I would work hard for her.

"You go upstairs to Martin in the morning," Rita said in heavily accented English, "eat breakfast and then go straight up to the wards. Help the nurses. Do whatever they say. Help bathe the children and change their diapers. At noon, go back to our good chef, Monsieur Martin, for his usual exceptional lunch."

Martin, blushing, bowed and saluted with shy pleasure. His little habit was to tap his smokes after scratching his chest.

"After your meal, back to the wards for the afternoons," continued Rita. "You will work some evenings and have some off. You may use the recreation room to watch TV. Perhaps some of the nurses may invite you to their homes, if they like you and if you are respectful."

"Let's hope there's TV in English," whispered Irene, who had recently become even skinnier and paler than ever.

That very week, our behavior began to change. Irene started hiding packages of biscuits and chocolate under the clothes in her top drawer. When Suzanne offered me a cigarette one morning on the balcony, signaling shared adulthood, I took it. Hungry for approval, I began to puff along with her, no matter how much I gagged with nausea and revulsion. I suddenly felt glad for the English books I'd packed, *Cherry Ames*, *Blue Fly Caravan*, *Little Women* and a new book, *Island of the Blue Dolphins*, all of which featured adventurous girls caught in unexpected situations. While Irene nibbled cookies in front of the TV, treats she declined to share with me ("Buy your own! You have money too!"), my books fired my imagination until sleep knocked me out.

Suzanne was proud of her knowledge, her efficiency, and her teaching skills. I tried to please her, to figure out from her gestures what she wanted me to do. When she showed me the rows of babies for the first time, a crucifix over each crib, I fell silent. Growing up in a house full of kids had not prepared me for the array of physical handicaps and deformities I saw before me. But as I watched Suzanne perform one soothing service after another, her love floating through like a yellow ribbon, I felt more at ease. I learned French quickly and provided Suzanne with translations. She'd say "one" and show me how to change a diaper, the first activity of my new routine. When she said "nest," I understood we'd moved on to the second item on my agenda. "Tree" meant the third most important activity.

In one cot lay baby Theo, his head an immense balloon. Small eyes, nose, and mouth crowded deep in a valley of swollen flesh, tufts of hair lost far away on the back of his bloated cranium. My heart drummed in my chest.

"*Bonjour ma chouette, mon chéri, mon adorable Monsieur Pompidou!*" sing-songed Suzanne with such sincerity, such genuine love that my shock melted instantly. When little Theo saw Suzanne, his face lit up and he smiled as naturally as any other baby, gurgling with pleasure even though he couldn't move his head at all. I noted how Suzanne placed herself at the end of his crib so that he could see her fully. Out of the side of my glasses, I observed a pinkish fluttering movement, like wings, and spied Theo's little hands emerging directly from his shoulders.

"Thalidomide babies," said Suzanne, pointing to dozens of cribs in the long row. At coffee break, I learned that many pregnant mothers had swallowed this pill, Thalidomide, to ease their morning sickness. Unfortunately, it caused deformities in their children.

"*Une erreur terrible,*" said Martin, shaking his head.

With much pride, Suzanne introduced me to other babies, some with short tails, others with exceptionally hairy pointed ears, and tots with missing arms or tiny feet wiggling directly out of the thigh.

"*Bonjour mon trésor, mon bijou, mon ange.*" My teacher caressed each baby with her heart, her voice, and her hands, lovingly stroking tiny wing fingers or sloped heads, one after the other.

"Big smile," she instructed me. "Look happy!"

Suddenly I had a mission. I would love them well! My time had come at last! At home, in Fergus, I cleaned. When Danny and Paddy were born, my sisters got to fuss over them. When Joey and Sheilagh came into the world, I wanted my turn and asked for it, but Mother just praised my cleaning. Under my care, the oak knick-knack shelf of miniature shoes gleamed. My floors shone. My faucets glowed. "I can't trust anyone else to scrub with the industry you bring to the task," she said. Pleased with her approval, I stopped asking.

In this new setting, I fell in love with one baby in particular, the one and only child Suzanne found difficult. To my surprise, the baby, Francine, was fifteen years old. She weighed less than twenty pounds. Franny made me famous because I was the only one who could get her to eat. Instead of tying her to a high chair, I fed her in my arms, sometimes out on the small balcony overlooking the street. I'd take my sweet time dolloping quarter-teaspoons of warm Quaker Cream of Wheat onto her tongue. Fascinated, I watched it slide down. Francine was a good girl and afraid of only one thing, water. Every night she managed to vomit and pee on her masses of long hair, and every morning she'd scream bloody murder when Suzanne shampooed her. The first time I heard Francine's pitiful cries of desperation, I ran to Martin in the kitchen. I couldn't listen to her gasping panic as Suzanne poured warm water over her soapy head, careful not to wet her tracheotomy tube.

"*Jésus-Christ et tous ses apôtres torturés sur leurs bicyclettes noires!*" spat Suzanne, her red face matching Francine's as she bundled the frantic child in a towel and shoved her into my arms.

"After this, you shampooing!" she ordered. Martin nodded to me from the kitchen, a salute as though I'd been handed a trophy.

"*Elle te fait confiance!*" he shouted, his hand curled like a fog horn over one side of his mouth, both of us pretending that Suzanne couldn't hear. She didn't contradict the fact that she trusted me, and my confidence grew. The very next day, a day so scorching and humid that I had to feed Francine in front of an electric fan at 7 a.m., I stuffed her volumes of vomit-reeking hair into my shower bonnet so that she could eat without it flying everywhere. And then I made a decision.

Francine stiffened as I carried her back to her crib. She knew the drill.

"No," I said to her. "No water, *pas d'eau.*" I removed the scissors I'd borrowed from Martin from my pocket and deftly cut her hair. I lathered her head with the Old Spice foam Martin lent me without question, and shaved the rest off with an old razor I found in the basement bathroom. Francine seemed to enjoy the soft coolness of the lather, and cried not a single tear since no water appeared. Finally, I sponged her head, creamed it with hand lotion, kissed it, and dressed her in a sleeveless summer dress. I carried her into the kitchen to return Martin's shaving cream.

"*Tabernacle!*" he yelped when he saw her. "*Une vraie dinde est sortie du tabernacle!*" He rolled his eyes upward, indicating the administrative office above. He enunciated slowly to make sure I understood the gravity of what I had done. "*Mon Dieu, le trouble, le trouble, mademoiselle,*" he said. Then he collapsed into laughter.

Francine also laughed, a strange jiggling chortle that made me laugh too.

"*Mon Dieu!*" cried Rita, and then, in her best English, "It's Visitor Day tomorrow! You perform this bizarre action without permission? You ask no one? The one thing Francine's parents are proud of is her beautiful hair! And now she's bald! I should fire you for this!"

Suddenly, I wanted to go home. With Martin's help, I called Mother collect, long-distance. "I want to come home, Mother," I begged. "Please!"

"No," she answered decisively. "Grow up. I gave you and Irene an opportunity to learn French, an opportunity other kids in Fergus would give their eye teeth for. Anyway, your father's not well. He can't have any noise around. I need you kids out of my hair while I take care of him."

"I won't make any noise, Mother. Please, I want to come home."

"No." Mother was firm. "I'll come for you in six weeks. And Rita won't fire you. She already told me you girls are doing a good job."

The following morning Suzanne woke me. "Francine parents upstairs," she said. "Get dress. Eat breakfast. Come to Francine crib. "*Dépêche-toi.*"

"What can they do?" Irene comforted me, and in a rare display of generosity, handed me a chocolate bar from her stash. "Let Rita fire you. Who cares? Francine's happy, isn't she?"

At the breakfast table, Martin smoothed the back of my head with a calming hand, not that I missed a single bite of the ample breakfast he placed before me. After tucking away two eggs, sunny-side up, two sizzling sausages, and toast lathered with Kraft Cheez Whiz and Habitant strawberry jam, I climbed *en haut* to meet my fate. Francine, sporting a polka-dot bonnet, let out a little yelp when she saw me.

"We want to thank you," Francine's father said right away. "Madame Rita told us all about it. Yes, we discussed it thoroughly and we understand. Our daughter is happier this way."

After the couple left, Rita warned me. "Suzanne is your teacher. After this, ask her permission before you take…" she sputtered, searching for the right words, "scissors into your own hands!"

As she strode away, I saw her exchange a wry smile with Martin and knew I'd been forgiven. Suzanne and I began to drink our coffee by Francine's crib every day. After all, the three of us were teenagers.

One morning, shortly before we took the bus back to Fergus, I watched Suzanne and an attendant slip Theo into a thick plastic bag, which they zipped up and removed from the ward on a small trolley. Suzanne pulled a chair up beside Theo's crib, put her head down on the edge of the crib, and sobbed with all her heart. I stood in silence as Suzanne cried piteously until Martin came from the kitchen and gently steered her shaking shoulders to the tiny upstairs balcony for the coffee he served her with his own trembling hands.

"*Merci, mon oncle*," she said as he plunked a third sugar into her cup with his tobacco-stained fingers. We all smoked a cigarette squeezed together on that balcony, curls of white smoke trailing baby Theo.

Soon after our return to Fergus in September, Irene was admitted to hospital with rheumatic fever and hepatitis. Then Dad checked in. Since his winter stint in the trailer, he looked like a thin old man. One Saturday morning, Mother answered the phone, untied her apron, and hurried across the street to the hospital. I followed her.

In my father's hospital room, Irene, Mother, and I watched Dr. Mason pump Dad's heart with great vigor until, finally, he stopped.

"Time of death: Saturday, September 28, 10:28 a.m.," he dictated.

A nurse led Irene back to bed in her ward and Mother left with the doctor. Alone with my father, I placed my warm hand on his folded hands and said the Our Father for him. Then I whispered into his ear, "I love you, Dad." I articulated those wooden words with no feeling whatsoever, but I knew someone should say them. I didn't shed a single tear for Dad on the day he died, or any day thereafter. Not a single tear for my father who, at age fifty, died of a massive heart attack. I slipped Dad's Du Mauriers from his bedside table into my own pocket and wondered, as I lit one, if there was something wrong with me. Back at the house, Mother assigned tasks.

"Brigit, you scramble eggs for the kids' lunch. Norda, people will be coming. Vacuum every room, and pay special attention to the downstairs bathroom."

By the evening, baked hams decorated with pineapple rings, scalloped potatoes, and tuna casseroles were weighing down our oak table. Mother didn't eat supper with us, but one of the Jesuit seminarians who visited did. At the table, he played a game of questions and answers with us, and one by one we took turns telling our favorite day of the week, favorite flavor of ice cream, favorite animal. When Brigit replied to his questions with "Oh, let me see now. No, I don't think I know about that!" we all giggled. We were so interested in each other's answers that the game went on and on. Our visitor wondered how kids who lived together could know so little about each other.

That night, I noticed Mother's bottle of Bright's Sherry standing boldly out on the kitchen counter instead of in its usual covert position behind the oatmeal sack. The following evening, three of Mother's Jesuit friends drove over for a laughter-filled supper.

"Excuse me," I said, interrupting their good time, "I don't think it is very nice to be having a party tonight." I felt so little. Mother said I was acting silly and told me to stop it.

"Stop it yourself," I talked back to her. "And you know what I mean."

Mother's eyes widened. She blushed to the roots of her hair. Suddenly she looked like a child herself. It struck me that I'd hurt my mother. I felt ashamed and sorry and slunk to my room until one of the priests came to get me. He asked me to come downstairs, apologize to Mother, and join the others, which I did.

~

Back in Montreal for Dad's funeral, I was dropped off at my Uncle Will's apartment on Harvard Avenue. Walking over to the funeral Mass together, we stopped for a candy bar at a corner store at Oxford and Sherbrooke. I finished the last bite of my Mars bar as we crossed Girouard Park and slipped into church.

"Where's Irene?" Uncle Will asked when we got to our pew.

"In the hospital," I whispered back.

The minute Mass was over, Mother took me aside. "Because you did so well at the hospital this summer, because you are fourteen and old enough, and because your French has improved, I've arranged a special opportunity for you, one that not many young people get. You'll live with a nice French-Canadian family here, go to a private French school, the Sophie Barat College on Gouin Boulevard, and become fully bilingual. You're going after lunch."

Uncle Will handed me some Kleenex to wipe the chocolate clinging to the corner of my wide-open mouth. "Here's a golden opportunity to run away if you want," he said as we walked back to Oxford for a second candy bar. "I remember visiting your family once in Galt. I wasn't even invited to your house for a cup of tea. Your dad sure was tense."

"Dad was always tense at home, Uncle Will." I asked my uncle for twenty-seven cents to buy a pack of Du Maurier, King Size. I tucked them into my coat pocket. "For tonight," I told him. He nodded.

I soon understood that I was to be a "mother's helper." Madame Choquette and Mother looked alike. Both had gray-blue eyes and raven black hair. Both radiated intense energy. Both had many kids. That first afternoon, Madame Choquette, large with her seventh child, shooed me outside while she and Mother discussed their arrangement.

"Go on, now," Mother said. "Be polite." Hesitant, I pulled on my boots and went outside to meet the kids: Pierre, Marie, François, Philippe, André, and Lucie. Moments later, Mother was gone.

"*Elle est partie… C'est mieux comme ça*," said Madame as my throat closed. Without delay, she escorted me to the kitchen and assigned me my first job— clearing out and washing the pantry shelves then putting everything back in an organized fashion.

"*Avant le dîner*," she said. "*Le reste, plus tard.*"

With a bucket of hot, soapy water and rubber gloves, I began to wash the pantry. I placed the soup tins in alphabetical order, labels facing out, each can precisely centered. If I failed to be exact, I was required to repeat the exercise until I learned what was wanted.

"*Maintenant, tu sais comment bien faire.*" No droplets of soapy water could be left in the bathroom soap dish; the three toilet bowls were to be sanitized with bleach every day; the soap bar wiped free of lingering liquid after each use; and the refrigerator given a thorough wash once a week.

Like Mother, Madame Choquette's cooking communicated all the feeling she couldn't seem to express otherwise. Her roast lamb and browned potatoes with sweet mint sauce, and a moist chocolate cake for dessert, gave me all the energy I needed to complete my cleaning. Before bed, the family gathered to pray the rosary, dedicating the round to my father.

"*On t'aime!*" the children said, kissing me goodnight and cuddling me like warm kittens.

I waited on my basement hide-a-bed for all signs of life to die down. Then I located my trusty smokes and slid out a basement door. "Thank God for you," I whispered to my paper-clad soldiers. I smoked two in a row and buried the remains. Before I fell asleep, I thought about Carlo and Nick and wondered what their first night in our house had been like.

On Monday morning, I was dropped off at the gates of my new French school. Sister Côté rang a small bell and smiled.

"We have an angel for you," she said as a girl half my age and height appeared before us.

"I'm fourteen," I pointed out, more alarmed than I'd felt at my father's death.

"*Oui,* but you do not speak sufficient French to be placed in a senior class," she said. We clattered down wood corridors and entered a Grade Five class. Small children looked up in curiosity.

"But Sister!" I tried again, "I'm in high school now!"

"You'll see," she said, closing the door.

I sat with a story book. I listened to the sounds of language, a sing-song of competency that excluded me. I wondered what my high school class in Fergus was learning this morning. At recess, enclosed behind a fence, I eyed girls my own age examining me, wondering, no doubt, about this tall girl in uniform surrounded by small children. Day after day, I stumbled to express myself in French. I clung to my four-foot angel, not wanting her out of my sight. She pointed to my chair at lunchtime, and because I couldn't name the dishes being passed around or ask for more, I left the table hungry until I learned to take big helpings the first time round.

One day after school, as I washed cupboards in Madame's basement, her husband came home, nodded in my direction, and hastened upstairs.

"*Elle doit jouer des fois, non, Marie? Est-ce qu'elle est une esclave ici?*" I heard him yell at his exhausted wife. At supper, he asked me about my interests, if I liked art or music. We spoke in English.

"One of my favorite things," I said, "is to go for walks. I like that. It's when I plan my future."

"Would you like to walk tonight?" he asked, "after *devoirs*?"

*Devoirs*, I thought, feeling sick. I sat in front of my homework every night. Every day my new teacher scanned my blank pages without comment.

"Yes, thank you," I said, as Madame Choquette banged serving bowls in noisy disagreement.

After dinner, I put on my warm winter coat, the one they'd given me. I hid my smokes and a pack of matches in my pocket. The older children begged to come with me, their mother encouraging them, helping them on with their boots and coats.

"You leave my children behind?" Madame asked me, in front of them.

"Well, how about we walk together for a while," I compromised, "and then I walk alone?"

Everyone smiled, except Madame. Perhaps she knew. Once the children turned back, I lit a smoke and hurried to a corner store with a public phone on Jeanne Mance Street. Out of my pocket I fished the number that Uncle Ed, Mother's brother, had given me at Dad's funeral.

"Any time," he'd said. "Call me at home or at the grocery store."

"Uncle Ed," I burst into tears when I heard his voice. "Can you come and get me? I want to go home!"

"Christ almighty," he said. "Where the hell are you? In Montreal?"

"Yes."

"Jesus Christ, did that sister of mine leave you here? Wait there. I'm on my way." The store clerk gave him directions and then led me to a back room where I waited.

"One parent dies and the other leaves you too?" he asked incredulously as my father's history repeated itself. We drove straight to his house in Beaurepaire, away from the Choquettes in Montreal North.

"You can stay with us you know," said Aunt Jane, as she served me a second supper of stew and dumplings. She poured a glass of red wine and set it by my plate, as Uncle Ed looked askance.

"It'll help her sleep, Ed. Drink it down now," she said to me. While I ate, I heard my uncle's voice yelling in the other room.

"She doesn't need a goddamned language! Her father just died! She needs her goddamned mother! What the hell were you thinking of, Ann?"

Uncle Ed came puffing out of his den just as Aunt Jane was pouring chocolate sauce over a bowl of vanilla ice cream for me.

"You have two choices, kiddo," he said, his blue eyes, so like my mother's, flashing. "You can stay here with us, where you are welcome, or I'll put you on the train to Fergus tomorrow."

I didn't need to think about it. "Home, Uncle Ed!" I cried.

I swallowed my ice cream, along with the thought of how much trouble I'd be in when I arrived at Mother's door.

∾

"Do you have any cotton-pickin' idea how much that Sophie Barat uniform cost me?" Mother greeted me from behind the kitchen counter the next evening. "You can bloody well wear it to school tomorrow and every day after that. Now get out of my sight. The commotion you caused the poor Choquettes! They were frantic. That's the last time I'm going to worry about whether you're bilingual!"

∾

Math class was, in many ways, similar to being back at the French school in Montreal. It was a language I didn't understand but instead of acute accents and gendered nouns, this was a language of xs and ys that meant different things in every equation.

"Don't you see that your solution to this equation can't possibly make sense?" my frustrated teacher asked me after school one day. "Do you have no filter to distinguish fact from fiction?"

I skipped math class the following afternoon, an act of personal survival, and jogged home through the back field behind our house. I opened the back door to Robert Goulet's deep baritone belting out "If Ever I Should Leave You." As I loped upstairs to retrieve my novel, I noticed something unusual. Mother's bedroom door, normally locked shut during her afternoon naps, was slightly ajar. I peeked in to discover her fast asleep in the arms of a hairy-chested man, an empty rye bottle on the nightstand.

"Oh!" I thought, my heart beating fast. "Robert Goulet?"

But it wasn't Mother's favorite singer whose pillow-creased face turned to see me standing in the doorway. It was one of her Jesuit friends. I fled to my room, the priest close behind. I locked my door and refused to open it. A moment later, Mother settled the matter.

"Open that damn door or I'll unscrew the hinges," she yelled, surprisingly forcefully for someone who'd just been napping in tender embrace. I opened up and the shirtless Jesuit grabbed my hand.

"I'm so sorry," he said in a pleading voice. "I'm so sorry to have upset you, Eleanor. We thought you were at school."

A little later, after he tore off in his car, Mother gave me a vastly revised version of the facts-of-life talk she'd given my sisters and me only a couple of years before.

"Come off it, Norda," she said. "Wake up and smell the coffee. Think about it. Can't you stop and think for a minute? These guys entered the Jesuits when they were no older than Gordie, when they were pimply-faced kids. Their simple-minded Catholic parents or their well-intentioned parish priests sold them a bill of goods about what God wanted of them, and they bought it hook, line, and sinker. They only wanted to please. They only wanted to be approved of. They only wanted to fit in. They had no idea which end was up, and it's only now they're thinking, 'Holy God, I've never known any physical warmth. I might die without knowing human love.'

"Especially these guys," she continued. "They live in their heads. They can talk ideas till the cows come home, but in fact, many of them are very lonely people. So don't worry about Father Jim. He's a nice, harmless man. Don't be mad at him. He likes you, and that would be an unfair punishment to a good but confused person."

"But what about his immortal soul?" I asked.

"What about it?"

"Well, he took a holy vow, didn't he? And now he's got sin on his soul. He'll be punished."

"Oh, Christ!" Mother rolled her eyes to a new kind of heaven. "Get off the pot! Those days are over. Forget that silly nonsense you learned. He no more sinned than I did. Stealing from your neighbor is a sin. Gossip is a sin. Love is not a sin."

"Are you going to marry him then?" I asked, still hell-bent on making this right in the eyes of God.

"No," she said definitively. "We'll be friends and leave it at that. Now let's get supper going. And let's not make a big fat drama scene over this."

I staggered downstairs, my head askew, and after supper. released my smokes from their hiding place under my math books. I pondered these new insights, puff by puff, in my room. After hours of deliberation, I decided that Mother was right. I agreed with her in my heart. She was doing nothing wrong.

"Everyone needs love," I sighed. I'd never seen my mother hold anyone in her arms before that afternoon. I didn't understand that alcohol was the agent that melted Mother's resistance to the affection she needed and wanted.

"Don't worry about what the Church tells you is a sin," said Mother, continuing our conversation later that night. "Worry about what you think is wrong. Think for yourself. Forget the Church." I stood there for a moment looking at her as she picked up her new library book, *The Catcher in the Rye*. I saw how Father Jim could love her. I did too.

"G'night then, Ma," I said.

"Goodnight. Now get out of my hair," she replied, a little softer than usual.

~

In 1963, in a hurry to begin her new life, Mother sold the Fergus house for a song. She paid cash for our next home with the money Dad left her, and the family moved, everyone but me, to Toronto. I stayed behind to fail my year.

"Father Ed's going to pay your tuition at a private high school for girls," Mother said when she picked me up in June. "Be sure to thank him when he comes over." Father Ed had been a friend of Mother's for years. I sensed he admired her even more than Father Jim did.

"Did you pass your year?" Mother asked on the drive to my fifth home.

"No, I didn't."

"Well, you can start fresh at St. Joe's in Toronto. Be the top of the heap."

Mother told me that she'd passed her real-estate exams and was now working as a top-notch real-estate agent with a grand company.

"I'm counting on you, Norda," she said as Fergus disappeared behind us. "You'll take over the cleaning. Irene's got the cooking covered, and Brigit looks after the boys and Sheilagh. I bring home the bacon. As soon as you're settled at St. Joe's, I'll help you get a part-time job over at the Bayview Mall. No reason you can't earn your own money for bus tickets and Kotex and lipstick. I'm not paying for your frills."

Now that she had a profession of her own, Mother appeared less dazzled by ecclesiastical brilliance than she'd been in Galt or Fergus. When I asked how her friend, not Robert Goulet but Father Jim, was doing, Mother said he'd left the priesthood and was having a rougher time than he'd ever imagined.

"I'd be depressed too," Mother said, "if I couldn't write a check or figure out how to pay my heating bill, or if I had no idea how to locate a can of tomatoes in a grocery aisle or how to open it when I did find it." I sensed Mother's pride in her new nap-free, pill-free, alcohol-free, and marriage-free life.

∽

Getting my younger brothers and sisters registered at Blessed Trinity elementary school was no guarantee that they would actually go to school. Starting that fall, my younger sisters routinely skipped school to cook and clean and look after the kids while Mother made a name for herself in real estate. Then something happened that changed my mother's life forever. A few months into her stellar career, Mother fell for Dad's brilliant childhood pal, the priest with the high, brainy forehead she'd admired for years. So began a compulsive and volatile relationship that, over time, brought out the worst in each one. All too soon, Stu began criticizing Mother, sometimes about her weight, her "girth" as he called it, or her penchant for garish Broadway musicals. He'd hoped she would at least appreciate *Madame Butterfly* as much as *Oklahoma*. Most unjustly of all, he began to question her intellect. He didn't like having her kids around, either. We didn't talk much about how Mother medicated her dreadful anxiety while she waited for Father Stu's next dose of approval.

If she locked herself in her room, we'd say, "Mother's resting," or if she shut herself in her office, we'd say, "Mother's working on her contracts." But we knew. We all knew she was drinking again. Although she rubbed shoulders with a lot of important people, Mother had not a single girlfriend she could call in the dead of night. She never called her sisters for help. She wept alone in her room. While she could fundraise to help others with their worthy needs, hers were doused with pills, cigarettes, and alcohol. Over these months, Mother's complexion got ruddier. Her hair thinned. When I stood behind her, styling her hair at her bedroom vanity mirror, I discovered dozens of small sores on her scalp. She'd grit her teeth, suck in her breath, and bow her head at the chemical sting of the hair spray, so I squirted it into my palms and then smoothed the artificial glossiness onto her hair. Until my steel comb could tease her fragile strands no more, Mother loved the beehive chignons I fashioned for her.

"There, you look beautiful, Ma," I said every time.

~

In late June of our first summer in Toronto, Mother announced her gift to me, Irene, Brigit, and Maureen, who was home from her West Coast convent school for the summer.

"It's a lovely cottage," she told us. "I'd like you girls to give the kids a special holiday while I work in town. You're old enough to be left in charge, and besides, you're lucky to get to see the Haliburton area. It's beautiful. Your Dad used to go fishing there."

"I can't go, Mother. I'm going out with Jordie Goldman. He invited me to go swimming when he gets back from a camping trip with his Dad. He said the second week in July. I have to be here for his call."

"I'll pick you up for your silly date, I promise."

"You'll forget!" I complained.

"No, I won't. I said I'll be there, and I'll be there."

After two weeks at the lake with no sign of Mother, Irene began rationing food servings. When Danny and Paddy accepted the barbecued burgers at a beach cookout, we were glad. When they came home with cans of beer, we told them to stay away from those strangers.

"Mother forgot my damn date!" I cried. I listened to "Unchained Melody" playing on CHUM Radio, in anguish over the love I might miss. What if Jordie called and Mother answered, or worse, didn't answer, or even worse, what if she answered with slurred speech and then forgot to tell me he called because she couldn't remember answering the phone?

"I'm hitching!" I decided in a panic.

"I'll go with you," said Maureen. "You can't get into a car by yourself."

"We'll be back with Mother, pronto," I told Irene, leaving her and Brigit with the kids.

"Bring groceries," Irene called after us as we headed off towards the highway. "We're out of toilet paper, peanut butter, bread, and cereal."

Half an hour later, Maureen and I were squished into the back seat of a red Ford with two guys in their twenties.

"What a couple of cuties," they said with a grin. They had styled their blond hair identically, coating it in grease and producing a single wave that arced from the center of their hairlines. The driver was an older man in his forties and the blond guys' boss at the salvage yard where they all worked. He boasted that this car, a Galaxie 500 XL Skyliner, had been picked up for a song after a road accident.

"A minor accident?" asked one of the men, smiling our way, flicking his smoke out the window.

"Lay off, guys!" said the woman in front—perhaps the driver's girlfriend— handing me a large newspaper. "Here, read this," she said with a wink as we covered bare legs.

"Our mother's sick, maybe dying. We have to get to her fast," I lied, hoping to gain the driver's pity. Hours later, dropped off on Bayview Street, we hailed a taxi, praying that Mother would be home to pay the fare.

"Thank God," said Maureen when we spied Mother's car parked at an odd angle in the driveway. Knowing Mother's policy of not answering her phone or door after 8 p.m. if she'd been drinking, we didn't bother knocking. While the burly driver rapped the steering wheel with his keys, Maureen climbed through a basement window and opened the front door. I found Mother's purse and, relieved to see the necessary cash, paid the nervous driver.

"Norda, quick!" Maureen flew out of Mother's bedroom and rushed downstairs to the phone just as I came back inside. It took me several seconds to recognize the still, swollen mound of bluish mottled flesh on the bed. A smoldering cigarette burned a sorry trail from the carpet up to a big O up the mattress. An empty vial of sleeping pills leaned on a fallen bottle of Crown Royal. Minutes after our call, two paramedics crashed into the bedroom, shifted Mother to a stretcher, and hastened downstairs to a waiting ambulance.

"Want to ride with us to the hospital?" asked the attendant.

"Not me," I said, suddenly remembering the purpose of our trip. "I have a date!"

"Oh, nice kid," he said, shaking his head. "Very, very nice kid." With the ambulance siren blaring down Gardenview, I called Jordie to confirm our date. His mother said he was still fishing with his dad. He'd be back in a week or so. It took the same amount of time for Mother to recover, shop for food, and drive us back to the cottage, where the kids were eating fish given them by fishermen at the dock.

"Just think," said Maureen after we hid Mother's car keys to keep her at the cottage for a long weekend. "That lie you told those guys was true. You saved Mother's life."

Months later, Irene and I began our babysitting careers. We started with the families on Gardenview and as our reputations grew, we expanded our services across the whole neighborhood. Sure, Mr. Spenser wanted a sickening kiss on the lips when he escorted us safely home as his wife asked him, but we got what we needed: cash and food. I learned to skim tubs of ice cream carefully and to pour cold water into a container after I'd drunk a glass or two of the juice we never had at home. I'd take ten chips or five cookies out of each of the bags in Mrs. Spenser's generous larder. She'd never miss them.

"Did he kiss you?" asked Irene one night when I came in.

"Yes," I said. "He smells of booze."

Together we hatched a plan. Irene would watch for the Spensers' car turning into our street and rush over towards their house to meet me, no matter how late it was.

"Oh, hi there," she'd say, casually bumping into us at 3 a.m.

"Mother was just putting on her coat to come and get you!" she exclaimed on another occasion, causing Mr. Spenser to drop my hand.

When another neighbor, Mrs. Evans, was rushed to the hospital for a Caesarean section, I received an emergency call from her husband. He wasn't good at feeding or putting their two-year-old to bed at night so he asked if I could help out while his wife was in hospital. I was glad for the money. After I put his daughter to bed that night, Mr. Evans called up to me from his basement gym. "Come down after you do the dishes."

"Lie there." He pointed to a gym mat when I descended. "When I say 'roll,' move fast! Rotate to the right and spin off the mat. I need to test my reflexes." When I failed to move quickly enough, he lay on top of me, crushing me.

"You can move faster than that! Try again!" He shook his head with apparent disdain for my lack of speed. Once again, I failed miserably. "Do you like how this feels?" he asked, his hands reaching down to stroke my legs.

"Oh, excuse me," I said, polite as could be. "I promised Mother I'd call her now."

"Sure." He chuckled, getting up to grab a beer from his cooler. "Sure."

Luckily, I found the front door and my way home. Mother said I should drop him from my client list. A few months later, Mrs. Evans found me at the drugstore where Irene and I had started working, a place with lots of people around. She handed me the overnight bag I'd forgotten at her house. "I thought as much," she said when I answered her gentle questions.

"I'm sorry about that, Eleanor," she added. "The more beautiful girls are, the more danger they're in. It's good you work here now."

When Mrs. Evans divorced her husband less than a month later, Mother didn't criticize her as she had Mrs. Roy back in Fergus.

~

Sometimes Mother didn't drink for weeks.

"I'm done with that stupid stuff," she'd say. "Alcohol's a drying agent. It's making my hair fall out."

She set herself a schedule and stuck to it. Grocery bags plunked on the counter meant bubbly tuna casseroles in the oven and clean laundry on dusted dresser tops. Library books hit the kitchen table, and Irene and Brigit got a glimpse of their classrooms. It seems that while the school would notify the Children's Aid if the little ones missed school, phone calls from the school administration about the older girls grew fewer and farther between over time and then stopped altogether. One weekend, a family down the road hired me to babysit on their maid's day off. At lunchtime, the teenager appeared in the kitchen, her pregnant belly huge, her hands and feet swollen.

"I'm Heather," she said. While I fed the babies their lunch, she told me that she'd been enslaved there and made to cook, clean, and iron despite her terrible fatigue. Heather said her employers frightened her about her shaky future as the unwed mother of an illegitimate child. She put her head down on the kitchen table and wept.

"Come to my house," I said. "You can stay till your baby is born, or even after if you want."

"Are you sure? What will your parents say?"

"My mother will say yes. I don't even have to call her about it."

After the unsuspecting couple got home and paid me, believing their maid to be resting in her basement bedroom, I strolled home to find her unpacking in mine.

"Thank you, thank you so much," she said. She looked exhausted.

"Yes, she can stay," said Mother, when I explained the situation. "But make sure that family doesn't find out. I sold them their house."

"Your mother brought me a cup of tea this afternoon," said Heather after school one day. "I asked her about giving birth. She was wonderful to me. She made me feel so much better. She said my life can be good from now on, that it's entirely up to me. I'm the one in charge."

"My mother's a good person," I said.

"Oh, yes," she said, her eyes moist. "Oh, yes, she's very kind."

"Do you think Heather will be okay, Mum?" I asked the evening our guest left for Grace Hospital.

"She's a maid. She'll be fine."

Mother's faith in a woman's capacity to work was indestructible. Her confidence extended to her own daughter Irene who, at barely fourteen years old, set off to earn a living for herself.

With her fine brown hair pulled into a bun, Irene resembled a cameo carving, a pale and quiet Beth from *Little Women*. Irene kept to herself. She loved to read romance novels, as delicious to her as the simple meals she cooked over the three years she and Brigit missed grade school. Once she completed the duties Mother listed for her, she'd dive back into her book, declining my invitations to church dances or walks to the mall.

My siblings had become private people. Perhaps they felt less hopeful than I did, or maybe they knew themselves better than I knew myself. While my sisters watched TV movies with bowls of buttered popcorn on Friday nights, I dressed up for dances, only to come home distressed, time after time. I would be in anguish about not being asked for a single dance. My sisters, who'd stayed home and enjoyed their seclusion, told me not to go to the stupid dances, but I'd make even greater fashion efforts for the next weekend and, with crawling anxiety, head out "to face another round of disappointment," as Irene put it. I was shocked when she left us to live on her own.

One evening after I finished my shift at Tamblyn's Drug Store, a week or so after Mother relapsed into her drinking, Irene was not at her usual place by the stove. Mother stood there instead, stirring tomato sauce.

"Where's Irene?" I asked.

"She moved out."

"She's fourteen, Mum."

"She'll figure it out."

I waited. I looked at Mother's slumped shoulders and at a little red sore on her closed mouth. After a stubborn pause, she filled in the missing piece.

"The Children's Aid visited again today. I don't want them nosing around here again. That damn Blessed Trinity called them. Joey went to school in his pajamas again."

"Did you blame Irene?"

The only reply I received was a ringing silence as Mother retreated to her room. I heard the hated click of her door.

∼

"Mr. Armstrong gave me a full-time job!" squealed Irene at the drug store the next day. "He's teaching me accounting!"

"Me too," I said. "He asked a clerk to teach me the cash. I never thought I could make change like that!"

"Yeah, maybe we're good at math after all." Irene and I turned to admire the kind owner of the drugstore, a generous man hell-bent on getting us trained.

"I told Mr. Armstrong I moved out yesterday," said Irene.

"What did he say?"

"He congratulated me. He said I'm smart as a whip. He said I'll be fine."

"Does he know?" I asked. "Does he know about Mother?"

"He does her prescriptions, remember?" said Irene. "He knows plenty."

"Where'd you go yesterday?" I asked.

"After my fight with Mother about Joey, I ran to the bus shelter. There's always a newspaper there. I thought if I didn't find a room, I'd rather die than crawl back to Mother. Anyway, a guy I called drove right over and picked me up. He lives close to the mall, so I can walk to work. My room is in his basement. He said he could wait till Friday for the rent money. I had to scrub his shower stall, but it's a start. Anyway, I have big plans." I'd never heard my sister say so much at once.

$\sim$

With a tell-tale whiff of rye through her Wrigley's gum and Lanvin perfume, her skin a little too red and her eyes downcast, Mother told us she'd quit real estate. She'd secured a better job in a carpet factory, with a salary and commissions. With Irene gone, Brigit, now twelve, cooked most of our meals, cleaned, and did the laundry. It never occurred to me to miss school, not even once. My dream of graduating from high school never wavered.

One afternoon, though, I did try to help out. I bought flour, brown sugar, raisins, even real butter, every ingredient for Raisin Delight, the only dessert recipe I'd made in the girls' Home Economics class in Fergus. I poured a creamy batter over raisins, lemon zest, and butter, baked it and invited the kids to help themselves before I left for work. My brothers and Brigit said it tasted delicious, just wonderful, that they had eaten every bite, even licked their fingers. Weeks later, on a rare impulse to vacuum, I found the whole concoction still in its baking dish under the couch, gray dust bunnies dotting the top. When my little brothers covered their mouths with small hands and squealed in delight at having fooled me, when little Sheilagh, with no understanding of the joke, copied their gestures with her baby fingers and giggled too, it struck me, as I viewed the spaces between their teeth and little gaps of wet pink gum, just how young they were. Stifling a strange dread, I invited them to the mall for ice cream. I also bought a tube of glossy white lipstick and, at Fashion Escapade, put a down payment on a velvet mini-dress dusted with a rainbow of translucent sparkles. That felt better.

I was fifteen years old when a girl in my class named Gabrielle asked if she could stay at our place for a few days. Her father had gone on a drinking binge and she wanted to avoid the inevitable fallout. Mother said yes. When Gabrielle washed her hair one night, it looked like a destroyed briar. Stripped of the tight skirt and heavy makeup she wore to the Catholic Youth Organization dances on weekends, she emerged a frail sixteen-year-old Snow White. Apparently, she had used Mother's pristine bathroom towels to remove her makeup. Surveying the black-mascara-streaked towels, I asked Gabby if she'd mind using Kleenex and cold cream to remove her makeup instead. She ignored my request, and I said nothing more as each stained bath towel hit the hamper. I wanted to, but for the first time, I'd lost my nerve.

Mother invited me to join her for lunch at the mall, just her and me. It began well. We ordered burgers. Soon, though, Mother's swollen fingers shook so much she had to put down her fork and order a double scotch.

"I gotta run soon," she said, ending my hopes for a special conversation. "I don't want to have another drink. I have commissions to make." She slid some money across to me and asked me to buy a bottle of rye at the LCBO and bring it to her car in the parking lot in ten minutes.

"Wrap up the rest of your burger and take it with you," she said, leaving money for our meal. Mother didn't want to be seen as a regular at the liquor store, nor did she wish to be seen buying a case at a time. Irene, when she still lived at home, used to pick up Mother's rye for her in smaller quantities, one or two bottles at a time, toting it home in brown paper bags.

"Thanks, Norda," said Mum as I deposited the bottle on the back seat and watched her drive over the tarred parking lot to the exit. The cloudy ache I had felt over our too-short lunch date dissipated slightly when Mother thanked me by name. From my pay check that day, I made a chunky deposit on my lay-away plan. Thoughts of my sparkly mini-dress helped.

Mr. Armstrong, my boss at Tamblyn's, asked Mother if I could help his wife, who'd given birth to their third baby. She'd fallen into a depression. She could barely function. Some mornings, he told Mother, she couldn't get out of bed.

"Unbelievable," said Mother. "A nervous breakdown at child number three? Don't get me started! Some of those femmes fatales have no idea what motherhood is all about."

Dropping me off in front of the Armstrong mansion, Mother pointed to their tennis court and back yard swimming pool.

"I have to laugh that women who have everything—money, two homes, cars, and vacations twice a year—still manage to have nervous breakdowns! Look at me," said Mother. "Do I have time to fall into a depression? Do I collapse in despair? Anyway, go help them out, Norda. Pay off those fancy clothes of yours."

I slipped out from the passenger seat, where I'd enjoyed the rare proximity to my mother.

"And phone Brigit and tell her to feed the kids. I'll be late tonight. Tell her I won't be home. Can you manage to remember that simple instruction between this car door and that front door?" Mother never missed a chance to question the accuracy of my memory. I closed the car door and watched as she ploughed down the driveway, stepped on the gas, and sped past the stop sign on the corner.

≈

One day in November, a year after Dad died, there was a knock on the door of my classroom at St. Joe's. Sister whisked over to answer it, her dark veil floating behind her. An instant later, her hand flew to her mouth. The president of the United States had been murdered. We were told to go home.

"Kennedy's dead," Mother said, sobbing in front of the TV screen in the family room, her hands full of Kleenex, red patches splashed over her neck and down her arms. I'd never seen Mother like this, certainly not when Dad died. No one had cried then.

"He was a wonderful, wonderful man," wept Mum, her face puffed with grief. "It's terrible, terrible, terrible... The first Irish Catholic president of the United States—an accomplishment so unbelievable and so great no one could ever have predicted it—such a brilliant, brilliant man. This is so tragic, so horrible."

Mother wept so hard her shoulders shook, and I struggled to understand why this death caused such a dramatic response. One by one, we crowded around her like chicks to a mother hen. At the surprise death of a stranger, I got to see my mother grieve naturally, without pills or alcohol, for the first time.

"It's okay, Ma," said Brigit, the only child Mother could tolerate laying a hand on her. "Mr. Kennedy is with God."

The next day, Sister asked us to express our feelings about the shooting of this wonderful Irish Catholic official none of us knew. "It's good to share our grief," Sister said, a tiny curl of red hair escaping from her wimple. No one said a word. Finally, I got up, stood at the front of the class, and talked about how sad it was that a Catholic family man, an Irish-American father of young children, had died on a business trip, in his car. My throat began to ache unexpectedly and I hastened back to my seat. "I don't even know him," I thought. "Why do I feel bad?" I wrote one question on the journal paper Sister handed out: "Am I a phony?"

Before and after class, I'd listen with interest as girls complained about being grounded for not getting their homework completed on time or for failing to achieve a desired grade or arriving home late from a movie date. On the one hand, I felt relieved I didn't have to put up with any such restrictions. The other hand pointed down my throat, to a bottomless abyss of aching.

～

Gail, a girl who briefly included me in her small clique, invited me home after school one day. She wanted to change out of her uniform and walk over to the mall with me, where the guys from a local boys' school also gathered for Cokes and smokes. In their small bungalow, I met Gail's mother. She stood ironing in the living room, three little girls playing close by her.

"A sandwich, dear?" she asked her daughter, who didn't answer.

"Gail," I said, trailing her into her bedroom, "your mother asked you a question."

"I heard her."

"Are you going to answer?"

"No, I don't feel like it."

I left Gail in her room to get changed and sat down at the kitchen table as her mother prepared a sandwich for me. She buttered both sides of the bread before spreading generous dollops of crunchy peanut butter. A journalist before she got married, she asked me about the novel I had with me, Taylor Caldwell's *Dear and Glorious Physician*. Suddenly Gail stomped into the kitchen, red as a beet.

"You didn't go press that same damn crease down my sleeve again, did you Mother?" she shouted. "How many times do I have to tell you I don't want creases! How many times, Mother?"

Gail's mother stood up for herself but I saw her humiliation. I left their house that day and rarely spoke to Gail again. When Sister asked us to pray for our parents the next day, I glanced in her direction, taking in her small glossy face, her hard expression. I wondered how such a warm-hearted mother could have such an ice-cold kid. Couldn't Gail see how lucky she was?

~

Since I was failing my year anyway, I decided I wouldn't waste any more time feeling stupid. I'd get busy training for my glamorous future as a Canadian fashion model. I could no longer bear sitting in a math class watching other kids calculate what I could not. I decided to subtract my losses and try again next year. "I'm going to study modeling under Dorothy Fleming!" I announced at supper one evening.

"You can study under a Mack truck if you want," Mother said. Everybody cracked up, including me. Mother's one-liners meant she felt well again, alert and sober. I wasn't offended.

"You'll soon see me strolling down a fashion runway," I retorted.

"You do that," said Mum. "We won't tell you it's a gang plank."

~

The Dorothy Fleming School for Models was a classy place featuring a glass French door sprinkled with golden stars. I learned to apply lines of dark color above and underneath my eyes and dust radiant blush over creamy layers of crushed pearl foundation. Under movie star lights, I glued top-quality false eyelashes above my own natural lash line.

"Value yourselves! Set new styles! Look at Mia Farrow! Her self-confidence made buck teeth look sexy! And always smile," repeated Miss Fleming, whose beauty also centered on her friendly, toothy mouth.

Two evenings a week, I'd catch a bus at Finch, novel in hand, read to Eglinton Station, and hop on the subway. "Keep your hips tucked under as you roll, roll, roll gently forward. That's the way! Lift your feet. Don't drag them! People who shuffle along with their feet do the same with their lives as well. Your walk speaks volumes about who you are!"

"She knows her stuff," Mother said when I reported Miss Fleming's comments at home. "She has a brain under all that bleached blonde hair."

One evening, I asked Miss Fleming if I could speak with her alone.

"Surely, most certainly, Eleanor," she said warmly.

When I told her that Mother had fallen in love with a Roman Catholic priest, my teacher extended her long index finger and hit the buzz button of her intercom. "Bruno, bring a Coke for Eleanor and a glass of chilled white wine for me!" She threw back her head of gorgeously sculpted hair and laughed, her eyes sparkling blue orbs of pleasure.

"Oh, Eleanor," she said, "It's all right! Be happy for your mother! Maybe she's in love! Don't you go spoiling it for her now! Oh! This is wonderful!" She giggled, clinking her glass to my can. "Perhaps the Catholic world is softening! Maybe that silly celibacy rule is crumbling now. See your mother as a pioneer of a better future, which she most certainly is!"

When I got home, I told Mother I hoped she and Stu would be happy together. The next day, I practiced my runway stroll all the way to the fanciest lingerie store at the mall and paid the first of a series of instalments on exquisite bridal lingerie for Mother. The negligee I chose for her featured six fluffy layers of apricot chiffon, each as delicate as butterfly wings. Mother loved it.

Weeks later, when Miss Fleming awarded me my modeling certificate, she insisted I go back to high school. "Graduate, Eleanor. Make sure your education is as high as your stiletto heels," she said. "My clients far prefer a model who can discuss world affairs to one whose mind is as glued as her false fingernails. Be a model if you like, Eleanor, but be an educated one."

Mother agreed.

~

In September, I slid into a seat at the front of the class. I shut up. I listened. I memorized facts on the recipe cards Mother gave me. I wanted to pass every exam this time. A week before Christmas, in a gym crowded with two hundred desks, my home room teacher located me writing a final exam.

"I'm sorry to interrupt you, Eleanor, but the Wellesley Hospital called," said Sister. "Apparently, your mother is having her stomach pumped. The nurse said she is highly agitated about the loss of her wallet. If you might possibly have it here at school, perhaps in your locker, we'll send it to her in a taxi while you continue with your exam."

I knew Mother and Stuey had fought terribly on the phone the night before and that Mother was beside herself worrying that he might leave her. Stu said he was having second thoughts again and Mother felt desperate. Sometimes, to thwart my mother's purchase of liquor, I'd hide her purse. Other times, as I did at the drugstore, I stole what I needed. I told Sister I'd go to see my mother after my exam and she let me be.

"Where's my purse?" Mother asked as I walked into a small room at the Wellesley Hospital in downtown Toronto. Beside her stood her Jesuit friend Father Ed, the priest who paid my tuition for three years longer than he'd planned.

"How could you rob your own mother?" Father pounced. "How could you steal from a widow, left with all you kids to raise all by herself? How could you be so unspeakably selfish?"

I fell silent before this big man with bushy eyebrows.

"I'll look for it, Ma," I said, observing Mother's inflated stomach and her swollen, blotchy face. I said nothing as I traced the plastic tubes of her stomach pump to a bucket of acidic yellow liquid bubbling under her gurney.

"How can you be so ice cold?" asked Father. "You don't love your own mother? Don't you care?"

"Leave her alone, Ed," said Mother from her horizontal position. "She doesn't know which way is up." Moved at this rare expression of my mother's protection, my throat clogged, I took the bus home, lost in my new book, *Five Smooth Stones*, purchased with the money I had in fact stolen from Mother's wallet the day before. I called the hospital when I got home.

"Mother?"

"Yes?"

"I found your wallet."

"Where was it?"

"In my room."

"I knew it. Did you take any money?"

"Yes, for cigarettes and a book. I'll pay you back."

"Oh, you bet you will. Father Ed is driving me home now."

"Please don't tell him, okay, Ma?"

"Okay," she agreed. "I won't."

While Mother rested in her bedroom, and before he left for his dinner at the rectory, Father Ed corralled us around the kitchen table and delivered a riveting lecture on the Fourth Commandment. Honor thy father and thy mother.

~

Mother's drinking problem was hardly a secret in our neighborhood, and instead of expressing concern or offering assistance, people withdrew. The Lionel family from up the street used to drive right past me on their way to school every morning, even in the bitter cold of winter, with an empty seat in their car. They turned their heads to the left when they saw me walking along the highway to the right, making my way to the school we all attended. I kept my head down, pretending not to notice the rejection.

Still, some people did care. One early morning, my classmate Patricia dashed into the school washroom to find me in front of a corner mirror, stuffing cotton batting into the small holes in my front teeth with a toothpick. I admired Pat because she talked a lot and said whatever was on her mind. I can still see her green eyes widen as she realized what I was doing.

"It's only temporary," I said, soothing her, as I tamped the moistened cotton into place. "Let's face it, Pat, you didn't notice my cavities till right now, did you?"

By noon, Pat had called her mother and by 4 p.m., I was sitting in their family dentist's chair. Without saying much, the dentist repaired six front teeth using white amalgam and then pulled out a molar that couldn't be saved. Pat did her homework close by and held my hand for the extraction.

"What a shame," the dentist commented to Pat. "She's in danger of losing all her teeth."

"I'm sorry," I garbled, my tongue lined with cotton. I couldn't help the tears that followed.

"Bring her back any time," he said to Pat, adding, "No charge."

~

When I visited classmates, their parents would inevitably shoo them off to do homework and indicate, gently, that I might want to be on my way now. Most of the time my friends did as they were asked. Not Michaela, though. When her parents urged her, more than once, to pass me over, to make friends with better-cared-for classmates, this stunning olive-complexioned beauty with the smiling brown eyes and powerful sense of humor stuck with me.

"Why don't your parents like me, Mick?" I asked her.

"'Cause you're an oddball," she said, giggling, folding her tall frame into her seat in class, right next to mine. "You quit school last year to work at a drug-store, you go downtown at night on a bus, alone, to a modeling school instead of doing your homework, you have family problems, and your uniform hem is always stapled."

"Look at your hem!" I retorted.

"Yes, but masking tape doesn't show through, dummy!" Michaela and I bonded through laughter. We talked about the future, about having children – I wanted two, she wanted three.

We gossiped about the characters in the books we read, what they should or shouldn't have done, how clever or utterly stupid they were. We talked about the importance of beauty, of making our homes and ourselves as attractive as possible.

"My mother says that makeup is not supposed to alter your face but enhance the natural beauty you already have," I recalled.

"Wow, that's inspired," said Michaela. "I'll remember that."

We discussed pregnancy and how, exactly, that happens, and how we'd love our children so much we'd never, ever tell them how much giving birth hurt. We whispered about the cute boys we'd seen and about the travelling we'd do.

"I want to see every corner of Canada," Michaela said.

We called each other to say goodnight. Michaela was permitted a two-minute post-homework phone call, while I was free to talk for hours.

"We're sisters," she said one day.

"Yes, we are," I said, feeling a boat anchoring inside me. I felt docked.

~

"Mick!" I shrieked into my pink phone one day, "I got a modeling job! They said you could come too!"

"What is it?" she cried, as excited as I was.

"A hair stylists' convention at the Royal York Hotel! We'll be the first in Canada to model real Vidal Sassoon cuts. Our pictures will be in hairstyle magazines everywhere! And they pay cash!"

"Oh, my God!" screamed Michaela. "Our lucky breakthrough!"

Pumped for action, we raced downtown on the TTC.

Before we stepped under the bright lights of a camera-crowded stage to face the clippers, we ate *hors d'oeuvres* from a plastic tray.

"Wow, this is show biz!" I said, eating egg salad sandwiches cut in four, crusts removed.

"I feel like doing the Can-Can!" giggled Michaela.

We had no idea our long hair would be shorn so exceedingly short up one side and chopped to chin-length on the other. We laughed hysterically at our cropped heads. On the way home on the subway, cash in hand, we observed passersby, visibly shocked at our wild appearance. We laughed with great abandon at our crazy bobs, the first of their kind in Toronto, and certainly at our school. Mother wasn't up when I got home that night and made no untoward comments the following day, but Michaela's parents were fit to be tied. Mick arrived in class worn out but victorious on Monday morning, and announced that her parents had said we could no longer be friends.

"Oh, no!" I cried in dismay. "Please don't tell me that!"

"Oh, that's what they say, kiddo," said Michaela. "That's not what I say."

My best friend had family problems too.

"When Dad replaced the solid door of my bedroom with a slatted one, he said he did it for better air circulation in the house," Michaela said one day. "But the real reason is he watches me get undressed every night. And he comes into the bathroom to pee while I'm the shower. He stands close to the sheer plastic curtain too long. It gives me the creeps."

"Has he ever touched you?" I asked, my heart beating fast.

"Not with his hands," said Michaela. "My dad devours with his eyes. And don't flatter yourself that your mother is the only one who drinks either."

It took me years to grasp the depth of love behind Michaela's graduation yearbook quotation: "All I ask of those I love is that they let me go on loving them." I learned that she and her younger brother had been adopted together when she was five and her brother three. Mick refused to leave the orphanage without her little brother and so her adoptive parents got two for one. She dreamed about finding her parents and a third missing sibling one day.

"My mother's from Quebec too," said Michaela. "Don't worry, I'll find her. I'll find out what happened."

It occurred to me that at least I knew what my mother looked like. I'd never have guessed in a million years that she had dark hair and blazing blue eyes, especially since my hair was auburn and my eyes brown, like my father. I'd never have to wonder about that. "Your mother must be gorgeous, Michaela."

"My father too, of course," she said, with all the loyalty of her loving heart.

$\sim$

That summer Mother asked me to housekeep for the ailing mother of one of her Jesuit friends. Weeks later, she drove me back to a new address, a brick house off Lawrence at Avenue Road.

"We live here now," she said, introducing me to my sixth home with no further ado. Brigit and the little ones, deposited in a new school, got lost several times after class.

"It's because Mother's closer to Stu's apartment now," said Brigit.

"No, it's because she's escaping the Children's Aid in that locality," said Irene on a rare visit. "You're out of their jurisdiction here."

During the summer, Mother returned to real estate. She stopped drinking. With Brigit attending school regularly, Mother hired a maid, Nina, who cooked wonderful food and did the laundry and didn't get paid for two months after Mother relapsed. We missed her when she left. We understood when Nina said her kids had to eat too.

$\sim$

One Saturday morning, I woke up to a weight sitting on my belly, like a five-pound sack of potatoes. It felt alive. I advised myself to keep my eyes closed, my hands still, and my breathing regular, to trick the foul force waiting for me to awaken fully before delivering, as I knew it would, a death blow into my face.

I remained inert, muscles passive, giving not the slightest indication of consciousness, desperately determining that I couldn't be mistaken, that indeed, a physical unmoving heaviness bulked on my stomach. There was. Over a full moment, one I won't ever forget, I slowly opened my eyes to this criminal presence. I sat up. Instantly, it disappeared. I felt my belly. I lay back down again. I closed my eyes to verify the heaviness, to feel it on me again, but no, it had vamoosed. Nor could the mass and pressing heaviness be conjured up. The unseen albatross had taken off.

"Where's Sheilagh?" I asked Brigit after school.

"Gone." I waited. I knew this would hurt.

"Mother drove her to Montreal. Aunt Maggie drove up from New York to take her," Brigit said. "Please don't say anything to her, Norda, please. She's sick. She's exhausted from the trip. She just got home. Her hair's falling out. She's been drinking."

Where there are no words, there are at least definite orchestrated motions. There are things you can do with your hands. There are routine gestures that create a sense of the unspectacular and the most coveted ordinary. I snapped open my purse, pulled out my cigarette packet, pressed a lever, and the predictable happened. I fished for my lighter. Brigit opened the cupboard and pulled down two mugs. She opened the cutlery drawer and extracted a spoon.

"Have a coffee with me," she said.

Thin and gentle, she reached for the jar of Nescafé I'd stolen from the drug store and dropped dry granules into the empty cups. She poured boiling water, added milk, and carried the hot drinks to the table, every precise action a slice of normalcy.

"It's better this way," Brigit said, pulling at the fuzzy tuft of hair on the back of her head.

"What if she doesn't like it there? She's only six. She's too young to run away," I said, remembering my escape from the French-speaking household where Mum had deposited me after Dad's funeral.

Brigit and I sat together in front of our cups, too clogged up to cry. The lifting, sipping, and descending of our cups allowed the briefest of reprieves. I smoked and Brigit tugged her fuzzy tuft. I took courage from my little sister's presence, her face a study of compassion. It didn't occur to me that Brigit, who'd cared for little Sheilagh every day of her life thus far, might possibly be hurting worse than I was.

"I better get to work," I said.

"Okay. I'll tackle the dishes then I'll make supper for the boys."

We normalized. We glossed over. We had to.

"After work I need to study for my history exam. I have to pass that sucker this time, Brigit. It's life or death."

"You will, Norda. You'll graduate this year," she said, her face a gift of encouragement. I felt no concern that Brigit wouldn't be passing her year, though, no anxiety that she barely attended school, no worry about her homework or that she was losing the hair on the back of her head as fast as Mother was losing hers. The physical symptoms of distress were equally distributed among us.

On the bus that day, my fingers ferreted for the tiny scab mountains hiding under my hair. It didn't help that I picked at them, but time and again my hand somehow slid over the dozen crystal hills, miniature incrustations waiting to be picked by the only hand that controlled their destinies – mine. Mick insisted I stop touching my head and I promised I would. Today I broke my word. Once the bus swung onto Bayview, the hidden decapitations began, sticky red blood streaming into my hair. Later that week, a horrified hairdresser at the mall refused to wash it, insisting she'd only cut it dry, with gloves on. How could it be that even though I didn't drink, I suffered the same physical symptoms as my alcoholic mother? I too would clench my teeth when I washed my hair or used hair spray. When the school nurse diagnosed me with shingles, Mother said she had them too.

Within weeks of Sheilagh's departure, I received a phone call from a Toronto-based volunteer organization that helped unmarried mothers keep their children. Both Michaela and I'd signed up at our high school and I got the first call to escort girls my age from the bus to their new residence, where they'd give birth. I was to meet Brita at the downtown bus station on Bay Street and escort her to her maternity home in Etobicoke, a long way off.

"Hi, I'm Eleanor," I said on the bus platform. "How are you?"

"Nauseous. Where's your car?" Brita, short and obviously round, answered abruptly.

"We'll take the bus." I smiled.

"A volunteer with no car?" Her freckled face fell. "I'm exhausted."

"Well, how about you come to my house and have a nap first?" I gaged Brita to be my age, about sixteen.

"Nice house," she commented after a snooze and a cup of tea. "With a decent place like this, you should have a car, no?" She opened my cupboard door. "Wow, top-of-the-line labels!"

"Really?" I was pleased. I chose clothes for originality of cut, for splash. I didn't know name brands at all. "I do the lay-away plan," I explained. "Two bucks a week."

"I'll never have clothes like this," said Brita.

"Start your own lay-away plan," I said.

"I'll be working for my father when I get home, for free."

"What?" I asked, surprised. "So move out! Don't go home after you have your baby."

"So easy, huh?" she said, staring into my wardrobe, her face suddenly old, cold, and crumpled. "No, I'll go back to hell when I'm done here. I can't talk about it. You wouldn't understand." She turned away from the closet, close to tears. Millions of ants began to crawl inside my stomach as I took in her face and sagging shoulders.

"Let's go now," she said, picking up her suitcase.

"Choose a dress," I ordered. "Once you have your baby, you'll fit into it just fine."

"Oh, my God!" she cried. "I love them all! I can't choose!" She stood, undecided, fingering this one and that, her happiness a warm light. "I can't decide between them. I can't." She laughed.

I swept past her and pushed all the hangers together. "Take them all," I said. "They're yours."

Glancing into my evacuated cupboard that night when I got home, I told myself that I had done the right thing. I closed the door on my discomfort and studied like a Trojan. With the money I'd make when I graduated in one more year, I'd replace that wardrobe and then some. I knew that for sure and certain.

"You passed!" said Sister that week. "You aced your history exam!"

"Oh, Sister! Thank you! I'm so happy!"

On the bus home, I imagined the slick drive to New York to get Sheilagh, with Brigit on the passenger side, the boys in the back. We'd stop for grilled chicken and Dairy Queen. We'd sing along to the Beach Boys' "I Get Around" in the flashy yellow car I'd easily pay for with my modeling money. That afternoon, Mother announced she was back on the wagon, that we'd never see her with a drink in her hand again, that she'd get stable, work hard, and bring Sheilagh home. The next morning she left early, briefcase in hand, her mouth set in a way that meant business.

Mother and Stuey were back on track, their engagement on again. Mother was at work. I passed my school year and, thanks to my mother's efficiency at matching people to perfect job opportunities, I landed a fabulous job in Montreal. Through my Aunt Jill, Mum learned that *Time Magazine* was in the process of hiring young hostesses cum housekeepers for their Habitat and Port Royal suites, beautifully appointed model homes where worldwide correspondents would come to celebrate Expo '67, the World's Fair. Mother volunteered me.

"It'll be good to get rid of you," she laughed when I fell over myself thanking her.

Mother's expressions of affection were always barbed, especially when she felt well. "How can I help you out?" she'd ask by way of a joke. After a pause, she'd answer her own question. "Which way did you come in?"

Mick and I performed a memorable Can-Can dance at my farewell party, ever more certain of our sizzling fun-filled futures. During those summer months when Montreal hosted Expo '67, I met fashionable, exotic men and women, journalists whose concerns for the world were genuine. I met people who fussed over their bodies, their minds, and their friends. I could hardly believe how one small detail could mean so much. Never mind that a flight from New York had been cancelled at the last minute and an entire agenda crashed. The critically important issue remained: "Did you get the fresh bagels for Mr. Greenblatt's breakfast in the Yellow Room?" The famous St. Viateur Bakery, my boss informed me, provided delicacies *"essentiel à une expérience de Montréal."* "A must," she translated in a tone that made me laugh.

I'd been dropped into another world; a world where butter could not possibly be served in formless slabs on plain plates. Instead, small crystal bowls of crushed ice chilled the fatty yellow roses. I learned to set the dining table of our suite on the twenty-third floor, remembering to place a tiny pronged fork beside the butter. I kept wondering, "Who cares?" while making hair, nail, and massage appointments for those who did. Still, after a while, I came to love tucking dainty doilies underneath bread plates the way my mother once had. I began to appreciate that a single touch could lend a sense of history to a breakfast table overlooking the Saint Lawrence River. After all, skilled hands had crocheted the complex designs that made an event of one cup of tea and a slice of buttered toast.

On the phone, Mother advised me to pin the doilies inside my apron pocket so they wouldn't be torn to shreds by the washing machine agitator. "And go for a walk to McGill. There are plenty of flower bushes where you can collect petals to cascade on the tablecloths. Line a cereal box with a damp napkin and keep the petals in the fridge till mealtime."

"Excellent," said the designer, who adored her job. "Your mother taught you to celebrate the moment with a hint of this or a feather of that, to transform the ordinary into something special!"

Soon I developed a taste for smoked salmon–topped salty crackers spread with cream cheese, caviar clustered atop thinly sliced mango, and herring rolled in thin pickle, washed down with what soon became my favorite drink, bright orange juice splashed with a transparent secret ingredient. Several times that summer, I fell into bed after too much of that powerful vodka, disturbances I dismissed as the folly of youth.

Brigit, now thirteen and a half years old, was excited to visit Expo, taking a brief reprieve from housework and cooking.

"How 'bout we get you some blouses and sweaters, a couple of skirts?"

We'd just had a disappointing lunch at a fancy French restaurant. The hot turkey dinner I thought I had ordered arrived in the form of a chilled slice of jellied pâté on crisp lettuce leaves. I didn't know what to say or how to say it correctly in French, so we ate it, disliked it, but finished every scrap. As we walked to a dress shop, I looked at my sister's tall, slim physique and her shoulder-length blond hair, nicely concealing the tuft at the back of her head. I realized that no one had ever once taken Brigit shopping. Not Mother, not Maureen, not me. No one. And yet

Brigit looked beautiful. She always did. "I'm glad you're my sister," I thought as I piled her choices on top of the counter.

"Thank you, Norda. Hey, maybe I will have fun at school this year." She giggled, covering her mouth with her hand, a new reflex action to cover teeth that needed repair.

"It's my pleasure," I said, just as the clerk informed me that my payment had been declined.

"I don't have room in my suitcase for all this stuff anyway," said Brigit. "It's okay."

My stomach burned with embarrassment as I apologized. I knew Brigit loved nice clothes and quality shoes. I'd seen the envelope stuffed with cut-out Sears pictures that she brought with her to Montreal.

"It's okay, Norda," Brigit said at the bus station. "I know you wanted to give me the clothes. That's all that matters to me."

I waved goodbye to her, small in her seat, and my stomach ached as she reached for her tuft, a motion that pushed the pain meter in my chest to unbearable. After she left, I bought what I could afford, a pack of cigarettes, and smoked two before heading back to my doilies and smoked salmon.

~

I returned home in September to an empty fridge and Mother drinking alone in her bedroom. I learned that I hadn't been the only one away that summer; one by one, my little brothers returned from Nova Scotia and New Jersey. Everyone had been deposited somewhere.

"Stuey wanted Mother to himself this summer," said Irene when I called her at her rooming house.

When ambulance attendants whisked her out the front door following an overdose not a month later, I sat and studied in the lovely living room Mother had decorated. I felt absolutely nothing as the gurney banged against the door frame on the way out. That very night I made two decisions. The first was to break up with Ken, my boyfriend. He'd begged to teach me about sex, how wonderful it could be, but Mick and I had already decided we'd only make love with men whose values we greatly esteemed. Anyway, what if I got pregnant? What if I got stuck with a hungry little baby and a big empty fridge? I'd made my decision. My goal was to graduate. After failing every alternate year of high school, matriculation continued to be my dream, my sure-fire ticket out.

"It's all you need to think about right now," Michaela reassured me.

Shortly after she hung up with me, though, she answered an emergency call from Ken. He asked her out on a date, and she said yes.

"What?" I shrieked when she broke the news. "Are you serious, Michaela? Well, you shouldn't have bothered telling me because I'm not jealous at all. So go ahead, date him. I think you'll discover exactly what I did, but go ahead. It's up to you. By the way, he doesn't like to read." Marrying passionate readers was one of the requisites we'd agreed upon for our future husbands. Michaela said something about my eating humble pie and we hung up on each other. As it turned out, they managed a single date and another two weeks passed before Michaela found me in the library.

"Hi," she whispered, a grin on her face. "I met someone else."

"Can he read?" I asked.

"Yes." She laughed. "And he can kiss too."

"Michaela, next time I break up with someone, I hope you'll let me do that without complicating matters."

"I promise," she said. "I don't know why I jumped in to help like that, but Ken said he needed a friend. Anyway, I sure as hell won't do it again."

It meant little to me to break up with Ken, but Michaela's friendship meant the world to me. I knew she cared about me. I felt her love and it warmed my life in a way I'd not experienced before. I knew we'd be friends forever. One afternoon as we were leaving her house, Michaela pointed to a cozy spot under the stairwell.

"That's where my sweetie and I cuddle," she said. "And it's absolutely delicious. You have no idea how wonderful sex with Bob feels. It's indescribable and transporting and blissful. I love him. You know, I truly wonder how I lived before I knew him. It was a half-life."

I was walking ahead of her, glad she couldn't see my face. As we slipped into class, I told her how happy I felt for her and was equally glad that our teacher was showing a film in the dark, a movie I missed. I felt as though I'd been hit with a rock, impaled with a grief I'd never felt before. Later I hurried home to curl up on my bed and weep, aching, all alone, until Mother found me.

"What's the matter with you?" she asked, standing at the door of my bedroom.

"I don't know. I feel terrible." I began to weep again.

"What brought it on?"

"Michaela showed me where she and her boyfriend make out. She said it felt so wonderful. She looked so happy and glowing."

"So? Are you happy for her?"

"Yes, I am."

"Are you sure?" asked my mother, her eyebrows raised high.

"Yes, I am, Mum. I am happy for Mick. I love her. I want her to be happy."

"So what's the problem then?" asked Mum. To her credit, she did edge inside the door. She did sit sideways on the rim of my desk chair across the room from me.

"I don't know. I don't know what's wrong but I feel like death."

"Maybe there's something you don't know," said Mum as she got up to leave the room. "Maybe you'll figure it out later."

I wept as I thought of those flowered pillows under the stairs, and it dawned on me that my best friend was out there enjoying what frightened me most.

My second decision that fall, once Mother was home from the hospital, was to leave the Catholic religion. I knew that in addition to boring me to death, Mass and all the talks about church doctrine gave me a stomach ache. I doubted that whatever the Pope said was as though spoken by God. After all, the Pope had once been a pimply-faced sixteen-year-old kid too. Maybe he had also been sold a bill of goods and bought it, hook, line, and sinker. Maybe he too just wanted to please his parents and feel admired and accepted. What did he know? After much thought, I decided that there was no God story I believed. How could a loving God authorize the death of his son and call that loving? How could a bird impregnate a teenage girl? I decided I would excommunicate myself from any religion, from any God story I'd heard thus far, be that God Buddha, or Shiva or Jehovah, or Jesus. Mick and I agreed that if we'd been born in China, we'd probably be Buddhist. If we'd been born in India, we might be Hindi. I decided to keep it simple from now on. I'd try to be a good neighbor, and leave it at that. That week, I chose my graduation quote from a paperback of famous sayings Mick found in the library, never dreaming of making up my own. I decided that the words of one Thomas Paine, a British-American political philosopher born in 1737, best summed up my personal dogma: "The world is my country, to do good, my religion."

"That about says it all, kiddo," Mick said. "Will your mother be upset you're leaving the Church?"

"Not at all. Mother says we make our own reputations in this world," I said. Standing outside the school gates, I made my declaration. "Mick, with you as my only witness, I officially excommunicate myself, by myself, right now. After this, I'll just try to be a caring person, and leave it at that."

"That's all there is anyway," Mick laughed, giving her assent with a grand show of elaborate motions over my head.

$\sim$

Days before my nineteenth birthday, we moved suddenly. This time there were no old-fashioned door frames or high ceilings to ease the transition from room to room in our rented townhouse, no elaborate moldings to decorate bare linoleum floors in need of washing. No back yard, no hardwood floors. Mother was having trouble paying the mortgage on our larger house, but Stuey couldn't move in and share the cost. The noise would be too much for him. Instead, Mother found a cheaper dwelling for us and convinced Gordie to leave his room near the university. She persuaded him, a responsible grown-up, to live with us. My brother's obedience made it possible for Mother to neglect her youngest children. With my brother as official head of the household, Mother could live downtown with Stuey. Should the Children's Aid come snooping around again, there'd be an adult presence in the home. Mother charged her stepson the same rent he'd been paying to his landlady, minus the fare he'd have to pay for his daily hour-long bus trips downtown.

I hurt Paddy once again, this time over a load of groceries: a big ham, a block of cheddar, a bucket of butterscotch ice cream, oatmeal cookies, brownies, and a bag of chips.

"We'll eat when I get home," I told everyone as I left our new digs with my date, Rick, a student at the boys' school near my school.

When we came home, I opened the fridge to see the gnawed remains of ham, barely enough for a sandwich. I saw no other food, not a scrap or a crumb. The other boys had smartly scattered, but not Paddy. I grabbed him.

"I told you to wait till I got home!"

"I was hungry," he whimpered. "We all were."

I slapped him. When he bolted, I flew after him and hit him again. Rick grabbed me, shoved me out the front door, and returned to comfort Paddy, now sobbing so hard I could hear him from my spot on the handkerchief lawn.

"Let me tell you one thing, Norda," Rick said, visibly upset when he came outside a little while later. "I never want to see you again. What a bitch! You choose potato chips over a hungry little boy, your own brother? What kind of girl are you?"

He didn't wait for a reply. I heard a door slam and his car tear away. After two calming smokes, I went in to apologize to Paddy, who had vanished. Filled with shame, I stole into Mother's room, pried open her tall white cupboard, and helped myself to her supplies. I poured myself the last of her precious rye and downed the lot, sitting in her room in the dark.

"It's okay, Norda," said Brigit. She sat close beside me, gently pulling at her hair.

Looking into her pale thirteen-year-old face, I vowed for the second time never to hit anyone again. Brigit continued to cook and look after the boys she'd been groomed to care for from her earliest years. When the baby bonus check arrived in the mail each month, Mother visited to cash it. She and Brigit shopped and cooked meals we ate together at a table covered in yellow plastic.

One night Mother came home after a full month's absence. I saw her tiptoe past my room, glass in hand, as I styled Brigit's hair. My little sister had made a new school friend and wanted to look snazzy for their Coke at the mall, an exceedingly rare social opportunity for my burdened sibling. We'd found a princess ponytail style that would cover the balding patch on the back of her head and I paused, holding her blond hair in one hand, watching our mother disappear into her bedroom.

"Don't, Norda." My sister just wanted peace and normalcy. I didn't listen.

"Were you at least planning on saying hello tonight, Mother, before you dipped into the sauce?" I asked, ready for a confrontation.

"No," she replied matter-of-factly. "Actually, I wasn't." She disappeared behind her bedroom door, closing it with a tiny click, a sound I had hated since childhood. That click set me off. I dropped my sister's hair, rushed to my cupboard, jammed on my heavy black school shoes, flew at Mother's door, and kicked it hard, three times.

"You're supposed to be our mother!" I screamed. No reply. "Why do you drink, Mother? Why? Why? You can walk, you can talk, you can lift your head off your pillow. You can save your own life! We suffer without you! Stop drinking, Mother! Do you hear me? We need you!"

Still no reply. Incensed, I crashed back to my room, barely noticing Brigit huddled on my bed, biting her palm, watching. On a length of masking tape, I scribbled "Poison" with a thick red felt marker. Racing back to Mother's door, I drew a four-foot tall bottle on it and slapped the label in the middle of my artwork.

"You bring annihilation home, bottle by bottle, to kill us all!" I screamed into the corner of her closed door. The only sound to emerge was ice clinking against glass.

Beside myself, a balloon ready to burst, I phoned Michaela. Her mother answered.

"Michaela's doing her homework, Eleanor."

"Please," I wept. "Five minutes."

"Talk at school," she said, sounding irritated. "It's late. Michaela's tired."

Then I heard some muffled sounds and Michaela came on the line.

"Three minutes!" I heard her mother say in the background.

I sobbed pitifully to Michaela that I'd screamed horribly at my mother, that I felt terrible, that my body was shaking so much my teeth chattered.

"I don't know what's next, Michaela, I just don't know."

"I'm coming over," she said.

"You are going precisely nowhere," Michaela's mother enunciated.

Minutes later, Michaela arrived at our front door, escorted by her mother.

"Fifteen minutes!" her mother said to both of us as she shook open her umbrella and dashed back to the car in the downpour. Michaela sat with me on the couch in the darkened living room. Brigit was now curled up in my bed, Mother was in hers, and the boys had taken off. The house was still. Michaela put both arms around me.

"Let's talk about after graduation," she said.

It took only a day to wish I'd behaved differently. I wished I'd done a lively swirl with Brigit's ponytail and tied lots of pink ribbons around it so no one could possibly spot her bald patch. When I saw the folded dollar bill on my dresser, I remembered the treat money I had intended to give her before I walked her to the mall to meet her girlfriend. I could have finished the geography homework I ended up failing to hand in and then waited for my sister to come home, cookies ready. I even imagined Mother wandering downstairs to join me. That week, Michaela came down with a terrible cold and I wondered if my rainy night disturbance had caused it.

"I wrote to Father Jim, Mother's Jesuit friend who I'd mistaken for Robert Goulet. I told him that Mother isn't living with us any more, that she's drinking too much and taking pills, that I hate that fat ass Stuey, that I slapped Paddy for eating my shopping, that one of my little brothers is coming home with a lot of cash from who knows where, and that I feel like I'm going nuts."

"What did he say?" asked Michaela, shaking two king-sized smokes out of my pack, one for her, one for me.

"He wrote back about baseball! Can you believe it? He talked about Babe Ruth and his way of catching the fast ball by dropping back a bit and loosening up his mobility, and how he had become the best baseball player ever. Now what would I, a girl, want to know about that stupid game? I'm so disappointed. It took me three hours to write that epistle to him."

"Men, so inept!" said Michaela, the vocabulary queen, rolling her eyes.

"Well, I'm not writing him again," I replied, the choppy wind batting my cigarette smoke away.

~

It always felt good to see Sister Charlotte, a retired teacher who would occasionally substitute in our class. She always allowed us private reading time, which we appreciated. One day in class, she asked me about my library book, Chaim Potok's *The Chosen*. I told her that the story dealt with family problems and a son who had a tough choice to make, one that would be good for him but would displease his father.

"Ah, universal theme," said Sister. "Offspring challenging parents' old ways. It's normal. It's natural. It's called evolution."

"What about Christ?" I asked. "He obeyed His father's wishes."

"Ah," replied Sister, unperturbed. "Yes, I see what you mean."

"What do you think, Sister?" I sensed my questions were welcome, that Sister liked me.

"Well, I answered that question one way when I entered this Order at sixteen years old. Today, I'd respond differently."

"How, Sister?"

"Well, I think I'd jump right into my own creative life, yes, dive right in, no hesitation. I hope you do that, Eleanor. All our answers lie there but each of us must earn her own autonomy, so I'll say no more."

I wondered how I'd be creative in my life. Observing Sister's complete and utter absorption in *The Feminine Mystique* by the open window, I knew it shouldn't involve slamming poor Paddy for stealing food.

One day Sister Fran, the principal, invited me to her office. As I made my way through the marbled hallways, I reviewed my conduct. Michaela and I talked non-stop in class. Had Sister discovered the cigarette in the gym washroom? Over the past eight weeks, German measles had increased my absences.

"There's a young woman named Carole in your neck of the woods," Sister began.

"Yes, Sister?" I knew the elegant girl, an honor student.

"Effective tomorrow, she'll drive you to school every morning. I want no further impediments to your graduation this year. You can do it. You have to do it. You will do it. What do you say?"

"Okay, Sister. Thank you. Yes, I want to graduate this year. I have to!"

"Yes, you do!" she said, compressing her lips. "You most certainly do."

She swung open her door to reveal Carole, bubbling about how perfect this would all be since she drove by my place every morning anyhow. I noticed Carole's staple-free, pressed uniform and her freshly washed short hair that fell, blond silk, over one eye. Her nails were polished pink, cuticles shaped round, and the long legs that pressed the gas pedal every school day were covered in smooth, hole-free black stockings and polished school shoes with unbroken laces tied in a bow. Soon after, when I babysat for Mrs. Purdy, I used her navy blue thread to hem my uniform properly and helped myself to her husband's black polish for my shoes. Sister Fran nodded her approval. The following week Sister Charlotte borrowed my copy of *The Chosen.* When I gave her Margaret Laurence's *The Stone Angel,* I briefed her that it included our favorite universal theme, an insistent father demanding obedience. She smiled and said, "Surprise, surprise."

As the school year drew to a close and graduation grew ever nearer, my headaches worsened. Lately, they'd become chronic. "222s don't help any more, Michaela. Something's wrong. I can hardly stand up. Even walking hurts." Michaela suggested I call my mother.

"There's something wrong with me, Mother," I said when I called her at Stuey's apartment, her main residence.

"You're telling me something new?" she quipped, and dictated the phone number of one of her doctors.

"You're eighteen years old," the good man said when I visited his office. "You're graduating soon. Do you have anywhere to go this summer? Any nice relatives?"

"I have my Aunt Jill in Montreal. I met her last summer at Expo."

"That's not so far away," he said. "Go. When you leave home, your headaches will stop. You don't need pills. You need a change."

～

I stood in line, alone, at Union Station.

"Hi." I heard her voice before I saw Mother beside me. She held out a small brown lunch bag containing a ham sandwich with mustard, two Dad's oatmeal cookies wrapped in cellophane, and an apple. "Congratulations on your graduation. I came to say goodbye."

"Thank you, Mum," I said, my heart thumping with shock. I hadn't seen her in weeks. Her swollen face was pockmarked with red dots, her thin hair wisped over her balding head. She was unemployed. "I asked Aunt Jill to give you a few tips about teachers' college in Quebec."

"Okay, Mum, thank you," I said. Passengers began to shuffle forward. It was time to board. My heart was thumping a mile a minute. "I love you, Mum."

"I love you too," she said, for the first time in my life. Our embrace was brief and stiff and awkward, but her blue eyes were as wet as my brown ones. "Be careful," she said. "You're like me. You wear your heart on your sleeve."

Glancing back, I caught only the retreating hemline of Mother's housecoat, the blue one with the white dots that doubled as both a day dress and sleepwear. Once I settled into my window seat, the stone in my throat began to soften. I began to cry. I couldn't stop. A gray-haired conductor gave me a package of Kleenex. Shortly after, he brought a cup of tea with milk and sugar, and a soft cotton cloth. He said nothing as I pressed it to my face and wept. An hour later, he brought more tea with two Peek Frean cookies, generosity that contrasted with my stinginess with Paddy. I wept more and received another absorbent towel, and finally, at Kingston, a soft blue blanket and a pillow. I slept for the last two hours of the trip, spent and exhausted, until I awakened in Pointe Claire, my headache completely gone for the first time in months.

"Next stop is yours," the conductor said. "It's a beautiful afternoon."

≈

That very night I called Bob, a handsome student teacher from Montreal I'd met at the farewell party Michaela had thrown me. I can still see myself standing at the black wall phone in Aunt Jill's kitchen, excited and confident as I dialed his number. Bob's curly brown hair, tall frame, and career goals had impressed me. He dressed like a man should, in my opinion—good pants, quality shirts, and Hush Puppies.

"You're gorgeous!" he said as we danced at the Edgewater Hotel on that star-filled night. "I can't believe you just turned nineteen. Don't worry, you'll get a job lickety-split."

That week I applied to waitress at the Miss Montreal at the Dorval Plaza, a short walk from Aunt Jill's house on Carson Avenue, but before my interview, I changed my mind. Instead, I took my young cousin for a walk to buy the *Montreal Star*.

"I didn't travel all the way from Ontario to serve fried potatoes in Quebec. I can do better than that," I told her, ordering two hot chocolates at the restaurant where I would not be waitressing. I gave her the cartoons and I circled possible job opportunities with a red pen.

"I love you, Norda," said my young cousin, stroking my arm as we enjoyed a slow walk home. Over the following weeks, I helped out at my aunt's house more than I ever had at home. I wanted to say thank you to her. When I washed my hair one evening, I noticed with pleasure that all of my scabs were gone. My scalp shone clear.

The following morning, I took the Greyhound from Lakeshore Boulevard in Dorval into Montreal and was hired on the spot by a dentist who offered to train me. I called Mother collect from a pay phone the minute I tumbled out of the interview.

"I'm making forty-five dollars a week on the most beautiful street in the world, across from Victoria Hall!"

"Where I had my high school graduation," said Mother. "Now you can save for teachers' college."

"I'm the boss of my life now," I wrote on a postcard to Maureen in big loopy letters.

My new boyfriend invited me to a staff party in Kingston, which meant an overnight trip. I wore a beautiful new dress purchased with my first pay check and treated myself to a copy of *Atlas Shrugged* for the train ride, a thick paperback I decided to read even though it was a slog. On that trip, I felt like the vivacious model I'd trained to be. Still, there was a tension, a gnawing discomfort during that ride. Bob was a full-grown man. What if he tried to kiss me?

I'd never made love before. I hoped it would feel delicious and wonderful and that it would be at least twice as beautiful as Bob reaching for my hand on the dance floor or a surprise phone call in the evening. My main concern was pleasing Bob, making sure he was happy with me. During the actual ordeal late on the first night of my visit, the real me seemed to disappear somewhere else, a bird on a high wire of tension.

"Stand on the bed. Straddle me," he said on the second night of that weekend visit. "Let me look up at you."

"What do you mean?" I asked, my heart thumping.

"It's called foreplay. It warms a man up. Get up. Put one foot on one side of my head and the other on the other side. Don't wear underwear. I want to look up, feast my eyes from here."

I gripped the headboard and stood up. Red-faced and awkward, I looked up at the stained ceiling as he examined me from below.

"Now lie down," he said. "I want to eat you up."

Voiceless, I pretended to participate in what now meant nothing to me. I obeyed his wishes. Not a peep from the boss of her own life.

That week, I was fired from my job as a dental assistant trainee.

"You're off in space," my boss said. "I need someone who listens, who connects, who responds. You're somewhere else."

Things went downhill with Bob. I couldn't express how disrespected I felt at his ogling my vagina, a sectioned-off part of my body he preferred to my eyes. It never occurred to me that speaking up might have been the best thing to do. One week night, Bob called to say he'd met someone else.

"I have tremendous respect for her," he said. "She's a real lady."

Utter relief was my first reaction. I wouldn't have to have sex with him ever again. Whew. Yet, even so, over that week, a slow, strange devastation set itself up inside me, a grief I couldn't understand. Bob's rejection of me, despite my loss of respect for him, got twisted around. I began to pine for him, to position him as someone wonderful. Slowly and surely, I began to blame myself. I should apologize. I was wrong. It was all my fault.

"I have great regard for her." Bob re-confirmed our break-up when I called him. "She's a teacher and easy to admire. Her self-esteem soars through the roof! You should try it sometime."

Will you invite her to straddle you ear to ear? I wondered, but didn't say. Somehow, I doubted he'd be peering up her nightie while she contemplated the ceiling above.

"You're passive," he summed up. "Not a big attraction. Men need self-respecting women."

I couldn't cry, though I felt bad. I ached in silence. I looked for a new job. I had bills to pay, teeth to fix, clothes to buy. Wooden, I moved forward.

≈

The first time it happened, I was washing dishes in Aunt Jill's kitchen sink; my youngest cousin was drying. A hand bearing a dirty plate appeared over my right shoulder, and for a brief two seconds before it slipped into the dishwater, Uncle Jack leaned the length of his body against me.

"Oops," he said. "Just dropping off a dish. A dish for a dish." He laughed as I registered alarm. When I served my uncle his meals on a little TV tray next to the couch where he always ate, he took to dropping a fork or a spoon and asking me if I'd mind picking it up, then peered down my blouse.

"You're one shapely lass," he'd whisper, his head close to mine so Aunt Jill wouldn't hear, as though the two of us were conspiring against her. Back in the kitchen, working beside my aunt at the kitchen counter, I felt my face redden. After that, I took to going to the washroom the instant Aunt Jill poured hot gravy over Uncle Jack's dinner plate so she had to serve him herself. Sometimes, in the hall-way, Uncle Jack stroked both my arms at once or patted my bum, letting me know that I wasn't just his special freckle-faced niece any more. I didn't tell Aunt Jill.

But when she returned from a three-week holiday with her sister in Nova Scotia, smiling warmly, looking genuinely happy to see me and telling me what a great job I'd done taking care of the kids and Uncle Jack while she was gone, the truth tumbled out. I told her all about how scared I'd felt. I blubbered about how Uncle Jack tried to get into my bed every night while she was away and how one night he cried on his knees at my bedside. I was shocked when Aunt Jill's sugary warm smile smoothed out like hard icing over a dark cake. In that instant, I knew I'd lost my aunt's love. She gave me three days to find a place to live and refused to discuss the issue again, even when I apologized for upsetting her.

"Save your apologies, Norda," she said, misinterpreting what I was saying. "You shouldn't have lied in the first place."

It took only a day to find a roommate in the *Montreal Star* classifieds. It took only an hour to unpack at Sutton Square and casually promise Lina I'd pay the rent tomorrow afternoon, "when my check arrives," and a brief moment to blame myself for lavishing all my money on new clothes for my Kingston trip. Now, in my hour of need, all I had were two bus tickets to get to one possible job interview. I called Mother. Sobbing, I begged her to phone one of her priest friends at Loyola College and ask him to meet me to lend me some money for food and rent. Slurring her words, she hung up on me. I knew she wouldn't answer another call, not even to tell me her brother and his wife lived mere meters from where I stood and would have welcomed me to their home with open arms. Standing on the corner of Sherbrooke and West Broadway on that blue-sky day, I was a match blown out. Relaxed shoppers casually passed me by, carefree kids bicycled along the sidewalk, and an elderly woman smiled and said, "Excuse me, dear." I wanted to run after her, sink to my knees, and beg her help. A big old IGA truck accelerated close by. How easy it would be to run a little too fast across the street. I could be dead in seconds. I knew, absolutely, that I would not, could not, tell my brand new roommate I had no money.

I stood outside the phone booth facing Loyola College, a place filled with the brilliant scholars Mother admired. That's when I had an idea. Shaking, I made my way over serene green lawns dappled with sunshine and shadow. I climbed the cement stairs of the Administration Building and asked for the office of the rector. When the secretary inquired about the nature of my call, I said, "Family business," and when she hesitated, perhaps about to tell me that his schedule was full for the day, I added, "It's urgent."

She looked at me over half-moon glasses, nodded her assent, and said, "The President will see you in the five minutes he has before his next appointment."

A minute later, I found myself face to face with a familiar sight, a Jesuit priest.

"Eleanor?" he read my name on a square of paper.

"I hope you can help me, Father. I wonder if you know my mother? She's engaged to Father Stu."

He lifted his head. "I was a young seminarian with Stewart. Yes, I heard he's leaving the Order." He invited me to sit down. "So, you are one of the children of the woman he is marrying?"

"Yes."

"How can I help you, Eleanor?"

"Well, the fact is that, right now, Father, and I hope this changes soon, Stu and my mother are drinking a lot. I need money to get to a job interview tomorrow. My mother can't help me today or any time soon, and I thought that since my mother fundraised for the Jesuits so much, I would ask you to help me now. I wouldn't ask you, but I have nowhere else to go. I have two job interviews tomorrow and only one pair of bus tickets."

Without hesitation, he reached into his back pocket for his wallet. He gave me all he had in it, thirty-three dollars, plus six worn bus tickets.

"Eleanor," he said, "I know a lot more than you and I are going to sit here and discuss right now but I want you to know that you came to the right place today."

"Thank you, Father," I said, tucking the money into my pocket. I stumbled out of his office and entered the first washroom I could find. I sat, fully dressed, on a toilet seat and muffled my tears for fifteen minutes. Then I hauled off to IGA and bought potatoes, lentils, rice, green beans, Tide (Mother said it was the best), toothpaste, and a big, plump chicken. There was money left over. Later that evening, when six bus tickets sat beside a fresh blouse ironed for my interviews, I treated my new roommate and myself to black cherry ice cream from the Elmhurst Dairy. I adored the two laughing cow heads on the outside brick wall.

"When did you arrive from T.O.?" asked Lina, an Irish girl with an English accent.

"Recently," I explained. "I was living with my mother's sister for the last few months."

"Free?"

"Yes. My aunt thought I was tops." A sinking feeling hit my stomach. "Not anymore."

"What happened?"

"Well, my uncle drinks a lot."

"Oh, I get it," she said. "He bothered you, did he?"

"How did you know?" I asked, astonished at her intuition. "My aunt went away for three weeks. She left me in charge."

Lina waited.

"My uncle began to creep downstairs to my room at night," I began. "He begged me to let him lie beside me. He wept that my aunt got upset if he ever came near her, that she pushed him away time and again. He told me that when they drank together as young lovers, they'd had a fabulous sex life, but without booze, Aunt Jill froze up like an ice block."

"Wow, he told you all that?"

"Yes, and there were bruises all over my uncle's legs from his stumbles to the basement."

"Did you tell your aunt when she got home?"

"Yes. She asked him about it. He said I must be nuts. Aunt Jill told me to pack up. She called me a colossal liar, a silly tart, and a big disappointment."

"Did you not point out the bruises on his legs to her?"

"No."

"Did you not think of installing a simple lock on the inside of the basement door?"

"No."

"Dumbbell," she said, hooking her arm through mine. "One thick padlock and some strategy and you could still be living on Easy Street."

That night, at my ninth new address, on the top floor of a gorgeous high-rise, I was glad that Aunt Jill had given me the boot. I could see right away that Lina was a good person. I felt safe now, safe and secure. "Now for a decent job and a pay check," I thought. "I'll never ask for anything else again."

The next day I was interviewed for my second dental assistant job and was hired on the spot. I hurried to Rossy's, the grand variety store on the first floor of my building, and bought a French-English dictionary with the last of my cash. I memorized key words and essential phrases that I would need for my job: *dents, gencives, la langue, où est-ce que ça vous fait mal?, traitement de canal dentaire, aiguille, plombage, désirez-vous un rendez-vous?, quand désirez-vous un rendez-vous?*

Lina quizzed me in the morning and I set out jubilantly for work in my clean white uniform. It wasn't long before I learned to distinguish between the instruments used for root canals, fillings, extractions, and cleaning. Dr. Beaudoin showed me the ropes, including how to heat Novocain under hot water so the freezing wouldn't cause as much pain, and how to tap just the right amount of mercury into dry metal powder to form a solid amalgam. It felt good to hold the hand of a nervous child and speak a little French to her. I opened the office every morning, made fresh-perked coffee, cleaned out the Canada maple leaf ashtrays in the waiting room, and booked early emergencies. I polished my employer's white shoes as well as my own.

Every morning like clockwork, the 90 bus showed up to get me to work on time. I waited in front of the tiny Elmhurst Plaza tucked behind the Montreal West train station, and noted that our French-Canadian bus driver looked like Jackie Gleason. While he greeted me with a nod each day, I could see he really enjoyed his regulars, who understood the fine French-language nuances of his riotous jokes so much better than I could. He greeted his favorite passengers, who laughed with him all the way to the saw mills. I got to know the regulars, where they got on and off, and as the months went by enjoyed the good-morning nods that acknowledged my belonging to this community on wheels. In my favorite seat in the back, I put my briefcase on my lap and tucked my feet onto a steel bar. I could relax for an hour each way. One day, I wrote my only goal—a university degree—on the inside flap of *Atlas Shrugged,* which I was still chugging through.

∼

"Stu's a bully." Mother wept on the phone.

"Why do you stay with him, Mum?"

"He's a brilliant man," she wailed. "He has a degree in Chaucer."

"Chaucer the saucer tips this way and that." I made up a little ditty. "What's his fancy education worth anyway, Mum, if he can't be nice to you?"

"I might spend a month with Irene," Mother sighed before she hung up our long-distance call. "I need to think things over."

That evening at Sutton Square, through their open doorway, I saw the janitor's wife dishing up mashed potatoes and sausages. I glimpsed two TV trays side by side, ready for the news hour, ketchup bottle at the ready. I wished Mother and her university professor could do that.

∼

In 1970, Lina raked in a hundred dollars a week on a Monday-to-Friday schedule as business manager of a small trade magazine. I made sixty-five dollars, working from Monday to Saturday noon. Lina said we pocketed about the same though, since she had to pay for an office wardrobe and I got to wear a uniform. One week's pay went towards rent, and there was enough left over for food, clothes, and bus fare.

Lina and I made a deal. Since she got home first, she'd cook dinner and I'd do the dishes. On Mondays, we ate tourtière (meat pie) smothered in ketchup, with boiled potatoes and veggies tossed with real butter. Lina extolled the virtues of flash-frozen vegetables.

"'Far more nutritious,'" she read out loud from her *Chatelaine* magazine, "'than the limp survivors of a long, hot truck ride from Florida.'"

We ate spaghetti on Wednesdays, and on Fridays, fish sticks with a tartar sauce of mayo and relish. On Sundays, the aroma of roasting chicken from the oven welcomed us back from the indoor pool. Once in a while, Lina served Del Monte fruit cocktail with pound cake for dessert. Most often, though, we'd settle for a cup of Red Rose tea, buying only the boxes containing nursery rhyme figurines to decorate the back of our stove. It was peaceful.

As soon as I got a raise, I registered at Loyola and began with a first course called Marriage and the Family.

"I'm so happy!" I wrote to Mother. Even though she didn't reply, I knew she was pleased.

One Saturday, I wrapped my copy of *Atlas Shrugged* in a brown paper grocery bag and addressed it to Sister Charlotte at St. Joe's in Toronto. "I wonder what Jesus would say about Ayn Rand's point of view?" I wrote in my note to her. "Rand says that if everyone sought their own happiness instead of sacrificing it, there'd be no bullies and no war. Everyone would be happy. What do you think, Sister?"

The following week I received a short note back saying that Sister had passed away in her sleep at the convent. I ached as I read it and then, out of the blue, I heard my own mother's voice in my head. "Figure it out yourself," she said. It occurred to me later that my book had not been returned with the note. Maybe Sister's friend was reading it.

$\sim$

Whenever there was a party at Sutton Square, I began to have discussions with myself about how little I should drink. I was most proud when I didn't consume any drinks at all. When I disappointed myself, when I drank too much and began to cry for no known reason, or worse, clung to someone I hardly knew, I suffered the consequences of confusion and anxiety that contrasted with my usual cool presentation. And not just once or twice. Over the two years I lived with Lina, I embarrassed myself a dozen times. After each humiliating episode of drinking too much, I'd make the usual promise to myself, and within weeks of a narrow unvaried routine of work and study, I'd feel better. I'd forget. I'd returned to my limited world, the one where I could cope — until the next time. The word *pattern* meant nothing more to me then than a dress design I cut out along the dotted lines.

~

Two years after I left home, Brigit called to tell me that Mother and Stu had gotten married at City Hall.

"I wasn't invited?"

"The whole ceremony lasted ten minutes, Norda. No big deal. They've rented a big house in Thornhill and we're all moving in together. It's what Mother wants. She looked happy all morning." Brigit sounded like a journalist, reporting events she had witnessed but hadn't been part of—until she whispered, "But they both drank too much last night. I don't think I'm going to stay here."

"Stuey's an asshole when he drinks," Joey told me when he phoned the next week. "I told Mother at breakfast that her scholar climbed into my bed again last night."

"What? What did Mother say?"

"She brushed it off. She said Stuey drank too much and maybe got lost on his way to their bed. Anyway, he found himself on the floor pretty fast."

Soon, Joey and Danny quit elementary school and found jobs at a factory, screwing propellers onto toy planes. Paddy, now twelve years old, was the next to call.

"I'll never forgive myself for not taking care of Mum," he told me, "but I got the hell out and I've advised Mum to do the same, though I doubt she'll leave her drinking buddy. As for me, I'm off to sunny Vancouver!"

Months later, I received letters from a hotel on East Hastings Street, with an English lord's name in the upper left-hand corner of the envelope. Paddy needed money.

"If you can afford to stay at a fancy hotel in downtown Vancouver, why would you need my money?" I wrote back, enclosing a few bills I knew I'd never see again. A year later, I received a call from the Salvation Army, saying that Paddy had suffered an "episode," not in his room but out on a sidewalk; he was both drunk and on drugs. He'd had a mild concussion.

"He's disoriented," said the volunteer who phoned me. "He needs to rest a while, but he doesn't want to go to his mother's house. Can we put him on a train to you? Could you wire us a ticket for him?"

"I live with two girls," I replied bleakly. "Can you ask him to call me when he feels better?"

∼

Over time, slowly, in my own unhurried way, I began to trust a good man. He took the time to teach me French. We laughed a lot. His good humor and daily welcome were important to me. I could hardly wait for Monday mornings. I was falling in love with a married man, someone who wouldn't challenge me to a next step, because he couldn't.

"Look, Norda, it isn't good for you to be mooning about Dr. Beaudoin all weekend," said Lina. "It isn't good that you like Mondays more than Fridays and that you're not dating or meeting people. C'mon now."

After I'd been exploring love from a distance for two full years, it was a woman who lived down the hall who jolted me out of my isolated make-believe state. Meg, forty years old, knocked on our apartment door one Saturday morning. Sitting on the couch, she told Lina and me that she'd been in love with her boss for twenty years. Between sobs, she said she'd turned down every other opportunity because of him, "because of our love." When her employer up and retired to Florida with his wife, with ne'er a backward glance, Meg fell apart over a man she'd never so much as kissed.

"He was crazy about me," she wept, her whole body convulsing. "I know he loved me as deeply as I loved him. I know it!"

"Has he not given you a ring, um, from a pay phone?" I asked.

"Not once. Not a peep. I don't understand!" Meg cried into her hands, sincerely incredulous.

The expression on Lina's face clearly said, "Are you listening, Norda?" as she poured tea for our devastated neighbor.

Seeing Meg a couple of days later at the downstairs *dépanneur* buying wine in a crumpled day dress I knew she'd slept in was the wake-up call I needed. Things changed fast after that. Lina got married. She offered me her job. I took it and quit mine. I rented a tiny apartment on Prud'homme Street, the first time I'd ever lived alone. I registered for three more evening courses. I missed my boss terribly, and we met once for a special and important talk, but thoughts of Meg steered me in the right direction.

~

In a letter from Carlo, I learned about the death of my beautiful Scottish sister-in-law.

"Barb died?" I said aloud, reading the letter in the lobby of my building. I examined the enclosed photo of the laughing woman who had inspired me as a child in Fergus. It was taken on a beach outing shortly before her death. Her stomach swollen, she waved at the camera, her children clinging to her matchstick legs. This could not be. This could not be.

"Do you think this is God's punishment?" Carlo wept on the phone. "For using contraceptives when we first got married, for disobeying God's law, like your Dad said?"

"Are you Catholic again, Carlo?"

"We went back to the Church when the kids were born. Barb stopped taking birth control pills on the advice of our parish priest."

"But Carlo, why..." I began then stopped myself. "No, I don't think Barb's death is a punishment from God."

"I do," he said, and wept more, his faith in a punishing God rock-solid.

Months later, when Carlo visited me in Montreal, my next-door neighbor and I decided to treat him to a night out. The evening that began so well turned strange and dark when, inexplicably, I dropped my head in my hands and began to sob uncontrollably. The next morning Carlo begged me to explain, but I had no reason whatsoever to give for my anguish of the night before, except perhaps too much beer. I rarely cried unless it was during a sad movie. Ashamed beyond belief, I apologized for the unaccountable scene on what had been a rare holiday for my stepbrother.

"Maybe it was about Barb?" I offered. "I'm so sorry."

Over coffee, Carlo spoke quietly to me. "I want you to marry me, Norda. I can take care of you, and together we'll take care of the children. You'd be a good mother to them, that I know. In time you'd come to love me too." Even he sounded unconvinced.

"Carlo," I said as gently as I could, disturbed that I had to point out the flaw in his plan, "you're my brother."

"Adopted, remember?"

"Yes, well, no, I can't marry you. I'm sorry." I apologized again, and yet somehow sensed his relief. I said he'd find a special woman in Toronto, someone he could love, and within a year he did just that.

~

In my second year as business manager, my new boss and I represented our trade magazines at a fire chiefs' convention at the Prince George Hotel in Halifax. I felt excited about the trip—the light lunch served on the airplane, the fancy hotel room with tiny bars of soap and little mountains of fresh hand towels in the bathroom, the pillows piled high on my bed. In our roped-off area in the convention hall, Mr. Normins and I set out our flyers along with dishes of chocolate to tempt good-humored firefighters and their families. Behind a cardboard advertisement of a blazing red fire truck, my boss tucked his Marilyn Monroe ashtray, the one I cleaned compulsively. It bothered me to see her lovely smile ground out by the cigarettes he smoked down to the filter, her body smeared in ashes and butts. When he wasn't smoking, Mr. Normins constantly shuffled his business cards.

"Always take a few seconds to jot down one identifying feature, one salient piece of information on the back of each business card right after you meet, say, Joe Blow," he advised me as we waited together for visitors to our booth. "So when Joe happens to blow by next year, you can ask him, for example, if his daughter, Tootsie, did well at school this year, or if his wife, Flossie, is still with Toastmasters. Little hooks work. Right away they think they're supposed to know you and, if you look a little slighted, why, that helps reel in the ads too."

The last evening of the conference, after a farewell dinner, I was ready to stretch out in front of the TV in my room when my boss knocked on my door to ask me a favor. Sucking on a cigarette, his mouth wrinkled into a corrugated grimace, he confided that tonight was the first anniversary of the death of his long-time mistress, Jean. He told me that her death meant, in a way, the end of his life too. Many years ago, he said, he'd made a mistake. He'd married an intelligent young woman, a bookish type who, over the years of their marriage, managed to develop Crohn's Disease.

"Problems with her female plumbing system," he explained. "But I wouldn't up and abandon ship completely. After all, this is the mother of my children we're talking about. Still, I lost my appetite for her, as you can well imagine, especially with her bathroom moans and groans every night. Finally, I moved to the guest bedroom and left her to it."

One day, he hired a new business manager. "Boy, could she hold her liquor," he said. Soon they fell madly in love. "So, tonight would have been our anniversary," he concluded his story. "I wonder if I could prevail upon you to do an old man a favor?"

I braced myself for his request, keeping my face blank.

"Would you have a nightcap with me? A memorial toast to Jean?"

My stomach cramped. My new book, *Valley of the Dolls,* was waiting on my bed along with a box of milk chocolate buds. How to word my refusal?

"I feel suicidal tonight," he pushed on, his head down. "I would take it as a great personal favor if you'd have a drink with me before bed."

I thought fast. "Okay," I said. "Right now? In the bar?"

"Oh, no!" he said. "Firefighters and their wives seeing me have a drink with you, such a young woman, would think it unprofessional. Too many tongues to wag, ears to hear."

"Well, we can have tea."

"No, no, you misunderstand. Jean and I always toasted with a shot glass of whiskey in my room. One shot and done."

"Yuck," I thought to myself. I wanted my Rosettes and my novel.

"Please, Eleanor. I ask you this favor, this tremendous service to me. Will you toast my beloved Jean with me tonight, a kind of private eulogy if you will? And don't worry, you'll get your beauty sleep, I promise."

In his room, Mr. Normins prepared our drinks at a tiny corner bar while I settled myself into a nearby armchair.

"I'll compose a prayer for Jean," I said, getting into memorial mode. I looked up to see him slide a small vial from his jacket pocket.

"I'll take my medication with this," he said, dumping the contents into a glass. He carried the two drinks over and handed me one. "All right." he smiled. "I can't thank you enough, Junior, but first," he clinked glasses with me, "down the hatch."

The next morning, I awakened in his bed to the close scent of his cologne. I opened my eyes groggily to find him standing over me, dressed in his suit and tie. He smiled down at me, a smoke in one hand. "You were a tigress, babe," he said. "God, I couldn't keep you off me. I tried to get you out of my room and into yours but you stripped naked and jumped my bones so fast I couldn't handle you."

Shame seared through my body, a hot rapier, a slash with every word. I needed to escape my body, to explode in spontaneous combustion, to die.

"I'll wait for you at the booth," he said. "I won't speak of your behavior to anyone and I strongly suggest you follow suit, for your own sake. You may continue, however, in my employ."

When the door closed, I stumbled into the bathroom, my body sluggish. The floor-length mirror reflected dozens of small blue bruises, round, the size of thumb prints, red lacerations, bites all over my breasts, abdomen, and back. My left nipple was bleeding. My buttocks were black and blue as though I'd been spanked. I crumpled to my knees in front of the mirror, spotting Mr. Normins's razor on the back of the toilet.

"In two minutes this could be over," I told my reflection in the mirror. "It would be so much easier than living with you. Mother was right. You're nothing. You're a big fat nothing, a colossal tart, a complete and utter slut." I knelt there for some moments, believing every word my boss had said. Suddenly, I wanted to chase after him. I needed to apologize.

"Get up," a calm, cool voice inside me urged. "Get dressed. Get dressed and get out of here. That's step one."

I made my way back to my own room. When I saw my book and chocolate sitting on top of my undisturbed hotel bedspread, I longed to turn the clock back to yesterday. Flying back to Montreal from Halifax was even worse. My internal organs ached the whole way. It was almost impossible to sit, even on plush Air Canada seats. Mr. Normins downed my complimentary drink and consumed my meal as well as his. "Why waste good meat?" he said.

As soon as I got home, I called Maureen. "Why did you go to his room?" she said. "How stupid can one person be?"

I blubbered into the phone that I had no idea.

"You've been through this before, no? There's always a bottle around these stories, Norda, as there is in this one. You probably got drunk, like he said, and one thing led to another."

"No! I know myself. That's not true at all."

"You know yourself and you're calling to me ask what happened? Take 1,000 mg. of Vitamin C to erase the bruises." She spoke tersely. "Drink lots of water."

Terrified at the thought of not being able to sleep, of having to sit up with myself all night long, I hit the *dépanneur* at Décarie and Sherbrooke and bought a six-pack of Brador, the new brand with 6.5% alcohol content. On the coffee table, I placed four 500mg. tablets of Vitamin C, four bottles of beer, a bottle opener, and a pack of Craven A, the foil cover shielding my little soldiers, all in their predictable order, always there for me, ready to take the edge off whatever I had to feel. I took the phone off the hook. I locked the door. With my record player on, and the alcohol, cigarettes, and a tuna sandwich all set out, I had something to look forward to. Now I could bear to remove my clothes and bathe myself, looking up at the wall tiles as much as possible. Afterwards, I dabbed zinc oxide paste onto the bite lacerations on my nipples, swallowed the Vitamin C, and felt an inch better, even as I watched the tiniest stream of blood marble the white medicinal paste. Jerry Vale sang "Al Di La" while I drowned my shame in two more bottles of strong beer. Finally, finally, at bottle number four, I broke down and wept until I stumbled off to bed. I decided not to tell anyone else about my shameful behavior in Nova Scotia and I promised myself I'd never be in this position again. Never again.

∽

"Mother's in detox," said Brigit, calling from Toronto a week later.

"Is that a hospital?" I asked, alarmed.

"It's a place where Mother can stop drinking safely, with medical care in case it's too much for her."

"How'd she get there?"

"By herself," Brigit said, a hint of hopefulness lighting up her voice. "She called up herself. She wants to get better. She wants to leave Stu."

"That's good news!" A gentle breeze flounced my lace window curtain like a dance skirt.

"She calls me every day," said Brigit, growing excited. "She met a wonderful friend there, the best friend she's ever had!"

"That's wonderful!"

"Yes, Mother says they laugh all the time together. They help each other live through the treatment. She said their counselors have a method, but it doesn't work for her and Madge."

"What's the method?"

"They shame you. They reduce you to nothing, to the lowest of the low."

"Oh, no!" said I, the door-kicker, the poison bottle artist. "How dare they upset Mum!"

"She's all right, Norda," Brigit assured me. "She has Madge. Mum said she's never laughed so hard in her life. She said she's never had a true friend before."

A trail of people marched across my mind—Mother's committee friends, the Jesuits, Mother's sisters, the Carmelite nuns. By fundraising for them, Mother earned her association with socialites, but she never let her hair down with them. No matter how much money she fed the church, a sharp divide persisted. Perhaps, with all pretense stripped away, friendship was easier in a detox center?

∼

That day I registered for three night courses and calculated that I'd finish university by December 1974.

"What do you want to do with your degree?" asked the registrar when I went to pay. I drew a blank. "Are you preparing for nursing or teaching or social work? What are your plans?"

"Gee, I don't know yet," I replied, surveying the scaffolding outside the Science building.

"Well, you're awfully enthusiastic for someone who has no idea where she's going," she said with a laugh.

Standing there, I imagined inviting Mother to my graduation ceremony. She'd wear her blue silk dress and matching blue satin shoes, my sisters at her side. That's what I wanted. That was my plan.

A month later, Brigit called again. "Mother can't stop crying. Madge died."

"What happened?" I asked. At times like this, I felt a heavy weight on my stomach, an instant pressure, a dark force that signaled terror.

"Her husband came home and couldn't find her. He was standing at the kitchen sink when he saw a strange lump outside the window and a row of sunflowers drooped over a curled-up mound on the ground. Her husband said he knew. He knew the lump was Madge."

"Oh, no!" I visualized tall yellow flowers bent in grief.

"Madge filled her watering can with Beefeater gin, rolled the empties into the *Globe and Mail*, and dumped them into the garbage pail in the garage. She took pills and drank herself to sleep in the garden."

"Why she didn't call Mum? Her best friend," I asked, blocking out the thought of how I'd silenced myself about Mr. Normins. I had also hidden in my darkest hour.

"I don't know. I'm going over to see Mum. She's fit to be tied."

∼

After a last-ditch effort to earn Stu's love, Mother was on the run. When she knocked on my door in Montreal early one Saturday morning, I wasn't alone. The night before her arrival, completely forgetting that she was coming the next day, I went to a party. While everyone else drank reasonably, I did not. I barely remember accepting a ride home with a guy I didn't even know. This was my mother's first visit to my new home, and she sized up the situation immediately.

"My friend is leaving now," I said. He tore off and I never saw him again, and wouldn't have recognized him if I did. I apologized profusely, drowning in shame, a terrible headache coming on fast. I'd been awfully drunk the night before.

"Did you forget I was coming?" she asked.

"I honestly don't know how I could possibly have done that, Mother. I don't," I said.

"Maureen told me you're having a rough time these days." Mother glanced towards the door.

Serving Mother a coffee and myself three aspirins, I berated myself. "If only I'd stayed home last night and studied. I could have done my laundry, gone to bed early, and today would be a sunny, happy day with my mother. I'd feel strong. I could take good care of her. Instead, I'm a mess, a mass of crawling nerves, and yes, a colossal tart. On top of it, I don't remember a thing."

Mother looked smaller than I'd ever seen her, almost shriveled. Her shoulders slumped and her head hung low over a shorter, heavier body. Her blue eyes, vestiges of dappled yellowish green around one of them, were tired and watery. She looked old. Mother told me that when he drank, Stu punched, his arms lashing out so fast that even he claimed to be shocked afterwards. On his knees, he'd apologize pitifully. He'd weep into Mother's open palms and she'd forgive him with all her heart. Within days, though, he'd lash out again. He'd torment her by mentioning another woman, a cultured madam whose skin wasn't splotched with red dots and whose familiarity with classical music surpassed Mother's meagre repertoire.

"She's slim to boot," said Mother.

"I hope you leave him for good this time, Mother," I said. "Please stay here."

"No," she said quickly, stirring my shame. "Irene's better equipped than you to take care of me right now."

Before she left, Mother agreed to hear me read my latest essay, about Portia, a character in *The Merchant of Venice*, out loud. Before I read it, I told her that in the children's section of the library, I'd found a book of Shakespeare's plays rewritten into children's stories. I explained that the simplified illustrated versions helped me to understand the themes of the original plays. Mother and I marveled that back in the 1800s, a brother and sister, Charles and Mary Lamb, sat at their farm kitchen table on long cold winter nights and transformed the dramas into simple tales.

"Your teacher doesn't mind you reading a children's version?" asked Mother.

"No! She wanted copies to read to her own children."

Pouring more coffee, I told Mother about another professor who'd asked our class about our favorite artists. When I replied that I liked Norman Rockwell's self-portrait reflected over and over again in a diminishing hallway of mirrors, my teacher had burst out laughing, the rest of the class joining in. I told Mother how hurt I'd felt before my friend Sandra stood up for me.

"What did she say?" asked Mother, lifting her cup to her lips.

"She asked him, 'Is Norman Rockwell beneath your contempt? Does this artist not fit into your time-honored old boys' club of preferred artists? All you have accomplished this morning is the public humiliation of one of your students, Eleanor, in front of her class. Now how artful is that?' Then she paused dramatically and added, 'I'd like you to apologize.'"

"What did he do?" Mother was rapt.

"The professor stood in front of Sandra, Mum. He stared at her. Then he turned to me and said, 'I am very sorry for my thoughtlessness, Eleanor.'"

"He apologized?" asked Mother incredulously.

"Oh, yes, he did, Mum. And he fell madly in love with Sandra too."

"That's something," said Mother, turning to gaze out the window. "A university professor apologizing to a student?"

"Yeah," I said, glad Mother seemed impressed.

I managed to put together a good meal before her trip back but self-loathing crept in as I watched her get on the train. My brain was festering with "could-haves."

"You blew your chance," I accused myself. "You and Mother could have lived together. It could have been wonderful! You could have taken care of her, watched her get better, and blossom. You could have bought a house together. The whole family could have had cozy Sunday dinners like other families do. How could you forget your own mother was coming? How could you be so damn stupid?"

I didn't buy beer the night Mum left, the last time I saw her alive. Instead, my cigarettes nestled in my pocket, I walked to the grounds of Villa Maria, over to Sutton Square and back home. The next day I quit my job. I insisted my boss fire me so I'd get unemployment insurance while I studied full-time. I got my hair cut short, a Vidal Sassoon cut. I did my laundry and cleaned the apartment. That night I took a bath and climbed into bed with a cup of hot milk.

"Whoever cares about me," I prayed out of habit, "please, please help me become a better person."

$$\sim$$

One evening after class, I spied a thick black arrow pointing to an AA meeting in the basement of Loyola Church on West Broadway Street. I decided to attend. I didn't want to drink again, ever. Perhaps such a meeting would strengthen my resolve. At the door, a gray-haired gentleman welcomed me and pointed to the coffee urn. Ahead of me, a woman Mother's age filled her cup only one-quarter full with shaking hands, afraid she'd burn herself if she shook the hot liquid out of her cup.

I took a seat off to one side and listened as the speaker described thirty years of alcohol abuse resulting in the loss of his four-door truck, his prestigious job, his house, his children's respect, and lastly, his wife. He described his parents, war survivors, daily drinkers too shell-shocked to quit until they were hauled off to a nursing home where strangers changed their diapers and fed them baby food. The speaker's new wife, pale and worn, smiled from her folding chair in the front row.

"I'm a lucky man," he said, beaming at her. "I have the best girl in the world behind me now, and I'm not going to screw it up again. With the help of my Higher Power, whom I personally choose to call Jesus Christ, the Big Book of Alcoholics Anonymous, and the Biggest Big Book of all, I'm saved from my disease for another twenty-four hours. Tonight, no matter what happened in the past, you are looking at the happiest man on earth."

"The Biggest Big Book of all is the St. James Bible," whispered the gentleman beside me, in case I didn't get it. The meeting closed with an Our Father. I was twenty-four that night, done with alcohol and likewise done with any religious cults. I was glad I went to the meeting, equally glad to leave.

~

At the end of the spring session, before the summer courses began, I decided to get away for a while. When he heard I'd decided on Scotland, a friend asked me to visit his mother there. When I met Ellen Mac at her home in Glasgow, we became instant friends. She laughed at my funny stories about her son's exploits in Montreal. She told me she was ill with cancer once again, and she doubted she'd recover this time. Soon she began recounting her own life, a gift of memoir shared with no one else but me. I'd planned a whirlwind ten-day tour, but ended up staying longer at Ellen's invitation. One afternoon, I noticed that Ellen's feet were alarmingly swollen and I massaged them as I listened to her stories.

"Look at your Nureyev feet!" said her husband an hour later, bearing a tray of demitasse cups filled with espresso to her bedside. As I lifted my cup to my lips, I had the warmest sense that we were a loving circle, a small family.

"I've never talked about myself, you know, never," said Ellen, shooing her husband away for hours at a time. "I wish I had. I'm having so many insights about my life. It's wonderful that you are here, Eleanor."

"Thank you," I said, depositing her words, one by one, into my heart. I felt their soft impact and warmth. Something important was happening, something far more valuable to me than bumping along on a tourist bus to see hills and flowers and stray sheep.

Days later, Mr. Mac carried soft pillows to the car and I held Ellen's hand as she settled into the back seat for our drive to the hospital. Soft blue veins beneath transparent flesh traced rough lines up her arms, yet I could see the child in her face and the beauty of a young girl, and I told her so.

"A right raving beauty!" called her husband from the front seat. "I've been besotted since the day we met."

"Yes," said Ellen. "Besotted is the correct word."

The doctor insisted that she remain in the hospital.

"But I'm here!" I said. "I can help look after her. I want to!"

"No," said the doctor. "You can't inject morphine. She'll be needing a steady supply now."

I regaled Ellen with more funny tales of her son, his wild epistles about British politicians, the Queen, Prince Charles, and an Australian woman at Sutton Square who, he claimed, swung her ample hips farther and wider than the Sydney Harbour Bridge.

"I haven't seen her laugh so hard since Douglas last visited!" said Mr. Mac. I wondered why their son had not been called. On our walk back to the car that evening, as he pointed out the filigreed façades of Scottish architecture, a heavily made-up woman stepped out of a doorway to greet Mr. Mac as though she knew him. When she saw me, she adopted a formal tone.

"Do you have the time, sir?" she asked.

He shook his head and kept walking. "A prostitute," he said. "If ever they're stopped by the police, they defend themselves by saying they were only asking the time. But we know what that really means, of course."

The car felt tomb-like without Ellen. After supper, he read Tennyson's *Iona*.

"Sit beside me," he said. "I'll tell you why." He pulled back the curtains of his bay window facing the street and we sat side by side. He slid one arm over my shoulders and juggled his poems in the other.

"My arch rival down the road will be driving home soon." He chuckled. "It will be my sheer delight for him to see me sitting here next to a gorgeous young woman. Let him take that news home to his stringent harpy of a wife, and long after their condemnations are done, he'll still wish he could be me."

I understood, in that moment, that Ellen had been living with a child all these years. As he read about craggy mountains that echoed the lament of Paris' lover, her sadness that his lust for power came first before love, I realized that Ellen must have been disappointed. His offer of brandy was easy to decline. Instead, I went to bed early, warmed by the gift of Ellen's friendship and her life story, and fell asleep easily. Hours later I awakened to the sensation of a warm paw on my breast and unmistakable brandy breath.

"Please," he said. "You helped my wife, now me. I'm a wonderful lover. I've learned from the best teachers in the world. I can make you feel things you've never, ever felt before nor will again, from any other man."

"No." I pushed him back into his room. "Now get some sleep." I heard him weeping until I fell asleep again, this time with my door locked.

"See how well things go when you don't drink?" celebrated my inner voice when I woke up in the morning, refreshed and hungry for the bacon already sizzling. Mr. Mac said not a word about his late night visit, nor did I, as we drove to my tour bus heading to the Isle of Skye. But first, a morning visit to Ellen. As her husband hastened off in search of tea, Ellen smiled at me, scanning my face.

"Did Himself try to crawl into your bed last night?"

"Yes," I said, "but I got him back to his room. I had a good sleep!"

"Good girl," she said. "I forgot to tell you to lock your door."

We rolled our eyes and smiled at each other, two women in the know.

"His boozing and sexing cost me plenty, I guess. That's the most I've said about it to anyone," she said, fingering the morphine tube extending from her arm. "I stuck with him, though. I honored my vows."

That afternoon, thistle bloomed purple against miles of green as my tour bus drove to the Isle of Skye. I sat beside a woman who smiled and introduced herself to me as a poet and teacher. Kindly, all that sunny day, she shared the country's fascinating stories, her Canada lapel pin sparkling as she talked. "Scotland is a country of rich erudition and murderous violence," she said. It seemed important to this generous scholar in her sixties that I understood and benefitted from my trip.

"Thank you so much," I said at supper. "I learned my Scottish history today."

In the wee hours of the night at the inn, I awakened to the sound of sobbing. I tiptoed down the hall. "Catherine?" I whispered. She opened her door, her face swollen with grief.

"I didn't mention that my husband died three weeks ago," she said. "My son thought this trip would be good for me. Well, it's not!" I went in and closed the door as she sat on her bed and wept. She got back into bed and I sank into a comfy armchair beside her.

"My husband was a wonderful, wonderful, wonderful man." She began to tell me about the first time she met her beloved in St. Catharine's, Ontario, a story of friendship and then love that gladdened her life for thirty-five years. Sipping midnight tea, Catherine detailed their lives together, so much happier, I reflected, than Ellen's.

"I'm so impressed," I said.

"I've known the best love this life could offer," she said, holding her still-warm cup. "Now, how do I find a way to live without him?"

"I once read that true love continues long after death. I guess you'll be experiencing that now, eh?"

"Yes, I hope so," she said with a smile, large tears spilling over deep laugh wrinkles.

"I hope I find love like yours, Catherine," I said. "That would be a miracle and a half for this cat."

Mr. Mac was waiting for me at the Glasgow bus depot. He was brisk.

"Let's head to the infirmary. My wife's not doing well." It was the first time I'd heard him refer to her as his wife. Things must be bad. When we arrived at the Royal Infirmary, Ellen lay exhausted. Her feet were huge again, two swollen boots. I began to massage them, trying to push the water back up her legs, until she lifted a finger.

"Thanks, my darling." She smiled. It would be our last visit. The next morning I unlocked my bedroom door and learned that Ellen had died at first light.

"We have to stop off at a friend's house," Mr. Mac said in the midst of making funeral arrangements.

I dressed for Ellen that day. I wore my purple velvet dress, high heels, a dark choker, and my gold chain bracelet I'd bought in Ireland two years earlier.

"Lady McKenzie is an extraordinary woman," Mr. Mac explained in the car. "And a wise one. No matter what stupidities I've managed to invent nor how frequently I've embarrassed myself in this sorry vale, she insists I try again."

On a tree-lined residential street, I watched him open her crystal glass front door with his own key. I sunk an inch into royal blue carpets over sparkling hardwood floors and followed him three flights up a circular staircase to her serene office. A wide couch, its back to the window, faced a small sofa with supportive arm rests. Leafy tree tops outside an open Tudor window tossed dappled shadows onto her book shelves, which were filled with selected biographies, history, and psychology books. I thought that one day I'd love to read them all.

"Dame McKenzie's my mentor," he said, placing an envelope on her desk.

"Is she married?' I asked.

"No, no, no." He was becoming impatient. "She's no time for that nonsense."

"Did she ever marry?" I persisted. With a mounting intensity I couldn't understand, I needed to know.

"Yes, but it didn't work out well."

"Are you in love with her, Mr. Mac?"

"Oh, God, no," he replied, reverentially. "She'd never uncross her legs for me, nor would I ever qualify."

That evening of Ellen's death and Lady McKenzie's absence, he shared parts of his story with me, including sex, as an adult, with real pigs at wild orgies in Cairo during his business trips, stories I listened to but didn't believe possible.

"I want to tell you something, my darling," Mr. Mac said, pressing a small gold ring into my palm. "I want to tell you what I see in you." I turned to face him.

"You're a thoroughbred," he said. "Like my wife. Like Lady McKenzie. Remember I said that, for that is what you are."

$\sim$

I looked forward to my flight home and to new beginnings.

As my plane sat on the runway, I peeked out the window for one last look. There he stood, a dapper Scottish gentleman clearly distinguishable at the head of the crowd, waving to me. He was alone now. Without Ellen. Within hours, a small blue ache in my belly would swell to a bruise of anguish that pressed the grief far up my chest and into my throat. I chose a liquid solution, and this thoroughbred arrived home a donkey, led out on all fours, a real mess. I had completely forgotten that Maureen and her husband were meeting my flight from Scotland. They'd travelled all the way from Ottawa to welcome me. Their disappointment clearly visible, they drove me to my apartment. Our welcome supper was cancelled. Maureen left me a bottle of Vitamin C and suggested I get right to bed. For months afterwards, I couldn't seem to cope with anything more emotional than office work and studying known facts in the library.

When I was ready to re-visit something resembling a social life, Maureen re-introduced me to the Reillys. "Remember the family in Amos we met on our cross-country trip in 1960?" she asked. "Remember Dad's old friend Stan, and his wife Edna?"

I did, vaguely.

"Well, they live here in Montreal now, and we're invited to a housewarming dinner."

Edna, now in her fifties, the mother of ten, had aged since she showed us how well her youngest, a handicapped boy, could pick up Cheerios from his high chair tray. Even though she cooked a fine spread for this celebration, the roast ham, pineapple rings nailed with giant cloves, and scalloped potatoes didn't fool me. The creases around Edna's eyes were not laugh lines.

"Call me Senior," said her husband, who appeared entirely unchanged.

The youngest son's constant refrain of "Yes, Dad, you're right, Dad," made me queasy, but I loved seeing Catherine and Gerry so grown-up, no longer babies snuggled on their older brother's lap. A young teen now, Catherine's blond hair shone bright and her attentive blue eyes noticed everything. Gerry, though, looked red-faced and embarrassed, as though he was keeping a secret, maybe a burdensome one he couldn't figure out. I asked after Stan Junior, Edna's eldest son, her right-hand man.

"He's studying to be a priest," she said, beaming. "We're very proud."

"Too bad," I whispered to Maureen as we filled our plates. "What a handsome guy."

Within weeks of that first visit, Edna up and left her husband. She'd wanted out for a long time, and moving to Montreal had opened up sources of help and support. Soon, though, things got nasty. Senior believed that if she left him, for whatever reason, she was no longer entitled to the contents of his wallet. Edna fell upon the good graces of social welfare, barely sufficient for a meagre apartment and food for the youngest three, who were still under her care. One day, Senior, the impressive friend my father once admired, called to invite me to lunch at the Jockey Club at Westmount Square. He made no mention of how he figured out where I worked nor of his recent separation. As I munched on a Jockey Burger, he detailed his life's accomplishments for me while I waited to ask how his youngest children were doing, and about my father. Before I had a chance, it was time for me to get back to work.

"Come for supper on Sunday. We'll talk about your father then. I have lots of stories."

That Sunday he looked confident. After the meal, I sat on the couch and he sunk himself precisely beside me, pressing close. "May I kiss you? You'd like that, wouldn't you?" Without any hesitation, he pressed his mouth to mine and held it there. "Did you enjoy that?" he asked.

I got up to make myself a cup of tea. Then I said I had to leave. I had a test on Monday.

"You can study here," he offered. "We'll be a team, me and you, you and me." He pulled me into his arms. "Let's not worry about the age difference. You know," he added, "I think your father would smile upon our union. Who knows, maybe he engineered this for me."

"I have an appointment," I lied, desperate to escape.

~

"What did you go there alone for?" asked Maureen on the phone.

"He said he would tell me stories about Dad," I said. "He was Dad's friend, Maureen."

"Oh, for God's sake, Norda. Do you think he'd have invited you if you were sixty years old? Use your head. Think. Don't ever go there alone again."

"Believe me, I won't!"

I understood that Senior had no desire to share stories about my Dad after all, no intention of honoring the best friend of his youth by being fatherly towards me. His only requirement was submission to command, and objections would have consequences. Even though Edna bore and raised their ten children, she was tossed aside like a gum wrapper for ever daring to complain.

I decided that living alone might not be such a good idea. I needed fun friends my own age. As soon as I could, I collected three people on the basis of their decency and availability and moved into my twelfth home, a four-bedroom flat close to the Loyola campus.

~

All my life, I've loved answering the phone, its ring jingling hope. What a thrill to find out who'd been thinking of me, the surprise person who'd dialed my number. In my new flat, I bought a tiny table for the hallway telephone, with an extra-long extension cord so I could wiggle it under my doorway and talk from my bed. I dashed out of my room early that Saturday morning in August, the French door grazing my leg in my eagerness to answer the early jangle. It was Maureen. My sister didn't waste words.

"Norda, Mother's dead."

"What do you mean?"

"She fell over her balcony in High Park." I noticed a chip off the orange paint of the telephone stand. I recognized rosewood in the exposed area and wondered why anyone would paint over good wood in the first place. I glanced at the bed I'd just leapt out of to answer the phone, the tie-dyed sheets twisted at the base, my rose blanket on the hardwood floor where it had fallen, soft and soundless.

"We'll pick you up in two hours," Maureen said. "Please don't keep us waiting."

With a terrible compulsion to make my bed, I moved fast. I grabbed the top sheet and stretched it to the head of the bed, smoothing out wrinkles and mitering the four corners as tightly as Mother had taught me in Fergus. "Tight, tight, so the whole thing doesn't fall apart the minute you lie down!" In one fell swoop, I resurrected the tumble of pink from the hardwood and flew it over the bed, wide wings falling gently and evenly on both sides. I placed my pillow precisely on the crease line of the bedspread and managed to cover it entirely, no part left exposed. Turning to the closet, I dragged out Dad's old plaid suitcase, filled with his heavy albums of our happy family. I dumped the lot onto one side of my bed and refilled the empty space with two packs of Du Maurier King Size, matches and, carefully, so they wouldn't clink, several beers and a bottle opener folded into a soft car cushion. I'd thought of everything.

I didn't feel a thing. Nothing. My heart beat a little faster, but that was all. I'd spoken to Mother the day before. She was agitated, upset about Stuey, a man she still called "Father" from time to time. Mother suspected he was running around, sleeping with women he met at drinking parties, just as her own father had done in St. Henri during the War. In my first hour of shock, which would last for years, the thought of seeing my brothers and sisters comforted me. It would be our first visit together in ages. I knew Gordie would be lending the boys money for their fares. My younger brothers worked only part-time, sometimes here, sometimes there, temporary jobs that never seemed to pan out. The girls did much better. We could cook and clean. We could type. Unlike my younger brothers, we knew how to be polite around rough-edged, thoughtless people without managing to lose our pay checks in the process. The boys lacked those skills. I wondered if Joey, now in his late teens, would be allowed out of his detention center for Mother's funeral. When a police officer failed to speak to my little brother with the proper respect and got punched in the face for it, Joey earned himself a ticket, as he explained it, to three squares a day and a clean mattress for four rent-free months. Joey said he'd never had it so good.

Leaning against the back seat of the car with a bottle of beer at the ready, everything seemed philosophically tolerable, something close quarters with reality didn't allow. I drank noiselessly. When I asked my brother-in-law to stop the car so I could pee in a field off the 401, I tumbled headlong into soft wet grass and lay there for a full moment, the scent of green fresh and good. I gazed up at wispy clouds sauntering across a blue sky without a care in the world. I took a deep breath. "Be a beacon of light to the family," I counseled myself, and staggered back to the car, where I emptied more bottles of emotional stability. I coughed when I pried off each cap to spare my relatives its gasp, and then settled down to a purposeful place of no feeling.

That evening Irene and I stepped out onto the cement balcony of the luxury apartment Mother had shared with Stu. We peered over the side. "How could she tumble over a railing this tall?" asked my sister as we surveyed the scene. At that instant, as I peered over the balcony, I viewed the most poignant art of my life, four thick lines, heavy scratch marks, powerful fingernails clawed into green paint. "Mum tried to save herself," I said. Irene's pale face whitened. Her dark blue eyes blazed the emotion she'd kept to herself. Irene was always a private person, a woman of few words whose questions often expressed doubt. At the funeral parlor, Mother lay in her blue silk dress, the flowered one she'd worn to convene the Daffodil Tea for the Cancer Society only ten years earlier. I leaned over her and, without prying her stiff hands apart, I examined my mother's fingers.

"What're you doing?" asked Irene.

"Mother wanted to live."

"How do you know?"

"Read the lines," I said. "Green paint under each nail."

He was no longer a practicing priest, but Stu was permitted to officiate at Mother's funeral High Mass. He began by shaking a liturgical implement over her casket. My stomach sank when I saw him submerge the aspergillum, an instrument with a round head attached to the top of a wand, a bald skull of holes on a steel spine. I observed his strong fingers gripping the stick and submerging its perforated face into a silver holy water bucket on the Italian marble floor. I watched his fist tighten around it to splash hundreds of water droplets over her coffin, all the useless tears Mother had showered over his sorry ass. Irene and I looked at each other and rolled swollen eyes as Stu fussed over Mother's closed casket, her last, lonely bed.

"He's damn lucky I didn't leap over the pew and bop him in the head with that damn thing, the pompous jerk!" Paddy said afterwards. "He's lucky I wanted my mother to have a quiet funeral."

We, her children, crunched together in the front pew and watched this Catholic ritual of goodbye. We said nothing. We left it to the religious men who knew just what to do. At the cemetery, we watched as Mother was lowered into the soft summer ground. Aunt Jill arrived and gave me a pot of yellow flowers to place on the mound. I wanted to ask Brigit if she knew where Mother's best friend, Mabel, was buried, but I forgot.

That night, Irene figured out what to eat and served chicken noodle soup to us all. I smoked constantly and drank compulsively. That way I could cry. There'd be no tears without booze, I knew that much. We walked outside to examine the grassy lawn area seven stories below Stu's balcony. The police had spray-marked florescent yellow around Mother's fallen form and we gathered around the fatal outline. There was no discernible human shape. We stared at the amoebic distortion, a giant ovary.

"Oh, Mum," said Danny.

"This wasn't her dream," said Irene.

"All she ever wanted was for all of us to be together under one roof," said Joey. His legal escort from the detention center nodded sympathetically.

"Why?" I asked, glass in hand. "Why did she drink? Why didn't she leave Stu?"

∼

I bumbled back to Montreal to pass my summer courses, an accomplishment requiring neither introspection nor reflective skills. I doubled my September course load. Home, classes, study—a safe and narrow life, though there had been one change. I took only courses that interested me, not for any particular profession, not to impress Mother any more, but because of a newfound curiosity. I still wanted a framed university diploma to cover the cracks on my wall, though. I still wanted to be able to pull up a chair and gaze at that piece of paper, the printed sheet that would proclaim my worth, my value, and my intelligence. I had no idea how fragile I was.

One October evening after class, on the 105 bus, I opened *Barometer Rising* to where I'd left off reading. As the bus passed the Montreal Institute for the Blind, I had an insight, gleaned from a frightened milk horse Hugh MacLennan described so well. I pressed the novel to my lap and considered the bizarre story. Even as buildings toppled under the intense pressure of the 1917 Halifax Harbour explosion, even as ancient oaks snapped like toothpicks in the air, the terrified milk horse stopped at every door along her habitual delivery route. Even as the iron railings of her customers' porches melted in the fierce heat, the obedient mare reacted to the disaster not by chasing to safety on four powerful legs but by accelerating the pace of her pre-ordained itinerary, full speed ahead towards her own destruction. How could this be? How could she participate so fervently in her own demise? She could easily have cut away to safety but no, during the furious detonation of a French warship loaded with explosives, the traumatized mare stuck to the template, the only one she knew. She got herself killed, flaming debris searing holes into her undefended flesh. I could almost hear the dozen milk bottles crashing onto the planks of the cart she hauled as she careened in the worst possible direction, not away from but towards the fire.

"What a dumb horse," I thought. "Why the hell couldn't that mare be an outlaw for once, why didn't she escape?" I got off at Prud'homme, my regular stop.

"I didn't sleep well last night." I heard myself pulling a time-worn excuse for what I knew would come next. I bought the beer I'd said I wouldn't buy and, convincing myself that two hours of homework entitled me to that sleep aid, I carried on with my routine like any other night. I took my customary bath, got into my nightgown, slipped into my soft pink mules—and drank the trinity down. The next morning, stuck in the same stiff spot I'd sprawled in all night long, I awakened, burning with shame once again. Still, I thought about that crazy horse, astonished anew at its stupidity. Why hadn't it galloped in a different direction?

A little over a year later, I'd successfully completed four more courses, each one a step closer to my first university degree. One of those programs was taught by a part-time professor at Loyola. I was surprised when I answered the door of my brownstone triplex. Months earlier, a woman friend of mine, a young professor at Loyola, had ended their intense, unreliable relationship and moved back to Ghana.

"Can you help me?" he asked. "I'm in a real spot. A member of the United Nations is arriving from New York this Friday and as it turns out, I stupidly forgot I have a faculty meeting in the Laurentians. Since my friend's already paid for his flight, would you have supper with him in my absence and maybe take him to the Montreal Museum of Fine Arts on Saturday? I'd be so grateful."

I told him I'd be happy to.

"I thought of other students," he said with a smile, "but I chose you because I know he'll enjoy you." He gave me an envelope of money for dinner downtown. He insisted. "After all, I'm on a payroll and you're not."

Flattered as could be, I said I'd include his friend in a supper with Maureen and her husband too; they'd be thrilled to meet a member of the U.N. When the New Yorker called me, he asked if I'd meet him at the apartment since he had no idea where he was. I dressed nicely and set out, proud to be an emissary to a man who in his own country was recognized as a prince. Tucking the envelope of money in my purse, I thought of an African restaurant downtown. The man, older than I'd expected, met me at the door.

"Come in, come in," he said, his accent sounding exotic to my ears. We chatted for a moment while he put on his sports jacket. "Shall we toast our evening with a splash of French wine before we leave?"

"Okay," I agreed. Within moments I sank to the couch, heavy and sluggish. My legs felt fat. I dragged my lead weight to the washroom and, groping the walls and barely able to stand up, I vaguely heard the gentleman chatting away softly in the other room. That dinner never happened. What did occur was a night of unwanted sex, over and over again, rape without any participation on my part. It took me a while after I woke up to orient myself. Was it still afternoon? What time was it? The U.N. emissary told me that I'd drunk a lot of wine and seduced him. He showed me the bottles. He asked me if I'd like another drink. I staggered out the door with no offer of assistance, no escort home, no concern for me at all. Trembling and desperate, I opened my back door to Maureen and her husband, Jake, both terribly upset.

"Where were you? No one knew where you were! Look at you! You didn't even call!" Maureen's voice shook. They packed me in blankets into the back of their car and we set out for their home in Ottawa.

"This is your fault. Your fault! You were drinking." Maureen turned from me to face the road. "You are in the process of exterminating yourself."

Suddenly I saw my drawing—the bottle of poison on Mother's bedroom door. I heard my steel-toed oxfords slamming against it as I interrogated my mother about her drinking.

"I don't know what happened. I don't know," I sobbed. "I only had one drink."

"Maybe I'll do myself a big favor at long last," I thought. "Death is an option."

How could one day be so fine, so hopeful, so fresh and light and the next so rock-bottom deathly? How could this happen, over and over again? I grappled with unbearable feelings of shame and self-loathing, blind to my part in all the mayhem of my life.

We stopped for gas and I handed my brother-in-law the envelope from my purse. Jake, an English teacher I'd always respected, was gentle. "American money?" he queried, counting the U.S. dollars.

"The professor gave me it to me before his friend came."

"*Before* his friend arrived? Hold on here, I smell a rat. Something is rotten in the state of Denmark. Why would a Canadian professor hand you American money? I'm picking up a distinct scent here."

"It's high time you saw a therapist," interrupted my sister. "There's a psychiatric outpatient unit at the Queen E. you should go to. Tell them you binge-drink. Tell them how easily you get yourself into compromising sexual situations."

My sister turned from me again. She remained cool for the duration of my stay. She fed me well. She gave me a bottle of 1,000 mg. capsules of Vitamin C to wash down with lots of water. I apologized for the trouble I'd caused. I thanked her for her help. I said I'd get therapy. Secretly, though, while I accepted her judgment of me, I felt sad that Maureen couldn't be a friend, hug me, or be close to me. She treated me respectfully, as courteously and as professionally as my sister dealt with all of her contacts.

I made an appointment with a therapist at the Queen Elizabeth Hospital. I told her what had happened with the U.N. delegate.

"What did she say?" Maureen asked when I called to say I'd followed her advice. I hoped my cooperation would appease my sister and earn me an ounce of redemption.

"She said whoever he supposedly was, he date-raped me. She said that I could have had a Coke or some freshly squeezed orange juice or a hot chocolate and my body would have swollen up like an inflated plastic dummy anyway because there were drugs in whatever I drank. She asked me for a lot of information. She wondered why one of us didn't call the police or go back to that apartment. She said that perhaps I'd escaped a far more dangerous situation, perhaps an organized one, worse than I could imagine."

"How could she possibly know all that?"

"I don't know. She said that possibly my Loyola professor never left the apartment, that maybe he was right there, hiding, camera in hand. She said I was very lucky not to be abducted, never to be seen in Canada again. I gave her all the information she asked me for. She called the police to investigate my professor and his friend."

Maureen said it all sounded awfully complicated to her. I wondered if she thought I'd made it all up, a dramatic story. Maureen's criticism weighed less upon me because the counselor reassured me over and over that it wasn't my fault. She said there was no sin in being helpful to a friend. I had done nothing wrong. She also said that sisters are often extra harsh with each other because they are so afraid the same thing could happen to them. Before my next appointment, I heard that the professor had been dismissed from Loyola, apparently for failing to provide the necessary documents about his academic status. The police told my counselor that the professor no longer lived at the address I gave and that there was no one at the United Nations in New York with the name I provided.

During this fiasco, I failed a course for the first time. My teacher said he wouldn't accept a makeup paper because I'd missed too much.

"I've been having a rough time," I said.

"I'm sincerely sorry about that, Eleanor, but the fact is you didn't fulfill the requirements of the course, did you? Imagine a student doctor missing a class in cranial surgery. Would you want to submit your brain tumor to the unschooled hands of a surgeon whose professor once took pity on him because he was going through a stressful time?" I knew I couldn't change this guy's mind. "So the question remains, do you merely want the credits or do you wish to master the content?"

"I can't fail this," I pleaded.

"Well, if failure is unacceptable to you, I suggest you pass next time. Now, thank you for coming to my office today."

On the corner of Belmore and Sherbrooke, I met another professor, who'd always been pleasant with me. I showed him my fatal university grade, my hands shaking, my only secure identity in peril.

"Oh well," he laughed, "relax, Eleanor, relax." He told me about a guest lecturer, Joseph Campbell, a mythologist invited to speak at Loyola. Under the leafy green trees on Belmore Avenue, my professor talked about mysterious and powerful energies that are always with us, supporting and inspiring us as long as we live.

"Don't worry about your mother any more, Eleanor," he said. "And look, take that course over again. In the grand scheme of things, you'll know more than you did before. No big deal."

I was glad I repeated the course because Dr. Gold was teaching it this time. But after the mythology lecture about the universal metaphor of young brides sacrificed to appease perceived gods, I spied my teacher entering the chapel for Mass, her daughters in tow.

"Why would such a smart woman convert to Catholicism?" I asked my friend Sandra as we followed the path of sunken stones, a set of gray teeth grinning at the chapel. "Doesn't she know the history of the Pope's refusal to help her own people during the war?"

"You judge, Eleanor," said Sandra. "You categorize everything into right or wrong.

Look, if you think she's so smart, why not trust her choices? Or better yet, talk with her, pose some questions."

We climbed the cement stairs of the Admin. Building and took our seats as Dr. Gold swished into class in her long English peasant dress. I couldn't bring myself to question my teacher. I couldn't do with someone else what I couldn't do for myself.

~

A young cousin I'd met only a few times had become ill. Dougie discovered over time and to his horror that the taut muscles he flexed on the football field at school no longer responded to his commands. He wept the day I visited him, a week after his terminal diagnosis.

"I'll never make love! I'll never have a family," he guffawed wildly, gooey saliva blocking the course of tears down his face. His nurse told me that laughing and crying are closely linked in the brain center and that Dougie laughed when he meant to cry and cried when he meant to laugh.

There was no mistaking the hilarity, though, as Dougie laughed during a supper we cooked for him that weekend. Maureen and Jake split their sides when I imitated my cousin cooking a guy kind of meal in a guy kind of kitchen.

"You observe people so accurately, Norda. You're a comedian!" laughed my brother-in-law. With supper on the table, Maureen suggested Dougie say Grace.

"Gimme a break," he drawled. "Let's just eat while we can chew."

Not even a good evening with people I liked could chase away the eerie sense of separateness that gnawed away inside me all the time. When I got home from Dougie's, I climbed out onto the kitchen fire escape with a drawing pad and pencil, an ashtray, and the smokes I couldn't be without. On that quiet summer's night, I sat still for hours. I thought about Dougie's terminal illness. I admitted to myself that I'd deny Christ as many times as necessary to save Dougie, or rescue a child from a spanking, or even for a smoke if I ran out. I was no longer part of that contrived Christian story, nor did I honor a father god who was content to see his own kid fry.

I did feel grateful for the opportunity to get an education, my faith anchored in the power of learning. I believed in good people, the kind who sat on their behinds for years and years, not to split hairs over a fictional God fable but to develop vaccines or help children in terrible trouble. That warm summer night, my back against my own wall, I glanced over to the university grounds across the road, my eyes drawn to street lamps casting circles of light against the red bricks of the chapel. Visually adjusting to the darkness below, I discerned large mounds, the bodies of sleeping street people, among them a motionless contour, a woman's shape, curled up, face to the wall. With soft light spilling out from my kitchen window onto my sketch paper, I began to draw a serious, thoughtful face, perhaps the silhouette of the mute woman below, perhaps a new face yet to come, yet to awaken to her own unique life. My drawing expressed all my good wishes, all my longing and hope for the woman asleep on the grass.

Transported to a place of consolation, I slept well that night. I decided not to rent out rooms any more. I'd be better off alone. I was short of funds, but I knew I couldn't call my family. I wouldn't call. I wouldn't embarrass myself again in front of Maureen and Jake. I'd given them enough trouble. I wouldn't bother Brigit and her new man in Edmonton because I knew my younger sister had been scraping by too. Irene and her husband intimidated me. I felt like the poor relative, but the truth was I didn't feel close enough to my sisters to ask for help. Even though gold nuggets of love were there, deep down, they were inaccessible to me. There was no picking up the phone for a completely relaxed yak. Even hearing each other's voices was loaded with memory and conversations were always strained.

The younger boys still owed me money, and I could predict their replies if I called in my loans. I begged Danny for my money back, the several hundred dollars I needed for my tuition, and told him I was just as desperate now as he'd been when he called me the year before. He apologized for the delay, but said he didn't have the money and couldn't get it. When I pressed harder, Danny said he'd always felt robbed, that the older family members got a far better start in life than he did and that I should know that. So I shouldn't be calling to bother him when I'd been the lucky recipient of the early care he'd missed.

"So why did you use the word 'loan,' Danny, if you had no intention of repaying me? Next time, say you'd like an envelope stuffed with money, okay?"

I still owed Gordie for my last tuition loan so I wouldn't call him for more. No, I'd call my family when my situation looked better, not now.

Entirely ignorant of the fact that the university would have given me a loan for the asking, I rented what I could afford, a cheap room in Notre Dame de Grâce, where Dad's family had once lived.

In my thirteenth home, I bought sticky roach motels to trap rampant cockroaches in a dirty kitchen. I set to scrubbing a shared hall toilet and thought of my sister Irene cleaning out the basement bathroom in her first digs away from home, a decade earlier. One evening, my neighbors, a father and his six-year-old son, invited me to supper in a room even smaller than my own, which at least had a tiny balcony. From the hot plate on his dresser, Pete served us hot dogs and Kraft Dinner on paper plates and announced he had two things to be grateful for on this birthday. First, he'd saved enough to rent a flat in the Pointe, close to his factory, and second, a volunteer was teaching him to read.

"I'm excited," he said, collecting our plates.

After supper, while his son played in the park playground, Pete confided that his wife had been murdered. A drug gang mistook her for the woman they intended to kill, one floor down. Pete said he found her in a blood-filled bathtub, two precise cuts in her neck and two behind her knees. I asked Pete if he believed in God.

"I'm a big boy now," he said. "We're all little ants pushing a wobbly wheel as best we can in this world. Even when it rolls through horse shit, we hang on if we possibly can. I keep going for my son, and that's about all I really know."

"You're leading him the best way," I said. "By example."

On our walk home, Pete reassured me that I could feel safe in the rooming house. "If anyone so much as disturbs a hair on your head at any time, all you have to do is tap on the wall. I'll take care of it."

I knew Pete would happily kill anyone who ever lifted a hand to hurt not only his son but any child, even if that someone was my father beating Gordie or an ambitious father inviting his son to be nailed to a cross. Who'd be inspired to follow that example? In my small room that night, I opened the bottle of wine I'd sworn I wouldn't touch. When the tears alcohol could and did generate began to flow, my alarmed new friend heard me through the paper-thin walls. He asked a woman down the hall, a nursing student, to find out what was wrong.

"I never heard crying so sad, so horrible, beyond awful, like you saw a murder!" the nurse told me the next morning. "We were ready to call the hospital. Then you stopped and we decided to let you sleep."

I thanked her. When she came home that evening and lingered a bit in the hallway, I waited until I heard her room door close. Then I slipped out of the building. I did the same the next night. A week later, I found myself standing next to her on the 105 bus.

"You're a funny one," she said. "Last week I comfort you in your worst nightmare. I'm right there for you. This week you don't even know me? No cup of coffee, no visit down the hall, no concern about how your crisis affected my studies or my sleep? You cried like you'd seen a murder and now you stroll on by like you don't even know me? Well, you know what, girl? You've got big problems, big, serious problems!"

I reacted to this direct confrontation the only way I knew how. I apologized profusely. Then I pulled the cord over the bus window and jumped off at the next stop. That evening, walking home from work, I found myself looking carefully in the windows and doors of houses close to Loyola and my heart thumped when I saw the "room for rent" sign I didn't know I'd been looking for until that moment. I rented a large sunny room on the top floor of an old house. When I opened what I thought to be a cupboard door, I discovered a sunny bathroom, sparkling clean, all my own. That move closed the door to any introspection about my noisy drama, my alcoholic drinking episode, and wonderful people who could have become my friends.

Good things began to happen. I intercepted the postman at the rooming house, and when he handed me my last unemployment check, I pressed it to my chest and ran all the way to the bank with enough money for a month's rent, groceries, bus tickets, and two spring dresses from the Turnabout Shoppe on Victoria Avenue in Westmount. I ate lunch at an Italian restaurant close to Girouard Park that served delicious chicken cacciatore, salad, dessert, and coffee for $3.75. My nearly-new dresses tucked beside me in the booth seat, I felt better. The waitress loaned me a newspaper, topped up my coffee half a dozen times, and shimmied the phone cord under the swinging kitchen doors and all the way to my table so I could make appointments for interviews.

I got a secretarial job at Loyola College. My new boss said I could start the following Monday but I begged to start right away, on Wednesday morning. He agreed. I met nice people. I learned the ropes. I still made morning coffee but I was not required to polish my boss's shoes. I worked hard, paid my rent and all my bills. I repaid my tuition money to Gordie, adding a box of Laura Secord chocolates to sweeten the thank-you. I got permission to take a morning English class, and when I discovered that the course was free, I jumped for joy. On weekends, I cooked big pots of stew that lasted a week of lunches. I munched on raw carrots and swallowed vitamin pills. I walked to and from work. Every day had become precious. Even though I'd only restored my impersonal routine of work and study, it seemed to be enough. I was grateful for stability and calm. I paid a final visit to my counselor at the Queen Elizabeth Hospital and announced to her that all I needed to do was not drink, simple as that, and all my problems were solved. I could tell by the way her eyebrows rose that I had impressed her.

~

Edna invited me to celebrate her eldest son's recent academic success at a dinner in the shabby digs that were all she could afford. I didn't tell her that her ex-husband had called my work place with invitations to parties and suppers. I had no intention of ever upsetting this brave woman, who still cooked meals for welcome guests despite being thrown into poverty.

"So what was your M.A. thesis about, Stan Junior?" I asked, as his mother served roast pork and baked apples. Little Catherine, Stan's young sister, placed a bowl of steaming mashed potatoes on the table and her younger brother carried in a gravy boat filled to the brim.

"Well, you're the first to ask," he said, glancing at his mother in admonition. Stan's thick brown hair gave a handsome, boyish look to the young Boy Scout leader I'd met in Amos on our family's cross-Canada trip fourteen years earlier.

Launching into an explanation that left us all far behind, he spoke as though delivering an academic lecture, a formal kind of speech, each word evaluated for its usefulness. He took few breaths during his monologue and seemed unaware that his siblings and I were hankering for their mother's strawberry shortcake, piled high with berries. I listened to the young man my father had once admired, the honor student who'd been his mother's right-hand man.

"Existential freedom for me, right now, would be to dig into that shortcake instantly," I said, interrupting him.

Even Stan laughed. After supper, he slipped into his little sister's bedroom and sorted his papers on her bed while the rest of us cleaned up in the kitchen.

"I don't like it when Stan uses my bedroom, Mum," Catherine complained. "Why can't he spread his stuff on the dining room table?"

"Be kind," said her mother, dumping dirty plates into a sink of hot water. "He's only here for the weekend."

A little later, I found Stan in Catherine's room. We chatted about how it felt for him to be out of the seminary now. He told me he was preparing to do a doctorate, perhaps in Europe. "Wow," I said. "If my mother were still alive, she'd be plenty impressed with you."

Months later, Stan confessed he'd set up that pre-test of my interest—going off to his little sister's room and waiting to see if I'd follow. Apparently, I passed with flying colors.

Later that evening, we went out for a walk.

"That's a dirty habit," he said when I pulled out a smoke. I took another puff and chucked it.

"One of the things I'm learning to accept about my family," Stan said with academic decorum, as though reading an essay, "is that they fail to understand my thesis material. Quite frankly, my insights are neither here nor there to them. Not one member of my family has ever inquired about the contents of my thesis, as you did tonight. Sure, they're happy that I got an M.A., but it would be easier for them if it were in plumbing."

"Yes, but your classmates understand, don't they?"

"No," he said. "Few people want to know the truth."

"Well, a dentist doesn't talk root canals with the family after work, right? And no one I know, outside my class, is interested in talking about English literature either. If I asked you right now if you wanted to hear about the casket theory in *The Merchant of Venice*, would you want to? I'd gladly tell you all about it right now." He didn't press.

"Exactly," I thought, my own test completed.

Then he said, "It's important for a philosopher like myself to lead people forward."

Suddenly I craved another smoke.

"He didn't ask me about myself," I thought when I got home that night. "I should have said I'm a plumber."

~

One day, out of the blue, I called Grandpa, my mother's father. He had not attended Mother's funeral. The last time I'd seen him, fourteen years earlier, we crossed the street to his grocery store together and he gave me sugary cookies for my train trip home to Fergus after I'd slept through the family party. Even though I'd lived in Montreal for several years, it had never occurred to me, not once, that my grandfather also lived in the same city and that he might want to see me.

"May I come over?" I asked. "I'd like to talk about Mother."

"Well, all right then," he said, with some reluctance in his voice.

"What's there to say?" he asked when I sat down at his kitchen table, serving us each a cold beer. "Your mother drank too much, simple as that. You drink too much, you pay. That's the math."

He was in his eighties now, his shoulders stooped, his blue eyes watery. I wondered if the same math equation applied to his other sons, all of whom drank too much. Except for one remaining son, my Uncle Dan, they'd all died of alcoholism, every one.

A clerk from Grandpa's store delivered a couple of T-bones and he began to lather the meat with barbeque sauce. Suddenly I felt exhausted. I asked if I could rest for an hour before supper. I lay down on the same bed I'd slept on so soundly years earlier, immobilized by the sleeping pill mother had given me. This time I woke up to find Grandpa on top of me.

"Is this what you wanted?" he breathed, his hands in my underwear. "You're a sly one, eh, asking me to nap on my bed? I knew what you wanted. I knew what you couldn't wait for." I pushed him off me.

"I gave it to my wife every morning of her life with me," he blurted as I stood up. "And when she was pregnant, I used the back door." Stumbling from his bed, I locked myself in the bathroom. Grandpa called his only surviving son, who lived close by.

"Get her out of here," he said. "She's just like her mother, good for nothing. Christ, get her out of my sight!"

"Two things," my uncle advised me in the taxi home. "First, steer clear of your grandfather. He's a complicated guy. And second, don't drink, honey. I wish I'd never started down that sorry trail myself. It's a wobbly walk to nowhere, I'll tell you that."

"What's wrong with Grandpa, Uncle Dan?"

"He's always been this way, honey. The only feelings he cares about are his own. It seems he doesn't know how much he hurts other people. He gets his back up at the slightest perceived offense but can't fathom how cruel he is himself, especially to his family."

Uncle Dan stared out the taxi window in the same abstracted way Dad had years ago, a solemn positioning of unseeing eyes. Within a year, he'd be dead too.

"Funny thing, though," Uncle Dan began again, almost as a reverie. "My good Irish father is always nice to strangers. You may not have seen this tonight, Norda, but in the living room is a framed photo of your grandparents sitting with two hundred strangers at a fancy ball at the Windsor Hotel. They're dressed to the nines, rubbing shoulders with all the other fifty-dollar-a-plate VIPs they'll never see again, as pleasant and friendly as can be for Princess Elizabeth's royal visit in 1951. That photo still covers the cracks in his wall, but look around some more, search the living room all you like, and you won't see a picture of us, his family."

The taxi reached my building and I stepped out, smack into a mud puddle.

"Don't visit your grandfather again, Norda," my uncle repeated. "Stick with nice people. It's the only possible answer."

∽

When Edna's son called on that confusing Sunday, it took me a few seconds to place the ex-seminarian, the M.A. student we'd celebrated a month earlier. Vaguely I knew that if Stan had called before my visit to Grandpa, I'd have declined. I'd have wriggled out of it. But today, a chance to chat with someone who liked me was welcome, even though I knew I'd be in for a lot of listening.

Stan had a small request. He asked me to tutor his little sister, who'd put off a writing assignment for so long that she was now in trouble with her high school teacher.

"Why is a memoir piece about her childhood so hard for her?" I asked, concerned for the child I once saw cuddled on Stan's lap.

"My parents' divorce has been hard on her," he said, his face flushing.

I visited Stan in Ottawa one weekend, and after supper we took a walk. I happened to mention the name of a government official suspected of sexual abuse. "Jesus Christ, what a bastard," I swore. "How do these pedophiles get away with it?" Stan dropped my hand.

"Filthy language like that is abuse in itself. Does Christ deserve to have His Holy Name sullied? You took the name of God in vain," he said, visibly upset. "The name of the Son of God, the man centermost in my life, the man, Jesus." We stopped in front of a Catholic church. "I think you should apologize."

"What?" I scanned his face as I felt my own turning red. My stomach muscles tightened.       "You should face this church and apologize to God for besmirching His only Son's name, for using vile language against Him."

I swallowed, turned to the stone face of the cathedral and said, "I'm sorry."

"Sorry who?" asked Stan.

"Sorry, God," I said, my humiliation complete.

"You're special," said Stan. "Not many women take responsibility for their wrongs."

Stan told me that a year earlier, he'd quit the Catholic seminary in Ottawa after three years of studies to become a priest. "You wouldn't believe what I saw take place behind those hallowed walls. The hypocrisy made me sick," he said, explaining the reason he'd left the seminary.

Shortly after we announced our engagement, Stan moved back to Montreal and my boss found a temporary summer job for him at the college. One day at lunch, Stan shocked me with the news that his mother hated the idea of our getting married.

"But I thought Edna liked me." I was surprised and hurt by this sudden turnabout.

"Well, Mother knows about your drinking and she's well aware of your mother's sad story," Stan began, removing his glasses. "And the other thing, and this may be the real, deeper issue, is that my mother is dead set on my becoming a Jesuit priest. She's been begging me to enter this order ever since I left the other one."

"Why? Why would your mother want you in a cell block all your life?" I asked.

"It's complicated," Stan hedged. "She wanted her first-born son to be a priest. It's fixed in her mind."

Back at work that week, my boss took me aside. "Look, I'll jump right in here," he said. "This isn't about your work. You're doing fine. I know your parents aren't alive, so I'd like to say something."

I wondered if he was going to offer to walk me down the aisle on my wedding day, but thought again, seeing his obvious discomfort.

"I'm worried, Eleanor," he said. "I sense there's something wrong, a disturbance of some kind with your fiancé. There's something off about him. I don't want to upset you, but I think you're heading into problems."

"He had a helluva rough childhood, sir," I said, leaping to defend my man, reciting the script I'd parrot for the next fourteen years. As I spoke to my worried boss, I felt stretched from head to toe, an elastic release from tension and rigidity. Defending Stan to the rooftops filled me with a surge of power, a sense of importance and a rush of fulfillment I'd never known before. I felt alive.

"You have no idea how much he's suffered," I argued. "But I promise you, with our marriage, all his sadness will be a thing of the past. Did you know that Stan's doing his doctorate in French?" I bubbled away.

"Eleanor, your mother died only months ago. Look, let's have you visit with a staff counselor to talk things over."

"I know what I'm doing," I insisted. "Anyway, sir, how mentally ill can a man with a doctorate be?"

Stan had told me all about his childhood, how abusive his father, Stan Senior, had been to him, stories I had no trouble believing. Stan said he'd nearly shot his brother, the sibling favored by his father, in the head with a loaded gun by mistake. Stan said his dad never missed an opportunity to call into question statements he made.

"I understand that. I know that feeling," I reassured him.

"I want you to know that once or twice I held my little sister," he said. "I cuddled her, sometimes a bit too long. I shouldn't have and I stopped it. Anyway, she doesn't even remember it. I also spent too much time with pornographic magazines during my adolescence, when I was a Boy Scout leader."

"Oh," I said, impressed by his honesty. "What does 'pornographic' mean?"

"Are you serious?" he asked. "You graduate from university this year and you don't know that word?"

"That's right," I said. "Is it some kind of writing?"

"No, it's pictures. Dirty sex pictures of cheap prostitutes, gutter whores, tramps. Anyway, I stopped looking at all that filth but knew I should tell you about it. After all, you told me about your binge drinking."

"Yes, but drinking wasn't part of my childhood. It's recent. It's serious business. You're stretching pretty far back, aren't you? Your adolescent behavior stopped so long ago, so why even mention it?"

"I wanted to be entirely honest with you," he said.

I considered Stan a truthful man, his forthrightness pointing to a better life. I said yes to a Roman Catholic ceremony because he wanted it. It made him happy. With uncanny exactness, I was drawn to a man who mirrored my past, the kaleidoscope of history I'd never faced. That fall, Stan left Montreal to begin doctoral studies in Europe. He'd return for our wedding in three months and then, together, we'd fly overseas to begin our married life. He made a rare long-distance call one day to say his mother had airmailed him the application forms to the Jesuit Order, along with a desperate note begging him to apply.

"I don't get it, Stan. Do you understand why your mother is so hell-bent on you being a priest? Those days when the first-born in Catholic families become religious are a thing of the past, aren't they?"

"It's about you, Eleanor," Stan said, cutting the discussion short. "She knows alcoholism runs in families. She knows how your mother died. She's worried about your stability."

I asked Father Bernard at Chaplaincy to call Stan's mother. "I know she'd talk to you, a Catholic priest, a man, more easily than she would to me. Would you call her?"

"Sure thing," he said. "Let's get the cards on the table."

A few days later, Father B. and I met in his office. "Did she tell you?"

"Well, yes, Eleanor. She's afraid. She doesn't want to see her future grandchildren hurt."

"Oh," I said, falling silent.

"You know mothers." He tried to comfort me. "Edna knows you've had some trouble with alcohol. She knows about your mother's shocking death. She's worried you might drink again."

"I guess I'll have to prove myself." I swallowed hard, burning with shame.

"You will." Father encouraged me. "She'll come 'round, you'll see. One day your mother-in-law will be thanking God Almighty her precious prize married a sorry lot like you." He chuckled at his own good-natured joke.

On a freezing cold day in December, my father's birthday, I married Stan Junior in a small ceremony at the Loyola Chapel on Sherbrooke Street. Edna greeted me and said that she wanted me to know that she wished Stan and me all the best. She gave me a hug. Perhaps if I'd blurted out all my fears and dread to someone I trusted, even at the last minute, I'd have had the courage to cancel the wedding, which remains a blurry, embarrassed memory of walking up the aisle in borrowed shoes that were too small for me. If only I could have talked to a friend. Instead, I began my wedding day with the kind of headache I'd first left home to heal. I got on the bus to go to my hair appointment at La Coupe. When Faubert, my hairdresser, asked where my maid of honor was, I pointed to the raging storm outside. "My sister said it would be crazy to slip and slide in this storm."

Two years earlier, when Maureen had married Jake, an educated ex-seminarian, a loyal man with a sense of humor, Irene and I did all we could to assist her for her wedding. It took me years to understand that Maureen's decision to meet me at the church had to do with her fears for all of us. Proximity to me had become threatening to her. What can befall one sister can surely happen to the other.

"Hmmm, natural red highlights," Faubert said.

"From my father," I said with a smile.

"Will he be giving you away today?" he asked.

"No," I said. "He passed away years ago."

"And your mother?"

"She died recently," I said.

"Oh, *mon Dieu*," he said, weaving a crown of miniature red roses into my long hair. "Do you know how many young people marry within a year of the *décès* of a parent? It is true. I know this."

My hair resplendent with real roses, I stood just outside La Coupe, on Peel at Sherbrooke Street, facing Henry Moore's stone sculpture of a mother and child, its details hidden under clumps of ice and snow. From behind the salon's ultra-modern glass wall, Faubert waved goodbye and I began to walk west along Sherbrooke Street. Across the street, a doorman at the Ritz-Carlton swept heavy snowflakes off a red carpet for special guests and a little farther along, the veiled face of the Montreal Museum of Fine Arts shivered behind squares of plastic scaffolding flapping in the wind. Excavation drills chain-locked to a crane lay under snow, while stormy winds loosed two garbage bins onto my path. I fell on the ice and salvaged my crown of roses from a snowdrift.

Back at my flat, I made toast and sat alone on the couch, my white dress, an empty form, beside me. I realized there was no one around to zip it up for me, and I'd forgotten to buy shoes. I had nothing for my feet. On the phone, Maureen said her friend had a pair of summer shoes, one size too small, but they'd do. She told me that her friends had prepared a wonderful turkey dinner with all the trimmings for her and Jake. I held back my thoughts. I didn't say how hurt I felt that she wouldn't be with me this special morning. An hour later, no one in my building saw me push through the glass front doors in my wedding dress and step outside into the blizzard, where I sank deep into the snow. No one saw the wet stains on the hemline of my dress, or how quickly they etched up my white skirt. I had only two minutes' leeway until my brother-in-law picked me up on Sherbrooke Street, the only ploughed road. I raced back upstairs and threw open the door that concealed my broom, dustpan, and a box of trash bags. Before I knew it, I'd crashed one booted foot and then the other clear through the bottom of a giant green garbage bag.

"Christ," I swore, stuffing myself waist deep into the sack. I twisted the plastic into a cone handle, adjusted my crown of roses, and steered myself into the hallway, bumping into a neighbor.

"*Mon Dieu*, Eleanor!" he said, obviously shocked.

"I'm on the run," I said. Soft sounds of plastic swept against wall plaster as I rushed for my ride.

Shortly after we were married, Stan and I flew to Paris, where he'd continue his studies. Within two weeks, I was hard at work too, teaching English at a local convent school. When Stan asked if I wouldn't mind working while he was busy with his studies, saying he'd had no idea Paris was so expensive, I said I was honored to help out. He was grateful when I paid all the bills, especially his student loans. One day he suggested a deal. I'd support him full throttle throughout his school years, and when he was done, he'd support my studies and our children. We shook on the deal.

"My hand is my word," said Stan.

Although I'd only shared my wish with my long-lost friend Michaela, I wanted to be a stay-at-home mother to my children, at least until they were in their teens.

In Paris that year, 1974, I washed our clothes by hand because one load in the tiny washing machine in the university laundromat cost the equivalent of three dollars. I could buy a jar of instant coffee for that and, instead of France's favorite spread, Nutella, I could also purchase chunky peanut butter from the American grocery store in St. Michel. When school finished for the summer, I worked as a part-time translator with the First National Bank of Chicago. I saved from each pay check for our return flight to Canada. One day I found myself doodling a caricature of myself, large with pregnancy, a little red-haired baby snuggled inside me. I picked up a pen and wrote "Hi, Teddy," and then penciled in his thrilling reply: "Hi, Mum."

I'd convinced Stan over the months that the time had come to start our family, that I'd be twenty-eight when our first baby would be born. Reluctantly, he agreed.

"I love you with all my heart," I wrote under that drawing, thus forging the strong bond I felt with my son long before his birth. I sketched, week by week, his growing sizes and shapes, from a grape to an apple to a melon, and counted the days to his birth in Paris, an exotic European beginning for my child.

One of my neighbors at the university residence, a hard-working Irish woman named Emma, was putting her husband through school too. "We're earning our 'PHTs'," she quipped. "That's short for 'Putting Hubby Through.'"

"I don't know what I'd do without you," said Stan when I told him I'd taken another tutoring job. "You've saved me." His words were my nectar. I was essential to the success of this brilliant scholar, a man who'd soon be a professor, a mentor to many university students back home.

"You get that doctorate, Stan," I said. "And when the baby comes, you'll take care of us."

"No need for reminders," he said, offended. "My word is my word."

When my friend Emma mentioned how reserved Stan was, I told her all about his difficult childhood. My eyes misted over as I described how terribly belittled he'd been by his father, how awful it had been for him to be so relentlessly criticized by a parent he needed and loved. I said that Gordie'd been treated like a workhorse and deserved to have some care in his life now. I burst into tears as I spoke.

"Gordie?" asked Emma, confused. "Who's Gordie?"

~

"My mother's taking note," said Stan, holding up an airmail letter from Edna. "She's impressed that you're putting me through school. My sisters are amazed too. Believe you me, Norda, you are fast becoming a star in my family circle."

In our small campus residence, Stan read long passages from his thesis and explained complex concepts at length. I took to knitting while he read aloud, always glad when he stopped talking. There was no sentence that didn't meander into a paragraph with all manner of asides, like tributaries from a fast-flowing stream, each racing in a new direction. I didn't understand a word of it. Stan said it was because I didn't have the academic background to grasp the highly specific language his thesis required. Once, when he asked me why I hadn't made a single query about the fifteen pages he'd just read to me, I didn't even hear his question. I was lost in my own thoughts about my baby.

"You don't care!" Stan got angry. "You don't want to learn about my work!"

"It's incomprehensible to me, Stan. The words are English but the way they are strung together, it could be Greek. I have no idea what you are saying. Can't you write simply? I've heard the best writing in the world can be understood by a ten-year-old."

"The world would fast come to an end if ten-year-olds were in charge I can assure you," Stan said, adding that he was now reluctant to read his work to me. I didn't apologize or promise to try harder to measure up. It was a tough ten minutes of silence, but I felt only relief at getting back to my book and my baby planning during brief weekends off.

Every Sunday, we travelled to La Gare du Nord, where the Little Sisters of the Poor ran a home for the elderly. Our job was to set dining room tables with real linen tablecloths and fresh flowers and feed the noon meal to those who couldn't feed themselves. One day, when a ninety-year-old man declined another spoonful of barley soup, I realized that I had a long rich life to live. Every time I volunteered, I appreciated my youth and vitality and all the educational opportunities ahead of me. I was grateful to be expecting a baby in such good health and without a world war to contend with. So much hope lay ahead.

~

One weekend, I picked up a book from among a pile of reference books on Stan's desk, a psychology text called *Love and Will* by Rollo May.

"What a name," I said. "Imagine a mother calling her son 'Rollo.' Let's hope he wasn't chubby." I read the first page and was hooked.

"Rollo says that today's technical man is schizophrenic," I reported to Stan. "…that he's missing part of himself. He says people have to love themselves first or else they'll always feel alienated."

"Christ says the way to love yourself is through service, through helping your fellow man," Stan replied.

"Yes, but that service has to have real meaning to the person doing it. You can't be a robot."

"Sometimes duty requires heroism. You sacrifice yourself for the greater good."

"Rollo May says that ordinary people seek refuge in conformity and traditional values but creative people are willing to go out on a limb. Wow, I like that idea!"

"Such people can also agree to give up such grandiosity for the greater good, as Christ once did," Stan said.

Three times a week, I tutored Lydie, a brilliant sixteen-year-old I grew to admire. One day after school, she pushed her catechism homework aside and blurted out, *"Jésus n'était jamais divin!"*

I learned that Lydie's grandmother, a friend of Simone de Beauvoir, barely tolerated her granddaughter's attendance at Catholic school. Tossing her red-gold hair out of her eyes, Lydie told me that the grisly tortures of women during the Catholic Inquisition far exceeded merely hanging from a cross for one day. She told me that millions of women had been tortured by Catholic priests for centuries, all the way up to the Reformation. This was all news to me. When I studied Descartes in Montreal, no professor informed us that innocent women were being burned alive in every town square at the same time that he was writing his *Principles of Philosophy.*

I was delighted when Lydie's *grand-mère* called and asked me to spend more time with her precocious granddaughter. While Stan studied on weekends, Lydie and I roamed the St. Michel art galleries, ate *Croque Monsieur,* fed the pigeons in Parc Montsouris and strolled the streets of Paris. My French improved (as, I hope, did her English), and I came to love this untamed young woman, who questioned absolutely everything.

I continued to read Stan's reference books, gaining ideas I squirreled away for later use.

"Rollo May says that going into a depression can be a good thing, a wake-up call, a sign you're changing. Listen to this." I read aloud to Stan. "'To be unhappy may be only the free will's demand for expression.' He says our problems help us figure out our values."

"Are you reading that whole thing? Word by word?" asked Stan.

"Well, yes, of course. Don't you?"

"I've never read a book from cover to cover in my life. I could never have advanced this far as an academic if I stopped to muse and ponder every single sentence like you do. I speed read. I skim and scan the indexes to sustain my arguments."

"That's so sad, Stan."

"How so?"

"You miss the beautiful turns of phrase, the lines that save your life."

That week I gave Stan a copy of *O Jerusalem*, a book I hadn't read but one Emma said her husband had found riveting. "This isn't a research book, Stan. It's to be read word for word, line by line, no skipping."

After work that night, I found him deep into it, a starving man at a banquet. "Great stuff," he exclaimed. "But I can't be indulging like that every day. I can't afford such luxury."

"Maybe you can read after you finish your doctorate," I said.

One school holiday, Stan and I took a trip to Belgium. On the train to Brussels, I was so absorbed in the novel I was reading, *Green Dolphin Country*, that a caring conductor suggested I might want to put my book down for a while and enjoy the scenery. He waved at the bright fields of golden wheat, edged like a birthday cake, with tall trees all round. I smiled politely out the window but returned to my book as soon as he moved on down the carpeted aisle. I don't think I moved until we reached our destination, when the aroma of potatoes sizzling in peanut oil made both Stan and me realize that we were as hungry as Canadian bears. That was when I discovered my purse was gone. In mere minutes, the conductor assured me that someone had turned it in and I'd have it in three hours. As we waited, starving, I controlled my first flash of anger towards Stan. The man had absolutely no money to share, not a centime, even to feed his pregnant wife. An ugly thought crept into my head as we walked through the fairy-tale setting of Louvain. What if Stan had planned for me to support him all along? What if he'd plotted out our "deal" long ago, maybe even before we got married, and then made it sound like a mutual decision? What if he planned to have me be the breadwinner for good? I scolded myself for thinking such a horrid thought in the midst of such an idyllic setting, and brushed my suspicions away.

~

It's astounding how much can be hidden in the background of a single day, especially under cover of silence. Up and out the door before 6:30 a.m., I'd eat a breakfast sandwich on the train. Thirteen hours later, at 7 p.m. I'd join Stan for supper at the Resto-U, the university cafeteria on the peaceful, leafy green campus of the Cité Universitaire de Paris, and then home to prepare for my next working day. The flurry of activity made it easier to conceal the little things that bothered me, little things that added up but that I failed to share with Stan. I didn't tell him how it felt to have him drop a pair of pants into the laundry basket or get back into them when they were all hand-washed and pressed without a thank-you. I didn't say how disappointed I'd felt with our lovemaking, how brief it seemed, and how Stan fell asleep so quickly. Was I so unattractive? Stan apologized, saying that his doctorate took everything out of him. Priding myself on my maturity, I said I understood. Yet, in a single second, in a split hair of an unguarded moment, all that had been denied, all the irritations I'd refused to acknowledge, burst out with entitlement all their own. Despite my presumed maturity, a meticulous record of subdued hurts did find a way out. Twice, before my pregnancy, I got badly drunk in Paris, my alcohol consumption triggering hours-long sobbing. Stan never asked me why I cried, never suggested I visit a counselor, never seemed the least bit interested in exploring my bizarre outbursts. Dreadfully ashamed, I apologized sincerely and promised to change. I would present no further impediment to our reason for being in Paris—his studies—and I'd try to become a better person. I wouldn't drink; I'd make up for my sins with good works.

For nearly two years, three times a week, I'd tutored Élisabeth, a senior teacher at the school. She was slim and tall, with short dark hair, slightly bent shoulders, and bright blue eyes that fanned a dozen laugh wrinkles. Judging by her tanned brown hands, I suspected, rightly, that this good-humored elementary school teacher was also a gardener. Sometimes we studied English in her kitchen, the walls cooled by ancient stone. I imagined the decades of French cooking in that solid reassuring space, where thick beams of gnarled wood over my head served not only as a kitchen ceiling but also as a bedroom floor.

"Imagine, your alarm clock is the scent of breakfast!" I laughed as my new friend presented me with two books, the first by a poet named Charles Peguy, a Catholic man who'd once owned her house, and the other called *We Have Been Friends Together*, by a philosopher and poet, Raïssa Maritain.

"Sit down and listen about the Maritains," Élisabeth said, serving fresh coffee and practicing her English. "Raïssa and her boyfriend, Jacques, were unhappy with their materialistic teachers at the Sorbonne. The two of them were so upset about the uniquely scientific approach of the university that they even thought of killing themselves in protest. Their suicide contract would be their personal solution to living in a godless world."

"Wow, even though they were madly in love with each other?" I asked.

"Yes, they couldn't accept that God allowed suffering and evil to exist. However, a small Catholic group advised them to wait a while, to be patient and trust that a message would be revealed to them." Élisabeth got up to snip herbs in her small garden.

"Did they receive a message?" I asked, following her.

"You tell me next week," she smiled, setting both books near my bag. "Now, we eat."

I caught the lemon she sent sailing through the air and together we ate an outstanding meal of fresh steamed salmon drizzled with garden herbs, lemon, and olive oil. I read first one then the other book that week. I read on the métro to work, on a park bench in the manicured green of Parc Montsouris, and in our room at the university residence. I asked a friendly psychology student, Marissa, a young British African scholar, guaranteed to be at the residence library every evening, to explain particular idiomatic phrases I had been unable to find in my trusty French dictionary. I wasn't consulting Stan any more. A dozen times he'd asked me to repeat back to him, in my own words, what he'd explained to me, so that he could determine if I'd managed to grasp the point he'd made.

"I'm not a child, Stan," I'd say, beginning to feel squeamish, a humiliated hostage nailed to the couch way too long. Why an hour-long lecture to a one-minute question? I preferred Marissa. She explained ideas to me in crisp ways that assumed I could understand her. The following weekend, I reported back to Élisabeth that Jacques and Raïssa felt betrayed. They felt their culture emphasized science and that so much outside of that discipline continued to be ignored.

"Yes," said Élisabeth, slicing ripe Brie. "Continue."

"Finally they met Catholic friends, poor people, who assured them of God's personal love for each of them. They were so deeply convinced that they established a prayer community, something like L'Arche."

"So it was a charming story of love and light?"

"Well, when I read they decided to live as brother and sister as personal penances to please God, it seems to me they did what they'd blamed God for earlier. They rained on their own parade. They darkened their own day."

"Do you enjoy being a Catholic?" she asked after we had eaten a delicious salad and fresh apple pie, "or is it to please your husband?"

"To please Stan. I don't like the Church, priests, or any religion for that matter."

"You attend Mass?"

"I'd much rather read in the park, a new story each week, not the same old dirge every Sunday morning. It's feudal to genuflect or curtsy this way and that, theatrics that mean nothing to me." I trusted Élisabeth. I went a step further. "And I always wonder what the priest is up to after his boring Mass. Who knows?"

"Yes, of course." Élisabeth nodded. "Have you shared these thoughts with Stan?"

"Yes, but he gets upset. I promised him I'd be a good Catholic before we married, so I want to keep the deal."

Élisabeth didn't roll her eyes or make any comment. We continued our lesson. She produced a poem called *Patriarchal Poetry* by Gertrude Stein, an American poet who had lived in Paris. She recited the lines several times, and each time she asked me to listen attentively to her pronunciation. At the end of our session, I congratulated Élisabeth on being a wonderful student, unaware that, in fact, my new friend had been trying to teach me. The next day at Mass, even though I felt a murky disloyalty to Stan, I sat in my pew and imagined my colleague out in her green garden, snipping herbs and picking apples and reading the books she chose for herself. As the priest traced the sign of the cross over his golden chalice, I visualized her, a free-as-a-bird, self-supporting teacher who had made a solid home for herself by the River Seine.

∾

"I can save you some reading time," said Stan when he saw me reading The Courage *to Be*, another of his reference books. "Paul Tillich's *New Being* is none other than Christ, the ultimate and only solution to human estrangement. That's basically all he's saying, so you can put down your pencil. No need to slog through the whole tome."

That evening, in the sparse wood-paneled Bibliothèque de la Maison Franco-Britannique, Marissa said she'd be more than happy to give me her take on the theologian.

"Look, Tillich's sister dies when he's twelve. Now he's fourteen and in shock when his father, a minister, abandons his only son in time-honored Christian fashion and deposits him in an orphanage boarding school, where the poor kid suffers wretched loneliness. Back home, his mother dies of cancer and he had no clue she'd even been sick. Later on, his wife leaves him for another man. So, yes indeed, estrangement was a hot topic for Tillich," she said, finishing her ten-second exposition.

"Stan said his book helped a lot of lonely people feel better," I said.

"Maybe a lot of lonely Christian people, but there are millions of people in the world for whom the Bible means diddly-squat."

"Really?" I asked, stunned. While I obviously knew of the existence of atheists and non-Christians, I had never thought of them as actual people, let alone millions of individuals who had no need or desire for doctrinal direction.

Later that night, when I shared Marissa's opinions with my husband, Stan said the Bible was indeed a source of comfort to many more millions of people than one would-be academic could possibly fathom. I replied that in all honesty I'd never found an ounce of comfort in the Bible either.

"That's because you've always anesthetized your pain," said Stan. "You fail to avail yourself of God's magnificent love, available to you in page after page of loving promise."

"What pain?" I asked. A flash of shame, like the hot sting of a slap, heated my body from head to toe.

That week, Edna airmailed my Bachelor of Arts diploma to me, with a small note saying that she'd taken the liberty of attending my graduation Mass for me. She said the altar had been beautifully laid out. I made a cup of tea and sat at the kitchen table to unwrap my framed degree. I waited for the big thrill. As I translated the Latin inscription across the top of the page, I felt some relief that a perpetual English expedition was now over. I wouldn't have to search for withheld meanings secreted away in ancient allusions any more. Endless queries and arguments as to what this or that bard meant by this or that phrase were officially over. As I left for work that day, I realized that neither my mother nor I had attended my graduation ceremony. Suddenly and inexplicably, I thought of Portia, Mother's favorite Shakespearean character, who even though she became a fancy lawyer, distinguished herself best of all by cleaning up her boyfriend's mess for him.

∾

Well into my eighth month of pregnancy, with Stan's courses nearly finished, I got off the métro at a Port d'Orléans clinic one day for a routine doctor's appointment. As I walked down a corridor near the birthing station, I was shocked to see a series of low wooden chairs with large toilet-sized circles cut out of the seats and a white tin basin under each one. In full view of passersby, right there in the public thoroughfare, a heavily pregnant woman adjusted her coat to cover herself, her skirt folded neatly beside her. As she lowered her head, my eyes fell to a trickle of blood and fluid oozing into the pan beneath her. If she stood up to alter her position, blood would trickle down her thighs and her bare behind would be exposed to public view. Perhaps it was her shyness or her personal dignity that prevented her from moving, other than to muffle her groans behind the only private place she could find, her own hand.

"Why isn't she behind closed doors so she can cry?" I asked my doctor. "She's in agony."

My physician explained that France, unlike Canada, endorsed natural childbirth, and that a drug-free birth would be far better for the sake of the baby.

"But what about her?" I asked. "What about the mother?"

He answered that there were serious space constraints at the clinic. As I dressed in my baggy polka-dot maternity top after my examination, I wondered why a woman who made sufficient room inside her own body and even distended it to its bursting point was denied similar consideration. I recalled what Mother had told me years earlier, when her parish priest asked her when she'd be making another soul for God. Mother said that if a priest ever spent so much as five minutes on a labor table, giving birth would become a mortal sin. I imagined the doctor sitting on that torture chair. Would he insist on pain killers? Who'd dare refuse him?

The following day, with the savings from my three jobs, I booked my own solid, comfortable seat on a plane that would fly to Toronto, where Stan's mother now lived. I'd have my baby in Canada.

I had enough cash for three months' rent, food, and expenses. We'd be okay while Stan looked for work anywhere that was reachable by Toronto's vast subway system. There'd be no desperation about job hunting, no panic about bus fare, rent, or food. Stan was nearly finished anyway and could fly back to Paris to defend his thesis when the time came.

We found a tiny attic flat on Albert Street, clean and roach-free. The mice I discovered later. Stan's mother gave me a stew pot, a potato peeler, material for curtains, and a brass curtain rod. Every time Edna visited, she brought a useful gift for our tiny nest. Proud of the care I took during my pregnancy, I followed Adele Davis's book, *Let's Eat Right to Keep Fit,* which Maureen sent in the mail, along with a beautiful card saying that when she was free, which she hoped would be "before the snow flies," she'd visit.

Irene and Brigit lived in Western Canada, Sheilagh in the U.S., the boys struggling in Vancouver, all of us in very different worlds. My younger brothers had no phone but when Danny called to borrow money that summer, he said he'd see the baby when he next came east. Joey lived in Toronto and we visited twice, but it was clear that alcohol ruled. His pregnant wife told me she'd leave my brother soon unless there was a major turnaround. There never was.

In our upper flat, I took all the vitamins and folic acid tablets that were never available to my foremothers. I ate well, our table a rainbow of green, orange, and yellow every day, and I drank a special concoction called Tiger's Milk. I couldn't wait to meet my baby, a child I already loved with all my heart. One sunny day, while Stan subbed for the Toronto School Board, I sat on the carpeted floor near our small attic windows, a pillow to my back, and gazed at an astonishing *Time / Life* photograph of a baby inside a mother's womb. I had no idea how such a photograph could have been taken, but it inspired me to draw a woven basket so full of spring flowers they toppled over the sides, a welcome-home card for my soon-to-be-born baby. I got lost in art and wondered, as I had a hundred times before, whether I'd give birth to a daughter or a son. My idyllic hour was interrupted by a call from our local priest, a cleric we'd met at his parish on St. Clair Avenue soon after our return.

"Is your husband home, Eleanor?" he asked.

"No, shall I have Stan call you, Father?"

"Actually, I want to speak to you, which is why I am calling you at this time."

I wondered if he wanted to book the baby's baptism.

"There's been a complaint from a parent of one of our little girls from the First Communion group," he said.

"The one Stan is volunteering at?" I asked.

"Yes, well," Father hesitated. "His service is now, most clearly, at an end. The child told her parents that Stan touched her private parts."

"Touched her?"

"Yes, fondled her inside her underwear when he took her to the washroom to pee." He blundered on as though my heart wasn't beating a mile a minute, as though I was Stan's lawyer and not his wife. "Stan had no business escorting her to the bathroom. There was a female volunteer available right there in the same room. He should have deferred to her."

"Yes." I watched my belly ripple.

"Please have Stan call me. I have some suggestions I hope he'll follow." I hung up and lay flat on the carpet. I watched my belly undulate. I waited for Stan.

~

"What a foul-mouthed liar! It's not true!" Stan roared, outraged. "That priest suffers from an authority problem! My success with the kids irritates him. It bothers him to have the competition of a former seminarian from a prestigious order, not an uneducated, dime-a-dozen country frock like him!"

"Stan, did you take a little girl into the women's washroom?"

"You never lived in residence with seminarians like I did," he shouted, jabbing his finger, still talking about the priests he once lived with. "*Playboy* magazines under beds, clandestine dating and, oh yes, the call girls, slutty prostitutes secreted under cover of night into residence bedrooms! Oh, yes! Believe me, I had to live with blatant immorality, night after night! And no one liked me. Why? Because I made waves, because I reported their screwing around! And here, a priest is accusing me?"

"Stan, why didn't you ask the woman volunteer to take the little girl to the washroom?"

"I didn't think of it! It didn't occur to me! And it's not true! I did nothing wrong!" Stan began to cry. He sat on the couch, covered his face with his hands, and wept genuine sobs, an undeniable testament to his innocence. Who could generate real tears, unbidden?

"Let's go, Stan. Let's discuss this with Father and the little girl's parents."

"No! We're not going near that filthy liar. I need you to believe me! Is that too much to ask of my own wife, my own spouse?" he asked, tears streaming down his face. "I would never, ever, have done what he accused me of, never, never, never, never. It's just not true!" Stan's back and shoulders shook as his tears fell onto his shirt. I'd never seen him this upset. "I'm a good person," he cried, the corners of his mouth flecked with white foam. I did not question why a grown man would steer a little girl into a women's washroom, or think that he must have made sure the coast was clear, chosen the moment his co-volunteer was busy, just as his mother had been occupied in the past, and my mother, fast asleep.

"I believe you, Stan," I said. "I believe you." And I did. I'd learned not to question early on. While it's grueling to stifle such inquiry early in life, eventually, with practice, rationality subsides.

"That's all I need to know, then," he said. He stood up and sighed several times, deep breaths of relief. "All a man needs to know is that his own wife backs him. That's all he needs. I'm going out for a walk in the park," he said. "Thank you, Eleanor, for your confidence in me."

When I called Father back, he declined my request to drop by the flat that evening, perhaps with another priest, and talk with Stan.

"He's upset, Father," I said. "Please come to our place, since he won't go to you."

"No, Stan can present himself at my office, with you, if you wish. I will see him here. Otherwise, I have only one suggestion for you, that you tell your husband to seek therapy immediately." When I relayed the message Father could not bring himself to deliver, my husband also delegated a message, through me, his pregnant handmaiden. He told me to call the priest and recommend similar therapy.

"That country frock is an outrageous liar. Anyway, now that you fully support me in the truth, Eleanor, let's leave it alone. We have a baby coming into the world now. Let's focus on that special joy in our lives."

∽

As I held my newborn son close to me that summer, two thoughts held sway: first, that with Teddy, I'd never be lonely again and, second, that I felt happier than I'd ever been in my life. Over the next weeks and months, little Teddy and I gazed at each other for long hours and I felt my heart expand with love. I was a mother now.

"We rarely see a newborn so pink, so oxygenated!" my nurse congratulated me, her words an award. The morning after I gave birth, she handed me a beer. "The hops will rush your breast milk in, you'll see!"

And it was true; bluish milk dribbled out in minutes and Teddy knew what to do. I didn't finish the drink. I neither smoked nor drank during my pregnancy and had no intention of starting up ever again. A committed mother with a universally admired new identity, I had a goal and a reason to live. The old Eleanor was gone, the impossible page of bad memories forever turned.

"He's going to be one good-looking man!" said my hospital roommate.

"Thank you," I replied, taking full credit.

～

I longed for my mother. I needed her more now, it seemed, than I ever had. One morning as I held Teddy to my breast, it came to me at last that my mother was dead and that she had died an unhappy woman. The birth of my baby made tolerable a fact I could only now accept, that I'd never see my mother again in my lifetime. With Teddy in my arms, I wept freely and naturally. It was bearable now. At home, Teddy's little cot stayed next to my bed. I kept a small hand mirror under my pillow and sometimes held it under his nose while he slept, checking for the two tiny reassuring circles of moisture. My son gained weight and showed great curiosity about the world around him, but maintained a serious countenance for weeks until the morning he displayed his first genuine smile, directed at me. The same joy I felt when I learned that I was pregnant warmed my body from head to toe.

"Thank you, my darling," I said at his first affirmation.

～

One morning in July 1976, I was nursing Teddy while watching the Montreal Olympics on the TV our landlord had kindly loaned us. In an instant, the pillows that supported my back against the wall felt like stone as I listened to a flash news report.

Teddy was asleep when I whispered to Stan, "A child's been sexually abused in Guelph. What a horrible, unspeakable thing." The words tumbled out, faster and faster. "That freak deserves life in prison!"

Standing over me, Stan replied, "Are you aware that judgment is the sole recourse of the simple-minded?"

"What?" I asked, my hands breaking into a sweat. "What would you do, Stan, if that poor kid had been our Teddy? What would your response to that travesty be?" I looked up, a screaming viciousness rising in my chest.

"I'd inquire," replied Stan. "I'd approach the situation in a spirit of inquiry. Please remember in your haste to condemn, the creature you accuse is also a child of God, a struggling human soul."

"Then before indulging himself, would it not be incumbent upon that ravaged addict to seek help?" I was trying to accommodate Stan's stiff academic style.

"I suppose you could ask the same of an alcoholic," Stan answered. "Sometimes the solution involves a conversion experience between God and the tormented individual. You think you know so much. Everything is so simple to you."

"A child in Fergus was fucked," I said, my voice breaking out of a whisper. "What's complicated about that?"

"I'm not going to attempt a rational discussion with someone whose emotions flood logic," he said. "And your language, especially for a mother, is filthy."

I stifled revulsion as he shut the flimsy door behind him.

"In future," he shouted from a distance, "if you wish to make a point, kindly address my intellect without the vile emotional vocabulary that so easily escapes your mouth. And by the way, the locale mentioned on the newscast was Guelph, not Fergus."

Once again, just as Stan had done at the Ottawa church several years earlier during our engagement, the topic of political sexual abuse had been replaced by a new topic: *my* guilt, *my* filthy mouth, *my* topple from the mother pedestal.

After his bath that night, I bent over and kissed Teddy's face, his tummy, and his little penis. Instantly, I wondered, "Why did I do that?" but I didn't get to answer my question before I heard Stan's voice behind me.

"Right now I could accuse you of sexual abuse," he said. "I could say that kiss you gave Teddy constitutes a violation."

I stood in front of him, red-faced and speechless.

"Things aren't always so simple, are they?" he said, as he left for a walk.

"Costa spoke disrespectfully to me," said Stan, storming back upstairs moments later. He'd confronted our landlord, who lived on the first floor with his wife and new baby daughter. Costa, a construction worker, had offered to get Stan a job on his work crew. "His barely contained sneer, every time I pass by, says it all. I suggest you cool it with them, and by the way, I sense similar derision from your La Leche League friend too. Just because I'm unemployed, I don't deserve her barely concealed contempt."

"I never saw any of that, Stan," I said, a sinking feeling in my stomach.

"Look, when I say people are rude to me, I'd appreciate some support from my wife," said Stan. Our landlady appeared when Stan left the house.

"Sorry husbands fight," she said, handing me a peace offering of baklava. A blue bruise formed in my throat as she placed a finger to her lips, kissed Teddy, and crept downstairs again.

~

"Can you come, Maureen?" I asked on the phone. "Come see Teddy!"

"I know this is hard for you to understand now that you're not working, Norda, but I'm deluged. Deluged! My work load never, ever ends!"

I called Irene and Brigit and Sheilagh too. None of my siblings were free to visit during the early years of Teddy's life. We'd all recoiled, it seems, each to their own corner, trying to fashion a stable life. Over the years to come, it remained that way, our relationships always pleasant, removed, brief, and cordial – and yet, decade after decade, maintained.

A month later, another phone call.

"Look, Eleanor," said the principal of the school where Stan worked as a substitute teacher. "I'll be frank with you. Your husband is fast becoming our least favorite choice of sub around here. He's Mr. Military in all his classes and isolates himself from the staff. We're more than a little fed up. He's too harsh. Knock some sense into him, will you?"

Fighting the storm in my belly, I agreed to speak to him that day.

"That mouthy student deserved it," said Stan after school. "The class was secretly happy I dealt with him, that brash know-it-all. He deserved what he got."

"It's not your job to deal with anyone, Stan. That's the principal's job, not yours, and furthermore, I doubt he'd have given the kid a clout."

When I answered the next morning's substitution call, I thanked the secretary for calling Stan. I told her that with a new baby, we very much appreciated the work and thanked her again.

"Why so profuse?" asked Stan. "Why mewl?"

"People are more likely to call the grateful person who says 'thank you' than one who doesn't, Stan. That's why," I answered.

"You're manipulative," said Stan. "The school should be thanking me. Not every sub has a doctorate."

It never occurred to me that I was compensating for my husband's lack of social skills, for his desire to draw away from everyone except those he considered, on a strict vertical hierarchy, to be less than himself. Like my husband, I was locked into my own limited perceptions, my own topical solutions of minimizing and normalizing. We were two frightened peas in a pod.

When the final call came from the principal, not even my social graces could save Stan's job. "I'm sorry, Eleanor. Your husband acted physically aggressive again today. He's fired."

"Oh, no!"

"I have to blacklist him so that other schools won't suffer his outbursts as well."

"Oh, no," I replied again, my anxiety mounting.

"I'm sorry it had to end this way," he said. "Your husband should work away from kids—far away."

Stan defended himself to the rooftops. I tried to reason with him.

"No, Stan. It isn't your job to dish out punishment. The problem is the principal's to solve, not yours."

"He's as weak as you are," said Stan. "He sugar-coats reality instead of dealing with it. I'm a person of integrity. I do what needs doing when it needs doing."

"You overstepped, Stan. That's disrespect too. "

That week at home, Stan asked me how long I intended to breastfeed Teddy.

"Eighteen months," I said. "La Leche says he'll have antibodies for life and a well-shaped palate for straight teeth. Why do you ask?"

"I ask because since you side with the principal instead of with me, since you think sugar-coating reality is the way to go, then maybe you should be the one out there facing the work world. I'd continue polishing off my thesis, the completion of which you interrupted."

"And who'd look after Teddy?" I asked nervously.

"I would," he said, as if it was the easiest thing in the world. "Don't feminists blare about fathers assuming a stronger role in the family now? Isn't that so?"

"No, Stan. That wasn't the deal we made in Paris. I supported you for two years. I paid off your student loan. You can scare up one job in this great big city. I'm staying with Teddy."

Weeks later, my savings used up, we applied for welfare. Support at last.

We moved closer to the Danforth, a busy, close-knit, working-class community featuring clusters of sidewalk stores that displayed all manner of goods, from shoes to fruit and vegetables to pots and pans, on wide wooden platforms several feet tall. While our clothes rinsed in the laundromat machine, Teddy and I strolled up and down the block, sometimes chatting with the butcher as he wrapped a half-dozen sausages, and then, once we switched our clothes to the dryer, off we went for our half-price vegetables, which I found fine for blended soup and rice dishes. To me, buttered pumpernickel bread or rye buns sprinkled with sesame seeds were as delicious as cake and ice cream.

"Please don't scrap with this Italian couple," I implored Stan. "They could have rented to working people."

"Why the disrespectful tone?" Stan asked. "You still don't believe that student deserved a cuffing, do you? Even after hours of detailed explanation, you still cling to your stubborn stance."

One Sunday before Mass, our parish priest asked me if I'd like to volunteer some time to help a young New Brunswick woman in her late twenties who had two toddlers. "You're a woman," he said. "You can help her far better than I can."

"Let's visit a bit out here first," I said after Father introduced us on the front steps and then hastened away. Kelly nodded at the Mass about to begin, the sun catching the darkest sea-blue eyes I'd ever seen.

"Let's take our time," she said. "I've about had it with that re-run. It's like watching the same old hockey game over and over and over again."

We laughed, bonding instantly over a stale religious ritual that bored us both to tears. That afternoon I minded her little Billy and Liz for the hour it should have taken Kelly to run around the corner for a prescription she needed. She wasn't back two hours later, or even after supper.

"I traipsed all over the Danforth looking for a pharmacy that was open," she apologized. "He had only half the dosage. Then I lost my bus tickets." I noted grayish holes in her front teeth and stains hiding in her yellow flowered dress. She declined the meal I'd saved for her, but when her little boy suggested I wrap it up for him to eat later, his mother agreed. Early the next morning, Teddy was delighted to see Kelly's kids back again.

"Is that breakfast offer still on?" their mother asked shyly, still in the same dress, one raggedy child on either side. Over our meal, Kelly told me that she and her children's father were from large Catholic families near Moncton. He was in a halfway house right now, she was on welfare. When Kelly left the kids with me again so she could fill the other half of her prescription, I suspected, rightly, that Teddy had friends for the day.

"Hold on a minute," said Stan after she left. "Are you a babysitting agency? Is she paying you for this?"

"She's on the same welfare we're on, Stan. She's all alone with two children, and sick on top of it."

Stan left for another day of job-searching at the library. The kids and I walked the several blocks to the local Birthright agency. With a mere glance, the volunteer accurately measured each child and filled a big bag with pants, new underwear and T-shirts, all in the exact right sizes. She tossed in a puzzle for Liz and Tonka trucks for Teddy and Billy.

"You're doing a fine job, Mom," she smiled, handing me a strip of bus tickets.

"I'm itchy," said Billy when we got home. "Mum said to ask you for a bath."

"She did, did she?" I laughed. Billy instructed me as I shampooed his hair.

"Do my sister next," he ordered, a real little boss. The sides of the tub were greasy gray when the children climbed into their clean clothes from Birthright.

"I suspect," said Stan when he got home for supper, "that your new friend is an addict."

Kelly stumbled back in the early evening, her face slightly green and shiny. "I'm on a bad slip," she said. "I've relapsed. I need to get to the Sally Ann tomorrow. Can we stay here tonight?"

"Sure, Kelly. What about Billy and Liz?"

"Intake will foster them 'till I detox. We'll look you guys up after."

In the morning, Kelly half sat, half lay, starkly awake in the den, her skin covered with tiny beads, hundreds of greenish tears weeping through her skin. "I'm god-awful sick. This is my fourth time kicking diet pills. Oh, I'm dying." She vomited into my cake bowl while we waited for the taxi.

"One day this will be the story of a victory, Kelly. Billy and Liz will be so proud of their mother," I said.

Billy stroked his mother's hair while she, a glistening twist of nausea, began her brave withdrawal.

"Please," said the cab driver, an older man, "if you need to throw up, tell me."

The instant we arrived at the Salvation Army center, Kelly jumped out with her kids.

"I'm sorry," she said. "I lost my wallet."

I thought the driver would ask me to pay, but he didn't. "Life is difficult," he sighed, as we both waved goodbye to Kelly, Billy, and Liz. A true philosopher, he insisted on driving Teddy and I home again, no charge.

"That could have been you, you know," said Stan. "You're lucky you have a husband to care for you."

The day after Kelly entered the detox unit, Teddy and I made cookies for two elderly neighbors, both recovering from surgery. The two women had been housemates for decades.

"Take some tea upstairs to June," Miss Rose said. At Miss June's bedside, I noticed a small gilt-edged photograph of a teenager, a young man holding a can of beer and laughing for the camera.

"Who's that handsome lad?" I asked Miss June.

"My son," she answered.

When I asked another question about him, she became agitated. "Ask no questions and I'll tell no lies," she snapped.

In an eerie, loaded instant, as though nailed to the floor, I hoped never, ever to be in her shoes. I held Teddy close. How could a mother have a child she didn't want to talk about? What had happened between them?

"Thanks for the tea," she said, her cue for me to leave. Downstairs, Miss Rose explained that Miss June's son had been beaten by his father as a kid but even so, the boy disliked his mother most of all. She'd divorced the man she should have rehabilitated. She'd abandoned his father. Even though his mother lived in peace with Miss Rose, even though she'd flourished and raised her son well, the boy claimed that she'd betrayed his father. She failed her marriage vows of "for better or for worse." She failed to stand by her man. Handing me her garden shears, Miss Rose asked me to cut some flowers from the yard before we left. "Her son's poor opinion of her is the only thorn in her side," she said, trying to reassure me. I held Teddy in my arms all the way home. How could a mother live with that torment?

~

There was no question. It was time for us to have a second child. I knew it.

"We're on welfare," Stan said. "I don't have a job yet."

"You will," I said, filled with hope. "With all your education, you'll get a great job soon."

The very next day, I felt a tiny motion, the thrilling flutter of a butterfly, the pop of a minnow's bubble, and I knew without a doubt that I was pregnant with my new baby, a dear person, a strong spirit, a beautiful energy. I couldn't compute that we were mouse-poor on welfare, that Stan wasn't remotely interested in working for a living, or in me personally, and that I too had serious problems, but I was thrilled to calculate that my new baby would be born in the springtime. It seemed that even if one part of me felt fenced in, the part that could not face reality, another part soared over all that to a bright new tomorrow. I was indeed pregnant with my second child.

I was always the one who instigated affection. I'd put my arms around Stan, give him warm looks, and suggest we make love. It became clear to me that Stan wasn't interested and so, after Nell's birth, I ended the humiliation. After our first years of marriage, the belief that my husband was busy with intense studies no longer sufficed. Stan wasn't attracted to me, nor had he ever been. Years later, when he accused me of having used him as a sperm bank, I replied that it was true, since he'd declined to give me more, he had indeed reduced himself to being a sperm bank. I had no idea he'd married me for his own reasons. I said nothing more about our early separation. Talking things over would have meant that stored-up feelings, horrible memories, and denied resentments would somehow be voiced and, like my mother before me, I had no permission for such honesty and certainly no experience of it. Still, even though I married the wrong partner, I got the exact right kids.

I knew how to be thrifty. I prided myself on how far I could stretch our monthly check after the rent was paid. I froze day-old bread and bought week-old vegetables that looked perfectly fine for the delicious blended soups I made. Nothing was wasted and desserts were rare, so the vanilla cake I baked for a friend coming in from Montreal would be a special treat.

"I forgot she was visiting," Stan said, moments before Vi arrived with her overnight case.

"But Stan, we talked about it this morning, and yesterday, and last week!"

"I have no recollection of that," he said.

That evening, while Vi and I set our supper table, I asked Stan to give Teddy his evening bath. Within minutes, high screams curdled from the bathroom. Racing to Teddy, I lifted him from the steaming water and screamed at Stan to turn off the shower.

"The water's hot! He's burned!" I screamed. Vi stood in the hallway, both hands covering her mouth. I bundled Teddy in a towel and held him close but he continued to scream. I ran to the kitchen sink, where Vi immersed a towel in cool water to wrap around him.

"Who used the shower last?" asked Stan. "Who failed to return the dial to its original position?"

"You, Stan, you did."

"Yes, well, as I say, the knob should have been turned back. I forgot to check it."

"How, Stan?"

"Are you accusing me?" he asked incredulously. "Is this an interrogation, a hostile cross-examination?"

"You put Teddy in an empty tub? Who gets into a tub and turns the shower on without testing the water first?" I shouted at him.

"You usually give Teddy his bath, not me. You're the one who revised the schedule. You're the one who invited a guest, not me!" he said, giving Vi a second shock.

I stayed with Teddy, comforting him in his wet towel until he fell asleep in my arms, little red patches mottled all over tummy and thighs. He was only thirteen months old.

"I didn't enjoy being humiliated in front of your guest," said Stan after Vi left early. "You owe me an apology for that hysterical scene in front of a complete stranger."

I stopped inviting friends over. I understood there'd be consequences for any intrusion into our isolated home. Had I been more aware, I'd have connected the dots from his behavior that night to his chronic unemployment, fear of authority, religious cover, and shameless sense of entitlement to the money and support of others. When the welfare agent visited us that week, she got to the point quickly.

"Still having trouble finding work?" she asked Stan, who handed over a thick file of applications to universities all across Canada and the U.S.

"I don't think there's a school in North America I've left out," he said.

"And what about you?" She turned to me.

"My husband and I made an arrangement that after our first child was born, I'd stay at home," I said.

She snapped closed her portfolio and stood up. "One of you works next month."

"Too bad substitute teaching is out, eh, Stan?" I said when she left.

"Am I hearing criticism?"

"You're hearing regret. We got by on that salary." That evening I worried about our landlords, who'd trusted us to pay the rent. They believed our promise, my sincere promise.

"I'm terrified," I said. "Our landlords have three kids. They count on us to pay on time every month without fail. We promised them, Stan."

"You can get work a lot faster than I can," Stan said. "You have common, marketable skills. There's plenty of work for secretaries like you, whereas for me, the pickings are few and far between."

With a single phone call, I found a job. Toronto's Kelly Agency confirmed plenty of available work, even for pregnant wives. I'd start at $5.35 an hour. I calculated that if Teddy slept later in the mornings and if I could be home by 4 p.m., the loss of our time together could be minimized to four hours.

"This is a temporary measure only, Stan." I said this for his benefit as much as to reassure myself.

"Let's face it," Stan said before I left. "It's a women's world now. Funny how you gals got your liberation and now all you want to do is stay home."

"I choose to stay at home with Teddy as per our deal," I said, as I made my lunch for work.

Teddy thrashed in his father's arms as I left for work, his little body twisting to free legs that weren't long enough to chase after me as I headed to the subway. I can still hear his desperate screams and feel the squeeze, the terrible moment of desperation. I wanted to grab him and tell Stan that no, absolutely not, I couldn't do it. But I kept walking, over the screams of my frightened child. I abandoned my little baby to rescue my big one. I sacrificed the son for the father, in seamless accord with my cultural and religious training.

While I worked downtown during the day, Stan wrote his thesis about maturation in a primitive world. After an early lunch, he put Teddy back to bed for a nap, one that lasted four hours.

"Oh, gosh," he said when I came home. "You back already?"

Teddy and I played till one in the morning, sometimes till two, certainly not the 10 p.m. bedtime I'd originally calculated. I'd sink into bed, exhausted, and sleep until the alarm rang at 6 a.m., when I dressed and tiptoed out of the flat, careful not to make noise. I began to live a double life: work routine in the daytime and a night-time schedule with Teddy.

The day I started my job, Jill, a member of our church, discovered she was pregnant with baby number four. She hoped with all her heart this would be the longed-for little boy, the son who would please her husband. Over tea at her house one Saturday afternoon, she told me how rudely Bryce spoke to her, how he demeaned her incessantly, even in front of their children. "Two of my daughters now boss me around like I'm their maid. 'Get me this, get me that, hurry and faster.'"

"How awful," I said, watching her dip into her ironing basket. "You iron his underwear?" I asked, astonished.

When I got home, I asked Stan to have a friendly word with Bryce.

"Mind your own business," Stan said. "She can talk to Father Fetrick if she wants. And you don't know the whole story either. I mean, she's clearly uneducated. He's far superior to her in intellect."

"So superior he married someone he couldn't talk to?"

"Maybe he wasn't interested in conversation."

"What do you mean, Stan?"

"Well," he began, but stopped himself. "I wouldn't get involved, that's all."

I was astonished to discover, the very next week, that Jill had flown the coop. Seven months pregnant, she went home to her parents in the Gaspé, leaving her man with the care of fledglings Regan and Goneril, her two demanding daughters, and the quiet youngest one. When I dropped by their house the following Saturday morning with Teddy bundled into his sled, I found the poor man up to his knees in laundry, the kitchen counter littered, the sink full, and his three girls parked around the TV, snapping orders.

"My wife left me!" he wailed, his face stunned, the news still fresh. "Maybe it's her pregnancy, her hormones."

"Maybe it's all those lovely compliments you give her day after day," I thought. I sensed he wanted me to rush in, roll up my sleeves, and help out, but I spent my day off with Teddy.

"I'm paying a fortune for the housekeeper," he reported the following week at church. "I even have to pay a neighbor to pick the girls up after school on top of every other damn expense! It never ends!"

The worst was yet to come. When he finally swallowed his pride and made the phone call he vowed he wouldn't, when he told Jill he forgave her irresponsible behavior and insisted she come home, she declined.

"She told me she didn't love me anymore," he said at our door that evening, pale and trembling, a different man. Stripped of his importance, he'd lost the one and only person who cared about him, the only person who felt proud of the fancy letters decorating the end of his name, the only woman who wanted a hug from him.

"I realize that I love my wife. I may have made a mistake," he ventured, incredulity spreading across his face. "She told me that if she'd treated me the way I did her, she'd understand my leaving her too. That's how she communicates with me, in a considerate way I never quite understood until now."

The neighbor charged a mint to look after his daughters for five days while he went to the Gaspé but he didn't care. The following week he reported, with even more alarm, that he was the one on trial now. Jill said she'd come home, but only for a test period. Even Stan seemed surprised.

~

One day Stan called me at work to say that our son looked pale and was unusually quiet. Teddy's doctor said on the phone that it was just the sniffles, and he'd soon be fine.

"I'll meet you at the Wellesley subway, Stan. We'll take him to the hospital. Please hurry."

"I can take him," he said. "You don't need to miss work for this."

"I'm leaving now," I replied, already anxious. When I got to the subway station, Stan was holding an inert Teddy in his blue crib blanket. "He's dying, Stan!" I screamed. "Look at him! Hurry! Get a taxi!"

The instant we exited the subway, a taxi driver threw open the back door of his cab.

"Hospital?" he asked as we got in, and tore away from the curb. This magnificent stranger leaned on his horn, ran a red light, and picked up a police escort to the emergency entrance of the Toronto Hospital for Sick Kids. The care was instant. A doctor grabbed Teddy and yanked off his diaper to reveal dollops of rectal blood. She ran down the hall with him.

"You can't come into radiology," she called back. "You're pregnant."

I lowered myself onto one of the hard plastic chairs in the waiting area, wondering what was happening in the radiology wing, and what the doctor would say.

"Good thing you got him here so fast," she said when she finally did appear, a lifetime later. "He would have died."

"Could this happen again, doctor?" I wept. Teddy'd been fine that morning.

"The intestines sometimes retract, but rarely in breastfed kids like Teddy. We don't know why this happened. It was a painful ordeal for the little guy."

I told Stan I couldn't go back to work; he had to find a job. But when my landlords grew anxious three weeks later, I relented and went back out to earn our rent. Slowly, I became exhausted. One evening when I arrived home at 5 p.m. to find my son still asleep, I burst into tears at the top of the stairs, a show of emotion Stan interpreted as manipulative. He reminded me that I could best appeal to him by engaging his intellect, not by emotional outbursts that reminded him of an alcoholic's temperament. I learned to speak to Stan in an emotion-free voice if I wanted to be taken seriously. But then he accused me of failing to communicate the degree of distress I felt because, as he said, my calm tone indicated nothing untoward.

"Stan, I can't keep burning the candle at both ends. I'm pregnant!"

"But what about the pressure I'm under," he retorted. "No one understands how far along I am with my thesis. Who cares about my critical gestation process?"

The next day, when Stan forgot to wake Teddy from his long afternoon nap before I got home, I was too tired to go through another harangue. I let it go the next evening too. Over time, the argument shifted to new terrain. The issue was no longer whether or not I'd work but how many hours of sleep I could be grateful for. When I broke down and cried, Stan accused me of using feminine wiles to make him feel guilty. My complaints about exhaustion were perceived as schemes to undermine his academic aspirations. His was a firm line of refusal. It was I who bounced up and down like a pogo stick, who gave him full support for his critical academic project one day and begged for sleep the next. It was I, not he, who displayed the jagged features of emotional instability. In mid-March, Stan's mother made a rescue call.

"A moving company needs muscle, Stan! A grocery store needs shelvers and a hotel is looking for a night clerk, all work you can do! Norda has got to rest in her last two months of pregnancy."

"Do you recall the summer you assigned me to replace all the insulation under our cottage, Mother? Do you recall how that grinding exertion injured my back and how, therefore, shelving or moving stoves might possibly aggravate that old injury?"

"Hotel clerk then?" Undaunted, Edna sipped tea at our kitchen table.

"My mother," said Stan after she left, "values manual labor far more than the academic forging ahead I do. Of course, she's not intellectually inclined, so why blame her?"

"Have you given birth on a labor table ten times?" I muted my anger.

"Have you ever lain flat out under a house for an entire summer?" Stan asked, adding, "You know, I'm beginning to feel disrespected by both you and my mother."

Not a week later, in the spring of 1978, Stan had an idea. Hundreds of disgruntled English families were fleeing Montreal and the Parti Québécois' promise to separate Quebec from the rest of Canada and make French the province's primary language. The looming threat of disconnection was causing an exodus down Highway 401 to Ontario.

"Hundreds of families who are terrified of losing their Canadian citizenship are leaving behind a lot of bilingual jobs, there for the taking," said Stan. "There's work in Quebec for me. Let's go."

What a price Teddy's grandmother paid for opening her mouth.

On April 1, I signed the lease for our apartment on Academy Road in Montreal, the city of my birth. The sweet scent of molasses from the POM bakery added to the marvel of a well-groomed park across the street. I considered how lucky I was, at thirty years old, to have my darling Teddy and my second baby soon to come. What a contrast to the vulnerable young woman with a binge-drinking problem who'd left for Paris three years earlier. And now, back in Montreal for some rest. Those last weeks of my second pregnancy, I slept in as long as Teddy, napped in the afternoons, and went to bed early, gray fatigue transforming to warm, pink energy. Teddy and I attended story time at the Children's Library before playtime in the sand box. "Feed birds!" laughed my son. Filled with excitement, he chased after squirrels with the new friends he made so easily.

Soon our daughter arrived, tiny pink hands clasped to her head as though she had a headache. I named her Nell, the Irish name of her beautiful great-grand-mother, the first-born child of Irish immigrant booksellers in the late 1800s and a woman who, I'd heard, loved to read and recite poetry. As I held Nell close, I admired her amazing ability to locate herself, to look around with her electric gray-blue eyes until she fixed on me, her rosebud lips voicing the softest greeting mere minutes after her birth. I found this extraordinary. I kissed her smooth cheeks and welcomed my daughter. Just saying the words "my daughter" was thrilling.

On the phone the next morning, Maureen told me she'd had a telephone misunderstanding with a nurse in the maternity ward during my labor. She feared I'd died. She sounded relieved to hear I was fine, but I noticed she hadn't rushed to see me in the hospital, minutes away from her apartment.

From my bed, I phoned Brigit in Edmonton, where she was working to pay for her studies, sometimes providing emergency support for Paddy in Vancouver. My brother's red liquid problem was now a white powder one.

"Don't be fooled," said Brigit, after congratulating me on the arrival of her brand new niece, "...by the fancy logo on the envelopes Paddy stole. The word 'fancy' in no way applies to his hotel on East Hastings Street in Vancouver. In fact, the one room he shares with six others is a hovel. I can't count the number of times he's overdosed and been rushed to hospital or sent to detox. I rarely hear from Danny any more. "

When Paddy called months later, he said he'd found God. "I'm in Alcoholics Anonymous now, and by the grace of God I'm clean and sober just for today. I have one main job in life and that is to stay sober. It's my only responsibility. The rest, all the rest, I leave in the hands of God." He began a job his AA sponsor got for him. When his girlfriend gave birth to their twins, one of them handicapped, she stayed with her mother on the west side of Vancouver. She and her sons never heard from Paddy again

Holding my precious, perfectly healthy child in my arms, gazing into her pink baby face while we talked about my poor lost brothers, I wondered why I was so lucky. I had a daughter now, and a son. I had a clean place to live, with a beautiful park across the street. I had so much.

Three months later, my savings used up, I agreed to a temp job to tide us over. Stan hadn't grabbed hold of a bilingual job after all. Even though he left every morning for the library, his central place of job hunting, he complained there were no jobs to be had.

I worked a mere five hours a day so I wouldn't have to give up breastfeeding Nell. I began as a temp clerk in an engineering firm on University Street for six dollars an hour, more than I'd made in Toronto. Stan brought Nell to my workplace during my lunch hour, and I rolled my office chair into the elegant carpeted women's washroom to nurse her and visit with Teddy at the same time. By mid-afternoon, milk would start to soak my blouse and I'd rush home in agony to feed Nell again. Fatigue ran me ragged.

It also resulted in major dental surgery for Teddy. I'd taken to splashing a little maple syrup into his milk bottle when he fussed in the wee hours of the night between Nell's breast-feedings. I knew that if I didn't get at least five hours of sleep a night, I'd be in trouble. The sweetened milk seemed the easiest solution. Teddy loved the sugary taste, emptied his bottle in no time flat, and fell right back to sleep. I got an essential two hours before Nell's next feeding. I hadn't counted on that syrup rotting poor Teddy's teeth though. Once we'd figured out the cause, the dental surgeon told me that all of Teddy's back teeth had to come out. I felt his contained anger, and noted that he avoided my eyes as he explained that maple syrup was an acid that bores through baby teeth. The color drained from my face as I promised the surgeon I'd stop this unacceptable practice immediately. Teddy screamed as he was pulled away from me by green-smocked adults who anesthetized him as he struggled on the surgery table, and I died a certain death by fire in the waiting room, a slow bursting balloon of toxic self-hate. I should have known better. I'd never read a parenting book in my life.

~

I saw the "Waitress Wanted" sign, and the word "evenings" handwritten below. If I worked nights, I could be with the kids all day, worry-free, rent paid. The friendly restaurant owners welcomed me, trained me well, and, like magic, life changed. There were daytime picnics in the park with my children, fresher foods on the table, and a grand luxury, sleep by midnight. For Teddy's third birthday, he laughed with his friends at the magic tricks of the funny clown I could afford to hire for his party. I pasted happy photos into our Montreal album. Our family was looking good.

One evening at work, I answered the phone, expecting an order for a gourmet pizza.

"Hello, Mum?" It took me a second to identify Stan, despite his repeated recent refusals to call me either Norda or Eleanor. "There's been an accident, Mum. Nell fell out of her car bed. She banged her head on the wood floor while she was asleep." Stan described Nell's accident as though our three-month-old infant had engineered the fall all by herself.

"No!" I flashed to the moment of Nell's birth, her hands clasped to her head.

"We're at the Children's. The doctors want to interview me. I don't know why." My heart drummed as I ran the few blocks to the hospital.

"I lifted her car bed to vacuum under it," Stan explained when I got there. "A side snap had been left undone by someone. She fell out."

"But who runs a noisy vacuum when a child is fast asleep in her car bed? Who does that, Stan?"

"Please let me hold her." I wept when the nurse said that I, Nell's mother, was not allowed to lower the railings of my daughter's crib. She, Nell's nurse, must remain in the room with me if I wanted to hold the little girl with the swollen face.

"Is she in pain?" I gathered my whimpering daughter in my arms. Nell's enlarged face reminded me of baby Theo, the treasured infant from Hôpital Notre Dame des Anges, not far from where I now stood. Teddy kissed his sister's hands through the railings.

"We gave her something. We took x-rays. We're watching the swelling."

"No, no, no," I cried as Teddy pressed against me. "If I were at home, this wouldn't have happened."

"Why aren't you at home?" asked the nurse, her sympathetic voice professional and reassuring to me. "Your daughter is still an infant."

I took a deep breath and launched into my time-honored refrain about my husband's struggle "He does get jobs," I added, "but has trouble with his bosses. He gets fired in the first week."

"Problems that fast, eh?" she asked, checking Nell's pulse.

"Yes, always, someone insults him," I noticed that Nell was struggling to focus, to match voice to face.

"Look! She sees Teddy!" the nurse exclaimed, patting Teddy on the head. "She recognizes her brother! You know," she added, "if I confronted my directors every time they managed to upset me, I'd be permanently unemployed too. If I didn't want to work, I could kick up a justifiable fuss any old day of the week, believe you me."

"So you say nothing when you're treated badly?" I asked.

"No, I call a friend. I call a trusted staff member. I contact a counselor. There's plenty to do before I up and quit. No one's going to offer to pay my rent for me, that's for sure."

The hospital insisted on a second meeting with Stan, a required interview for parents whose children present with bruises or head trauma, standard practice to rule out child abuse. When Nell breastfed that night, I felt untold relief and gratitude. When I got home, I threw out the car bed. When I mentioned to Stan that Nell's nurse had suggested counseling, he was offended that I'd spoken to a stranger about him.

"I don't need counseling. I need work in a respectful milieu, not advice from people who consider themselves my superiors."

When Stan got home from his hospital interview, he told me that an intelligent doctor had framed the situation in a way that left him feeling understood: Stan, a highly educated, unemployed father of two, unused to the art of housework, had simply been clumsy for a moment.

As I'd done when Teddy nearly died, I stayed home with Nell for two weeks before returning to the restaurant. In the meantime, Stan had applied for and got an interview for a job as a town house janitor in the West Island. He'd receive a small salary and we'd get to live in a two-bedroom townhouse, complete with five appliances and all utilities.

"That's great news, Stan." I rejoiced. The day of the interview, Stan and I left Nell with Maureen, a first- and last-time event, and took Teddy with us.

"Wonderful," I said, thrilled with the children's playground just steps away from the outside door of the sparkling, sun-filled kitchen. All the way home on the bus, I told Teddy about the wonderful new friends he'd soon meet in our new 'hood.

On our return to Maureen's apartment to pick up Nell, I could hear my daughter sobbing, even from the elevator. I raced down the hallway of Maureen's high-rise. This was only the second time I'd been to my sister's home, the first time having been earlier that same day, but I had no trouble determining which door was hers.

"I didn't hold her," Maureen said, without apology, as though to reassure me.

"How long has she been crying like that?" I asked, keeping calm as I gathered up my daughter.

"A while," she called from the balcony.

I said nothing to my sister as I held Nell close. Maureen gave me a plastic container of frozen soup, some quality English tea, and some panty hose for work. She wished me a good week. I knew I wouldn't ask her to babysit again. I knew I was on my own. I felt that this must be my fault, that I deserved Maureen's rejection. What I did not understand was that my sister had always been a very private person who far preferred long-distance phone calls with family to face-to-face visits.

Stan got the janitor job. I can still recall the joy, the disbelief, the thrill of our move to the sunny new home. But our grand good luck lasted only half an hour. Teddy was deciding which side of his bedroom he wanted his bed to be on when Stan crashed into the hall foyer.

"Pack up! We're leaving!"

Teddy started to cry.

"That bastard thinks he can disrespect me? He thinks he can up and revise our deal? Well, he can think again! I'm a man of integrity!" Stan bellowed. "I don't tolerate prevaricators!"     "Stan, please don't tell me this." I begged him to return with me to speak to his boss, to talk this over and see if we could come to some compromise. But no, it was over.

"I'm the real victim here," said Stan. "First the Children's Hospital makes their thinly veiled accusations about Nell's fall, and now Mr. Big Shot attempts to abuse me too? No. No. No. No."

I called Maureen from a pay phone.

"Consider it a dream deferred," she consoled me. "You'll have your home another time and in another way. It's not meant to be right now. "

Back in our old place the next day, I couldn't seem to get comfortable. A strange dull pain spiraled down my arms, back, and chest, from head to toe. Stan called an ambulance. I begged the attendant for some medication, but she refused, saying the doctor would be unable to tell what was wrong with me if I arrived pain-free.

"Oh," I said. "I never knew that." When she asked me again and again where it hurt, I couldn't seem to identify the specific location of my meandering pain.

In the emergency ward at the Queen Elizabeth Hospital, a young man groaned on a cot next to mine, his whiskey breath reeking through the worn curtain separating us.

"Look, you're still young," I heard the doctor tell him. "You can turn this sucker around. You can! You think you're a prisoner of your addiction, but you're not. You have choices. Problem is, no one else can make them for you. No one else can steal your freedom from you. Only you can build a beautiful life from scratch!"

I listened as the distraught fellow spoke. "I wish I'd been told that when I was a kid," he wept. The next moment I realized that my pain was gone. It snuck out as quietly as it came. I sat up. I swung my legs over the gurney. I stood up. I parted the curtains and stepped out, as from the Red Sea.

"Thanks so much," I said to the astonished ambulance attendants at the Northcliffe exit. Only moments before, I'd been begging for pain relief. On the sidewalk lay a bus ticket, just what I needed. Home again, I played car crash with Teddy and wrote invitations to his birthday party before settling down to nurse Nell. For the first time ever, my daughter turned away from my breast, refusing to eat. Was there something wrong? Should I call the hospital? I had twenty minutes before I had to leave for work, my breasts increasingly sore. As I expressed my milk into a cup, confused and upset, Stan explained that he'd never dreamed there'd be any physical consequence to me if he purchased a baby bottle and a can of liquid formula and fed Nell while I was at the hospital. He just hadn't thought about bringing her to me. He apologized, before adding, "You might have told me about engorgement."

I learned that talking to other mothers in the park was a good thing. A young woman, a college teacher, listened as I asked what to do if I was away from my daughter, or if I got sick. She said she had an electric extractor pump, and that afternoon she dropped off a dozen mini-bags of her own milk to keep in my freezer, ready for Nell at any time.

Within six months of Nell's birth, one of my regulars at the restaurant, a gentleman who took pleasure in gathering his grandchildren around a large all-dressed pizza every weekend, told me he'd bought a building in Westmount. Would I know of a janitor? Yes, I did. Stan would work independently and unsupervised, advantages I now understood were necessary to him. We could live in a lovely apartment in exchange for keeping the halls clean, putting the garbage out, collecting rent, and doing minor repairs. There was no question now that Stan would work outside the home. We'd never talked about it, but I knew. There would be no further discussion about my staying at home either — until, that is, I had a brainstorm, a way for me to be a stay-at-home mother that even Stan would approve of. We'd be foster parents. I made an appointment with Social Services, never guessing that I'd be on the receiving end of their care soon enough.

An older social worker visited us and, while Stan fussed over a tea tray, I talked on and on about my grand idea of a daily routine, with one educational activity after another.

"Why don't you take a breath and let your hubby get a word in edgewise," said the agent, nodding over at Stan, who smiled back at her with a relieved expression, one that acknowledged her astuteness and suggested that he was used to being drowned out by my endless babble. He leaned forward and engaged her in a direct, intimate colleague-to-colleague discussion, one that excluded me. He spoke in low tones, fanning before her his history of over-education, his hefty file of refusal letters from universities whose quotas were, for the moment, filled. He said he'd be more than glad to lend me a hand with foster children.

I escaped to the bathroom to crumple up in frustration and humiliation at the unspoken suggestion that I had failed to let a humble man get a word in edgewise. A purposeful punch in the stomach couldn't have hurt more. More and more, I was living with an unvarying degree of anxiety, tiny insects running up and down my veins, drowning in my blood, desperately batting their fragile wings and flailing legs in fear. One night after work, that strange body pain returned in full force, crashing through my legs, arms, and back. Every time I isolated the throb, it escaped, shooting off somewhere else, mystery pain as avoidant as I was at revealing the root of its trouble. While Stan and the children sat in the hospital corridor, I donned a blue gown, answered questions, and gave blood samples. It turned out I was anemic.

"How's your daughter's head?" the nurse asked, perusing my file. The attentive nurse was different, but my file was full of accumulated and transferred notes. "Your husband got himself a job yet?"

An inexplicable grief crept over me. I couldn't explain to her what I couldn't understand myself, that my husband's happiness required my self-destruction. To keep our family afloat, I had to submerge myself below a constant smile. To be a normal family meant denying everything that didn't fit with my own insistence that everything was okay. I wept on the gurney while the knowledgeable nurse who'd seen it all stood by, her hand warm on my shoulder. She didn't busy herself with something else or tell me to get dressed. I could feel her loving concern.

"When you're ready, Eleanor," she said, "you'll know just what to do."

Our application to be foster parents was refused, and I felt unexpected relief. Had the nurse zapped my plan? Or did that older social worker know us better than we knew ourselves?

∽

When I arrived home from work every night, I'd find Stan at his desk, the children fast asleep. I'd fill a bucket with hot water, mix in a cup of Cow Brand Baking Soda, and sink my feet into soothing heat. Nell slept poorly now, sometimes crying out in the wee hours of the morning that she saw a hairy spider crawling on the wall. An especially big one had crept into her bed. She cried that it had sneaked between her little legs and up inside her body. Nell often fled into my bed in the wee hours, clinging to me for comfort, cold and upset. Many a time, Stan volunteered to sleep on the couch and get our son breakfast in the early morning so Nell and I could sleep in a little. I said I appreciated his kindness.

Because I was bilingual, I could waitress at a larger, fancier restaurant with an international clientele. I jumped at the chance to double my income. The William Tell restaurant was a living culture, a sensual school of taste, scents, laughter, and conversation that opened my eyes to the banquet table life offers to those who feel entitled to it. I'd never peeled the bottom golden layer of baked cheese from a fondue pot or tasted real schnitzel drizzled with fresh lemon juice. As I deboned Dover sole or placed steaming plates of Veal Marsala on table after celebratory table, I noted the long lazy time lovers took, dawdling over their meals as though food wasn't the main attraction. On occasion, clients complained, which always upset the chef, and I wondered who'd want to nitpick about food. Why not down the lot and be grateful? I noticed their eagerness to listen to each other, to nod and smile and ask questions, to clarify, to deepen their conversations. I noticed warm glances, hands touching gently, overlapping or intertwining. I noticed love.

Confronted with contrasts every single day, exposed to the reality of others, as I had been at the Port Royal years earlier, my capacity for gratitude thinned as my eyes widened. I'd think about my customers after work, on the way home on the métro, speeding to my stark contradiction. The constant visuals of couples who made it a point to polish their love were plays I needed to see. Over time, I developed my own clientele, customers who asked for me to serve their table, and inquired about my health and about Ted and Nell. Among them were the Nadlers, who always reserved a corner booth in my section. As soon as I saw the hostess seat the couple, I ordered the cheese fondue I knew they'd share, followed by their favorite dishes. One night Mrs. Nadler asked me, as she always did, what I had been reading in my Concordia course, and I said it was *Alice in Wonderland,* which I hadn't enjoyed at all.

"Everyone betrayed her," I said. "Alice was tricked over and over, even by animals."

"Yes, it's true, that little girl lived a nightmare," said Mrs. Nadler.

"I don't know why on earth it's read to children as a fairy tale," said Dr. Nadler. "You're right, Eleanor. *Alice in Wonderland* symbolizes childhood trauma." Their support thrilled me.

In the wee hours on Saturday nights, I'd soak in a warm bath. I'd pumice my feet well before slipping into my foam mules, the only footwear possible after a busy shift. I had been taking one course per term at Concordia, an effort to slowly, little by little, move forward with my dream of becoming a teacher. That term I took a poetry class in my master's degree program and read language I found constrained and oblique.

"If you don't know the classics, you won't have a chance in Dante's hell," my professor said, wagging his finger in reply to a student's comment that some poems required a nutcracker to extract their meaning. I too wondered why the poets everyone said were so great made obscure, nuanced historical references that required even more study. Why couldn't they spit it out and be done with it?

"Yes," I said in support of my chastised classmate, as my friend Sandra had done for me years earlier. "Why not be as clear as 'Out damned spot'? Why so secretive?" I had no inkling of my own concealed grief.

One day I announced to my favorite customers that I'd be leaving the restaurant. Dr. Nadler offered to write a recommendation for me. Perhaps it was his wonderful reference, perhaps it was the seven-year accumulation of part-time courses, or perhaps it was that phone call from the student I'd supported in poetry class. She alerted me to part-time openings for ESL teachers at a local college.

"Is your husband an educator too?" Barbara asked as we walked to our classes at the Selby Campus of Dawson College. My stomach clenched slightly as I began my usual litany, my well-practiced speech about Stan's vast over-education. He was so overqualified he couldn't find a teaching spot anywhere in Canada. While Barbara remained quiet, I added how diligently he'd searched, for a decade now, with no success. She nodded and somehow, as had become my compulsion, I spoke faster and faster, perhaps to fill such silences and prevent Barb from saying something I didn't want to hear. I see now my many attempts to avoid personal introspection. I had no idea then that Stan was my cover too. After all, the more the focus was on him, the less it was on me.

The following week, Barb asked if I'd be interested in teaching at a local private school, one a friend of hers had helped establish. I replied, my heart racing, that I'd love to. The two schools offered me enough work to support our family, without my having to waitress ever again. I treated myself to a green silk dress for the end-of-term party Barb and I planned for our students. Nell wore her pink silk and Teddy his gray flannels and a new sports jacket. Too busy to attend that day, Stan was absent from the lovely photo of that celebration I tucked into our Montreal album.

∼

Nell wanted a baby sister. With Teddy and Nell, there'd been absolutely no hesitation, no question whatsoever, but now, a cloudy feeling emerged. I was thirty-seven years old. Could I work as hard as before and still nurse a new baby? Would I be putting us into financial jeopardy? Every time Nell asked about a new baby, I was in anguish. Finally, I decided to speak to our family doctor. Was I strong enough to have a third baby, nurse the infant, and continue working full-time? I made an appointment, one I had no idea I would soon need so much.

"At school today," Nell said one afternoon, "the visitors in our class said no one is allowed to touch your private places. Maybe Daddy doesn't know. Can you tell him?"

Less than four feet high, in her navy blue school uniform and crisp white blouse, her face red with embarrassment, my daughter looked up at me. We looked at each other and I believed her. There was no question. It was as though she'd flipped a switch and I had suddenly become automated. I felt like I had stepped behind a thick cement wall, but my daughter must not know this or sense my shock. I thanked Nell for telling me. As though mouthing the words from a distance, or under water, I told my little girl that she had done the right thing to come to me and that I would speak to her father.

"I'll tell Dad he's not to cuddle you, he's not to touch your body at all. I'll tell him that you're not a baby any more. I know he'll promise me he'll never touch you again. If he forgets, I want you to tell me, Nell, okay? You must tell me right away."

"Okay, Mummy," she replied.

While Nell played Holy Mass with her friend, their dolls draped around a soup-box altar, I fumbled for the phone book. Stan wouldn't be home for several hours. In that window of time, I could speak to someone, anyone other than him. I dialed the number on the back cover of the phone book and experienced an eerie incident, one I have since come to understand and even expect. The woman who answered my call listened to me stumble on about my daughter's disclosure, and then, incredibly, she began to yawn before all sound disappeared. Total silence. I waited. What had happened? Another emergency caller? Long seconds later, perhaps half a minute, the volunteer returned to me. She apologized. She said she'd slipped off there. Spaced out. Fallen asleep.

"I don't know what happened," she said. "I guess I nodded off." She apologized again for a dissociative reaction not uncommon to those who've been abused. "Anyway, this isn't a sexual abuse hotline," she said, her voice bristling with irritation. "This is a suicide prevention line."

Stan didn't deny that he had molested Nell. He didn't burst into tears. He didn't call our daughter a liar, nor did he criticize the school program that alerted our daughter to her rights. He apologized. He said it was a mistake and that "it" would never, ever happen again. It took years for me to make the connection with Nell's night-time terror about a spider that continued to crawl into her bed.

I taught my class that night because it never occurred to me not to show up. Like a sleepwalker, I issued robotic answers to questions about grammar, pronunciation, and articulation, language I should have been employing at home on Nell's behalf. As from a distance, far, far away from my authentic voice, I taught pronunciation at school but was inarticulate at home. I detailed grammar rules in the classroom while basic life rules were broken in Nell's bedroom. In the washroom stall at break, I sat on the toilet lid, dense, dark, heavy, soundless, and sick. When I got home, I told Stan not to talk to me. In the morning I kept my appointment at the Seaforth Medical, the one I'd made a month earlier to ask about the possibility of carrying a third child. As I dressed that morning, I knew I'd be relieved if I could tell Nell that the doctor had advised against my bearing another child at my age. Unable to assume any personal responsibility, I wanted to reassure Nell that it was the doctor who'd said a third child would not be a good idea, not me. But here was a chance to talk about something else, and I hoped I could find a way to speak.

Without a murmur of what was on my mind or heart during a uterine examination, my doctor and I sat on opposite sides of her desk. She said that yes, I could indeed have another child if I wanted to. After all, I'd given birth to two healthy children already and there was every reason to believe a third would be the same.

As if from a distance, I heard my own reply. "Let's hope it's not a girl then."

"Pardon me?" she asked. "Why on earth would you say that?"

"If it's a girl, Stan may touch her the way he has Nell."

"How do you know this?"

"Nell told me yesterday."

"You must send her father here today," she said. I felt a giant pressure lift.

"I'll tell him," I said and then made my decision, a privilege denied my foremothers.

"I won't have a third child, doctor. I'll take care of the two I have."

"My own wife betrays me?" shouted Stan when I got home. "You told your doctor? Do you have any idea how such data could be misconstrued? You told me you had an appointment about a new baby! You lied. You lied to me!"

"Your appointment is in an hour," I said. The hall cupboard door slammed, a signal that Stan wasn't going anywhere. "The doctor said she'd file a police report if you don't show up." This time, the front door slammed. Stan was on his way out.

"I'm sorry, Mum," Stan said to me when he returned from the doctor's office two hours later.

"Did the doctor assign you a therapist?" I asked.

"No, why should she? I explained to her that my snuggling Nell while getting her off to sleep was a one-time event, an unfortunate aberration, the result of being unemployed and frustrated about my life and work. She understood. Like myself, she's educated. I had only to explain myself once. I said it won't happen again and I mean it. Unlike my own wife, your doctor believes in me. Unlike my own wife, that MD is able to comprehend the facts."

Stan picked up his mother at the Berri-de Montigny bus depot that week, but said nothing to her about his molestation of Nell. I told Edna myself, after Nell's birthday party. She quietly closed the kitchen door, sat down and faced me. Did I imagine that my mother-in-law would react differently than I had, that she'd insist on confronting her son, or call Stan's sister, Meredith, a nun, and maybe one of his brothers, and that they'd grab Stan for the showdown of his life? Actually, the mere fact that Edna and I were sharing information about Nell's sexual abuse *was* evolution, historical progress at a snail's pace. In my own history, the door to such talk had been slammed shut before it began.

"I'd hoped this kind of thing, Stan's trouble, was over after Catherine," Edna said, staring into her empty tea cup.

"Stan touched Catherine?" I asked, avoiding the correct term: molestation. I vaguely recalled Stan saying he had cuddled his baby sister too much, and another memory surfaced, of Catherine's strange teenage depression over writing a memoir piece about her childhood.

"I hoped with all my heart that Stan would be safe in the priesthood." Edna's tone escalated. "I sent him the registration papers. I begged him. I'd hoped this kind of behavior was over. I am so deeply sorry for Nell's situation," she added, with great sincerity. With our muted vocabulary, Edna and I could have been discussing parking tickets, not a criminal offense against a child we claimed to love. I noticed something new. Edna had gnawed fingernails. Each mini-face was bitten down to the quick, a shiver away from bleeding.

"I did everything I could before Stan got married," she said. "I told Father at the Chaplaincy, when he called me in to discuss my opposition to the marriage. I told him how worried I was about my future grandchildren."

"But Father said you were also worried about me, about my binge drinking in my twenties, and about my mother."

"I couldn't say more at the time, Norda. I couldn't," she said, her fingers pressed in prayer position over her mouth.

I jumped when the whistle screamed out over the blue flames of the gas stove. At its boiling point, the small kettle hissed what was impossible for Edna and me to voice. After a walk with her grandchildren, Edna returned with a package of sixteen thick sound absorbers, pads for each foot of each kitchen chair. "To preserve the life of your floor," she said. I thanked my mother-in-law for one more small act of thoughtfulness. Like me, Edna never dreamed of questioning our doctor's decision to give Stan another chance. Who were we to disagree? My mother-in-law could not lead me to where she'd never been. Instinct-injured together, our only collaboration was to silence chair feet instead of running on our own. We stifled noise instead of making it.

"I am praying for you with all my heart," Edna said the afternoon she left, without confronting Stan, our silence giving him permission to escape censure. Soon after her visit to us, she moved closer to her daughter's religious order in Northern Saskatchewan. "Know that you are in our hearts and prayers all the time, Norda," she wrote in the birthday cards she always remembered to send on time. "Trust that God has you all in the palm of His Loving Hand."

∾

When Teddy refused to return to school after lunch and I learned that his teacher had placed a Pampers diaper on his chair as punishment for undone homework, I was furious. I raced to the school. "That's not right at all!" I confronted her with all the self-righteous umbrage I'd never dared to direct at my husband.

"Your son's on the moon! He lives there!" she shouted at me. "He lives in outer space!"

"All you had to do was call me, his mother!" I said. "A diaper on his chair is no solution!"

On the way home, my nerves a-jangle, I talked to the mother of one of Teddy's classmates, who comforted me.

"The Pampers Lady looks after her elderly parents day and night. She's all alone with two dozen kids all day and now she's sick herself. Forgive her," she said. "She's losing it. She's a slave. She's wiped out."

When I got home, I called the principal and had Teddy transferred to another school. I declined her invitation to wait a day, come over, talk things over, and reason things out. No, thank you. I was on the warpath, a path drastically diverted from where it was really needed. Even though Nell was doing well, comfortable and secure in her class, I transferred her out too, without any discussion with my distressed daughter. Oh, yes, I handled that problem, lickety-split.

"Mummy fixed her clock," I boasted to my children at supper. "No one's going to bother my kids and get away with it!"

～

When Nell came home with problems she'd never had in her old class, when she cried that she missed her friends and her old classroom, where she'd been happy, I felt desperate. Teddy was badly bullied over at his new school. A steel gate, a lot harder than a Pampers diaper, was slammed into his face within weeks of my radical reaction. I showed us all right. I showed us how to avoid any exploration of why Teddy was so detached and "living on the moon." I flipped my children on their backs, where they flailed like two baby turtles in helpless misery, just like their mother.

Our insurance agent, Stan's only friend, visited us once a year. Mr. Gupta brought gifts. Russian nesting dolls for Nell, an ancestry of female figures, each enclosed inside the diminished next one, and a Rubik's Cube for Teddy. The children fell to absorbed exploration as we told Mr. Gupta about the resale of our apartment building, a real-estate flip that had left Stan without his part-time janitor work.

"Maybe it's time you became homeowners yourselves," he said. "Maybe it's time the children settled into a permanent community. You've already moved seven times since Teddy was born."

Seven times? At nine years old, Teddy had lived in seven different homes; at seven years old, Nell had lived in four.

"You've paid off Stan's loans," our agent said. "Now a mortgage. What do you think, Stan? You'd have the biggest job of all, of course, to find the best house." He looked directly at Stan. He knew to employ a question, not a statement form. He appealed to Stan's authority. Any other way would have been a mistake. We waited in silence for Stan's approval. "I can do that," Stan said. That autumn, we moved to an old house only blocks away from where my mother grew up. I was the only one of my family who lived in the birthplace of our parents.

~

For the first time in many years, Brigit paid me a visit. A year out of a disastrous relationship that had left her paying her partner's burdensome debts, my sister completed her university degree at night. While I missed her and wished our visits could be more frequent, they were not. I didn't know it then but Brigit and I both gravitated to angry and sometimes violent people. Instead of spending time with each other, we worked out our problems by re-living our dramas with damaged people.

On this rare visit to Montreal, Brigit invited me to a special supper, just the two of us. She told me that she'd met and had been living with a wonderful woman in Edmonton. She praised her unreservedly. I nodded and smiled. When she disclosed that she was in love with this woman, that they made love and found each other irresistible, I searched her face. I could see only happiness. Brigit talked animatedly about her volunteer work, teaching prison inmates to read. She said that one woman, a fundamentalist Christian, had made homophobic comments about "diesel dykes" and later asked my sister to Christmas shop for her kids and take them out for supper and a movie.

"Did you let her know your orientation?" I asked.

"No, I didn't. My personal life is none of her business. Anyway, if she keeps reading, she may well read herself to sanity, all by herself," said Brigit. We smiled at each other and she told me that she'd never known a quality of love like this in her whole life.

I climbed into bed that night and fell into a troubled sleep, awakening in a sweat somewhere near 4 a.m. My heart was pounding, my skin burning, every nerve from head to toe feeling alive with sexual desire — not for Stan, but at the thought of making real physical love with someone I loved. Agitated, I tiptoed out to speak with Brigit, but she was asleep. I drank a glass of freezing cold water and climbed back into bed for another restless hour before I fell asleep again. The next morning, I invited my sister to join us for Mass and learned that she would not enter any church. It had become a matter of principle.

"Why should I bow and scrape before priests who were happy to see our mother flat out on labor tables once a year, the ones who told Grandma to silence herself while her sex-addict husband 'worked the parish,' the same religious cult that still denies condoms to African women whose many babies starve. Need I go on?" she asked.

"We'll talk later then," I said, hurrying out the door. Stan hated wasting gas on an idling car. As I sat in our regular pew up front with my husband and two children, images of making tender love with a wonderful lover obliterated Father John's sermon. I finally had to sit down, claiming to feel faint, which was true.

"You're lucky it didn't happen to you," said Stan on the way home. "It easily could have. Females coming from disturbed family backgrounds often experience sexual confusion. Just be grateful you're normal and married. And how sad that your sister won't ever have children." He shook his head. "That's the real kicker."

~

The following Sunday at Mass, Brigit safely back in Edmonton, I met the "Pope of Verdun," an off-the-wall, middle-aged man who dressed up as a bishop, a cardinal, a priest, a seminarian, a page and once, as on this occasion at church, a pope. His colorful robes, long, flamboyant gold-threaded dresses and capes, foot-high crimson pointed hats, and stiff birettas etched in gold and silver, were eye-catching, especially since he wasn't an ordained priest and was not entitled to dress up this way. When he swept into church in a royal blue gown stamped with a golden cross, all heads turned. A young male page in skin-tight pink stockings and short toga skipped lightly behind him, lifting the papal raiment off the floor. A red velvet camauro, a cap with slender ermine lappets, hung down his back in two furry tails. The congregation collectively turned its attention from the customary ritual of Father Conner raising a gold chalice to watch the alternate spectacle. The Pope of Verdun swept down the center aisle, pivoting on his heel, his arms raised high. As one, we followed his index finger to the open front doors of the church. He pivoted once more, his gartered page scampering behind, and sank to his knees in front of a potted plant. He bowed deeply before the clump of growing green and took a single iris into his hands. He raised it towards his spellbound flock.

"The word iris," he proclaimed dramatically, "means the dot in the middle of your own eye. Look to each other. You, and you alone, are the God you seek."

He carried the plant to the front door, placed it to catch the light, and withdrew. He never once looked at the priest shuffling cups at the altar, nor was he acknowledged by the attending priest. After Mass, parishioners commented kindly about the poor fellow's antics, his obvious mental instability, and his most-likely disturbed childhood. I thought about his instruction to look inward and how he had honored a single plant. I felt moved by his words and performance.

"He's like Jesus," said Nell, holding my hand on the way out.

∼

I wondered why my son was doing poorly in school.

"Where's your homework, Teddy?" I asked one night.

"I did it in school," he said. "It's done."

"But your teacher said he was sending extra work home with you from now on."

"It's done," Teddy said. "I finished it in school."

"Okay, let's see it."

"I left my books in class, Mum."

"You're lying to me," I said. "You didn't do your homework in class!" I removed my hands from the soapy sink water and turned on my son. "You're lazy and you're a liar!"

"Mum!" said Teddy, his eyes bright with fear.

"No!" I exploded. "You don't do your homework! You don't copy it down. You don't bring your books home. You don't sit at the table and study like every other kid. You refuse! You're completely irresponsible!"

"Mum, please, no!" my son cried, stunned by my tirade.

"I'm sick of it! I'm sick of worrying about you, rushing to school with the lunches you forget! I'm sick of begging you to remember your homework! I'm sick of all of this, Teddy!" I watched as my son collapsed. I'd never seen him cry so hard. His shoulders shook as he sobbed uncontrollably.

"I'm sorry, Mum. I'm sorry. I'll try harder! I'll try harder!"

"We've been having this same discussion for too long, Teddy!" I screamed as he ran to his room.

At supper that night, Stan put in his two cents. Together, we heaped the detritus of our own failings onto our son, an innocent scapegoat.

"Where's your bus pass?" Stan demanded. "Where's your homework book? Where's your locker key this time?"

Teddy started to cry again and then suddenly, things became worse. He couldn't stop. He gulped for air. His face turned first blotchy and then far too white as he slunk down on his seat. Nell wept in her chair.

"It's okay, Teddy," said Stan, suddenly alarmed. "It's okay. Calm down. Calm down. You'll bring your homework home tomorrow, and tonight you can watch *A-Team* on TV. Relax now, relax."

"I'm sorry, Mum." Teddy hiccupped. "I'll try harder."

I grabbed a cigarette I'd hidden, lit it, and smoked it in the bathroom. "Unfair," I addressed myself in the mirror. "You went way overboard there."

I had no right to expect Teddy to be perfectly normal when he was living with two disturbed parents. I was expecting my children to look like poster kids for a happy home that didn't exist.

I found Teddy sitting at the end of his bed, shoulders slumped, staring out the window.

"I'm sorry for my explosion, Teddy. I'm so sorry."

"It's okay, Mum," he said, throwing his arms around me.

My shame was enormous and long-lasting. I hated myself for hurting my son. My style of anger was accurately named "bottle 'n' blast." I had hoarded all my reactions and resentments, most of which had nothing to do with my children, for far too long and then exploded. Sometimes, I could project up to a year of niceness so sweet my children called me "the marshmallow." I congratulated myself on my patience, but it wasn't patience at all. I held my tongue for protracted periods of martyr-styled retention. I controlled my stored-up resentments until I could no longer. While my blasts were rare, they were memorable to my children for that very reason. Regular, honest, trusting communication was unknown to me.

# PART 3

## *Fall Prey No More*

"You can ask for a second opinion," said the nurse. She offered me a fourth blanket to warm me as I lay shivering on a narrow gurney in a corridor of the LaSalle Hospital. "You're entitled to a second opinion before undergoing a major incision, even with a diagnosis of cancer. You're entitled to see another physician if you want one." She spoke so kindly to me, as though she cared about me personally.

"Yes, please, then," I said, frightened and overwhelmed. Even though I could hardly bear the pain, the diagnosis of intestinal cancer was much worse. An hour later, the chief resident, a Chilean doctor, arrived.

"I got here as soon as I could," he said. He pressed my sore belly. "How are things at home?" he asked, reading my thick file.

"Not good," I said. "I'm falling apart. I shouted at my son. I'm exhausted. I can't sleep."

"Are you happily married?" he asked pointedly.

In that silence, I looked up at the dark-haired man and read only concern in his eyes.

"You know," he said, allowing me a moment to gather myself, "I come from Chile, the most beautiful country in the world. I was raised by beautiful parents. I never knew that one day things would change, that I'd be a political refugee, an immigrant without a home. Never once did I imagine what was to come." Then he added, "You don't have cancer at all. You're severely impacted." He cancelled my surgery order.

After an embarrassing and painful treatment, I slept in a small side room until Stan woke me up. "What did the head doctor say?"

"Severe constipation."

"Prunes," said Stan. "I'll get some today. By the way, I hate to say this, but we're short on cash."

"Go away, Stan. Don't activate my pain again."

When the Chilean doctor came to check up on me, he told me that we are the captains of our own ships, and that perhaps I'd like to think about the course I was on, especially with young children involved. I promised I'd do some serious thinking.

"Not up here," he pointed to his head, "but down here, in the body that resists the dictates of your head."

Back at work, I was assigned to tutor a young man in his early twenties. Despite the brain injury he'd suffered in a car accident a year before, Evan had registered for a course at Dawson College. When he told me he was studying James Joyce, I worried. Stream-of-consciousness stuff was like pinning a jelly fish with a darning needle. Like dealing with moody people, it required tremendous patience. We began with a story about brown houses, all in a row, each facing the other.

"What do you think?" Evan asked.

"To tell you the truth, I find row houses depressing," I answered.

"Street people wouldn't though," he replied, slowly formulating each word with immense concentration.

"What about the color of the row houses?" I asked him.

"What does brown mean to you?" he asked, a grin playing on his face. "Chocolate?"

His palsied finger pointed to the last house in the illustration, the one at the blind end, detached from its neighbors.

"That's me," he said. "Not one phone call from my friends since my accident. It wasn't the fall that hurt most. It was being dumped from a great height by them."

That day at our weekly meeting, I asked our staff psychologist, Leah, how Evan's school friends could possibly abandon him in his worst hour.

"Where there's trauma, immature people scatter," she said. "They blank out. They take off. They run from what could so easily have happened to them." Out of the blue, I thought of Maureen's blame when bad things had happened to me in the past, rapes that must have terrified her.

"Evan's friends can't cope," Leah added. I considered my brothers living in Vancouver, calling me only when there was a crisis. I thought of Nell, so quiet now, and Teddy on the moon.

"Evan needs to make much more mature friends now," said Leah. "He must take that brave leap into a new life. It will be like falling backwards off a cliff," she added, "but dramatic change requires dramatic courage—and strong support."

⁓

It was Parent-Teacher Night at Teddy and Nell's school. Stan went by himself because I had to work. When he got home, Nell ran to the door, eager to hear what her teachers had said about her.

"You're failing French," he told her, not beating around the bush. "I'm disappointed in you."

With that swift verbal punch, Nell crumpled to the floor, her skirt covering her knees like an umbrella mushroom, her head bent down. Mademoiselle Natalie was her favorite teacher, so the failing grade felt like a personal blow. I chose that moment to tell Stan that a marriage counselor could see us the following night.

"I'm sure you had no problem telling the kids' teachers how you excelled in French," I said, after Nell had cried herself to sleep. "No difficulty letting her teachers know how well you distinguished yourself in school. You have no trouble lecturing our children on the nature of sin, so why not a report card for us?"

Our appointment at the Catholic Family Services was one I intended to keep.

"If you're forcing me to visit a therapist, I'll drink this fortification first." Stan surprised me the next day with his purchase of two bottles of strong beer.

"I'm not forcing you to do anything, Stan."

"Yes you are."

"I'm going tonight whether or not you come. I've been feeling sick for a long time. There's something wrong with me. I may die early, so I'm going to save my life."

⁓

"What do you want, Eleanor?" asked Mr. Sauvé, our lay counselor. "Say what you need."

"I've never had a chance to stay at home with my children. I want what time I have left."

Stan explained to the counselor that I was a friendlier, simpler person than he was, so it was easier for me to maintain superficial contacts with people. "And in view of gender equality," he continued, "who cares which parent stays at home?"

"Your wife does, Stan," said Mr. Sauvé. "Look, let's cut to the chase here. Let's take a giant step forward tonight. Stan, you go first. Can you honor that original contract you made with your wife in Paris? By our next appointment, can you tell me you'll work as a waiter, or pump gas if you have to?"

"I've always made sincere attempts to find work, efforts my wife is quick to discount, but yes, I'm willing," Stan said. The evening before our next appointment, our counselor called and asked Stan if he had found a job. Stan explained that he'd set up an interview for late next week sometime.

"Then don't come tonight," Mr. Sauvé said. He hung up.

"You're not going without me, are you?" Stan asked.

"Yes, I am. You made a deal with Mr. Sauvé and you didn't keep it."

Stan insisted on accompanying me.

"No," said Mr. Sauvé, when Stan tried to slip into the session as though he hadn't been told explicitly not to come. "I want to speak to Eleanor privately."

"She's my wife," said Stan, pushing past him.

"Is Eleanor your property, Stan, to direct as you will, to earn that pay check for you?"

At that, Stan sailed his fist close to our counselor's head and smashed the wall.

"You fail to understand, sir," he said.

"Yes, everyone fails to understand, Stan," said the counselor, throwing open his door. "But there's such a thing as fairness. Your behavior has nothing to do with women's liberation and everything to do with exploitation. Now get out of my office. Wall-banging is not permitted here."

Stan's agitation was so loud that I knew it would be better for us all if I went home with him. On my way out, I quickly made another appointment for myself with Mr. Sauvé.

"What an officious bastard!" said Stan on the métro, bits of white foam at the corners of his mouth. "Look," he continued, "I promise you I'll get a job this week. That's a firm commitment on my part. There's only one condition: these sessions with that ignoramus must end."

"How can you guarantee that, Stan? How can you promise now what was impossible before?"

"Because I said so. You can stay home from now on."

I looked at him and knew, for the first time, that it was absolutely true. He could have worked at any time over the past fourteen years.

"I'm waiting," said Stan. "Do you agree to dump that arrogant bastard?"

"Let me rest," I said. "I feel sick."

The following morning, I called Mr. Sauvé, who agreed to see me right away.

He didn't mince words. "Make your move as soon as possible, Eleanor. We don't often make such stark recommendations, but I've discussed your situation with my supervisor and we both advise you to get out. Don't walk; run from your hostage-taker, for that's what Stan is. He's not well. He has problems you can never, ever fix."

"Thank you," I wept. "Thank you for telling me what you see."

"And, Eleanor, for the past fourteen years, you've helped Stan to stay isolated. That's a long time. You need considerable help too," he said, scheduling my next appointment.

That night I offered to sleep on the couch, but Stan said he'd sleep there, and I thanked him. In the wee hours, I awakened with a feeling of alarm and tiptoed down the hall, my heart pounding. I stood at Nell's bedroom door, which was slightly ajar. I saw his bare back. He sat on the side of her bed in his underwear, one hand over her, the other hand working on himself.

"Stan?"

His back stiffened. He leapt behind Nell's cupboard door to adjust himself back into his pajamas and stole out of her room as quietly as he had stolen in while our daughter slept.

"I'm sorry, Mum," he said. "I got carried away. You dress Nell seductively. You do it on purpose. And now you're thinking of leaving me. I know it."

I had long since perfected the art of speaking calmly while a blood rush of feelings boiled inside me. But this time was different. This time I was as honest as I was composed. "I don't love you, Stan, and I have no respect for you. I want you to leave. I will keep the kids." There, it was done.

Bending his face to his knees, Stan wept. His shoulders shook. He told me that I'd stabbed him through the heart, that I was killing him, that I was merciless and vengeful. In the past, Stan's powerful emotional outbursts, especially his tears, had convinced me he was genuine. But this time I unraveled the bizarre twist that had confounded me for so long. I realized that Stan's feelings were, in fact, a hundred percent authentic, but they didn't extend beyond himself. He wept with deep feeling only when his own safety was threatened. He wept only for himself. Even as his tears fell, he blamed me. His predation was my fault. I dressed our daughter in flannelette nightgowns he found seductive. Mere seconds after I'd caught him molesting her, I was the guilty one. I should apologize.

The next morning, before he left for his new job, Stan said he'd rent a room somewhere and contribute financially to supporting the children and me. I could hardly believe it. By that evening, though, his mood had changed.

"Did I ever beat you?" he shouted. "Did I slam you on the floor or pitch you against a hot stove? Did I run around with sluts? Did I cheat on you? No! None of the above! I never laid a hand on you! Read the paper or watch the news to verify how good you've had it!"

Later, he changed the channel again. "I'll go to counseling now," he promised. "And I got a job, Mum. I got a full-time job!"

The following evening, Stan crashed into the kitchen again. "I'm not going to be bullied out of my own home by a man-hater."

"Okay," I said. "Then the kids and I will leave."

"And don't think Catholic Family Services will let you keep the kids either. I'll tell them about you and your mother, and your crazy, alcoholic, mentally-ill family."

Stan retreated to Nell's room and stretched across her bed as though it was his right. I recalled, years before, his study notes strewn across his sister's bed, as if he owned it.

"I want to speak to Nell," he called to me in the kitchen moments later.

"No, Stan. Enough." I hurried down the hall to Nell's room. He looked like someone I'd never met before—a clear, childlike, vulnerable man with Stan's facial features. I was taken aback.

"I beg you for another chance," he said, sitting on the edge of Nell's bed. "I am deeply sorry for my lapse in morality and I promise you with my life it will never, ever happen again in our lifetime. I appreciate who you are, Eleanor. I never want to live a day without you."

I stumbled back down the hall to the kitchen, on the verge of explaining to my ten-year-old daughter that maybe, maybe, at long last, something good had happened. Maybe her father had had a transformation. Maybe I'd try one last time.

"Nell," I began, hesitantly.

"Mum, if you change your mind, if you stay with Dad, I won't ever trust you again," my daughter said quietly and clearly. She sat still, pale and shaking in her own nightmare. "I can tell you're changing your mind again, Mum, and if you do, I'll never believe you again. Oh, I'm so disappointed!" She lowered her forehead to the kitchen table.

"Nell," I said, not knowing what else to say.

"You always do this, Mum. You always, always, always give in," she said. Her small face almost disappeared behind her fogged-up glasses. I stood, one foot in the kitchen, one in the den, a deer caught in the headlights of grotesque indecision.

I opened my mouth to speak but she raised her hand in front of my face.

"Just stop," she said. "I don't want to hear any more."

"It's all right, Nell," I heard myself say. "We're leaving."

Nell's mouth dropped open. "Really, Mum?"

"Yes, and I'm so, so sorry, Nell. You're a little girl. You shouldn't have had to help me with this, but you did. I'm so sorry, and I thank you."

I let Stan imagine that things had returned to our usual kind of normal. He dressed for work. "I'm going to keep this job," he said, heading out the door. "You'll see."

Less than a minute after Stan left, the phone rang. A friend had recently rented out her house and left Canada for a year of study. A problem had occurred. The renters had summarily picked up and moved out, claiming they saw fleas.

"I'm leaving Stan," I told my friend. "If you'll rent your house to me, I'll move in today."

The surprise arrangement was sealed in minutes. I dropped Nell off at her friend's house and drove home to pack. After I'd delivered many hastily packed boxes to our new home, a congealed mass of blood fell from between my legs and onto the wood floor. There was more blood after the next load. A jellied necklace of scarlet dripped down my legs. My period had arrived two weeks early, with frightening force. "I'm going to live," I thought as I showered and changed for the second time that morning. When Stan got home that night, Nell, Teddy, and I had left. When he saw a droplet of blood on the floor, and despite our non-existent sex life, Stan's first thought was about abortion.

"You're demonic, just like that Daigle woman," Stan screamed at me over the phone.

That year, 1989, the Daigle vs. Tremblay case had made headlines across Canada. Chantal Daigle had decided to end not only her relationship with her boyfriend, Jean-Guy Tremblay, but also her pregnancy. Tremblay contested her right to an abortion and a legal battle ensued. The law ruled in Ms. Daigle's favor, declaring that in Canada, men do not have the right to prevent women from obtaining an abortion.

"You're just like her, Mum, defying the sacred law of God, aborting your unborn child, taking life and death decisions into your own sinful hands!"

I listened to Stan's outrage and wondered what he was getting at. "Are you my unborn child, Stan? Is that what you mean? Are you saying I aborted you?" I ended the call with the man who called me Mum, the one who was supposed to be my husband, not my child.

He called again the next morning, offering to try therapy again. "We'll go together, twice a week if you want."

"You go, Stan. Go by yourself for a year or two then call me."

"No, together under one roof or not at all." His voice quickly resumed its authority.        "So not at all then," I said and hung up. There were no more chances.

It was good not having to monitor night sounds any more. It was wonderful to sleep deeply after a warm bath, with clean soapy scents still present in the morning. It was a holiday not having to beg Stan to bathe. His lack of personal cleanliness had intensified over the years, a sure sign of decline. Nell was ten years old, Teddy twelve, I was forty. A marvel had happened: I had made the decision to leave Stan and then I'd followed through. I was out. And I knew I would never, ever return. Unexpected joy and excitement kept surprising me afresh, every hour of every day.

∼

"If only your son had a positive father figure," said Teddy's gym teacher. "A man friend."

I had called three men from the church, fathers whose kids I'd tutored for free. The first two gave me a flat-out no. They had jobs. Their available time was nil.

"There's no point showing up for a baseball game once a year," said Derek. He had backed off, even when his girlfriend, Stacey, encouraged him to befriend Teddy.

"Derek had a bad relationship with his father," Stacey explained. "He gets depressed around kids."

I appealed directly to Derek. "One baseball game a year from you, and some manly warmth, is better than nothing at all. We'll take it! I'll look for other men to help too." Derek didn't call Teddy but Stacey did. She brought decals and paint for his room, rented movies he liked and encouraged him.

"Stacey's nice, Mum," said Teddy.

One day Teddy and I talked it over and, at my suggestion, he went to where the men were. For a while, it was a dream come true at army cadets. My son perked up. He came home for supper with new friends. He instructed me to call him "Ted" from now on. He slept better and laughed more than I'd ever seen in our argumentative household. We installed an exercise bar in his cupboard, and his workouts signaled a new beginning — until, that is, my son told me that an adult officer had insulted a kid on parade drill.

"It was the worst insult, Mum," said Ted. "It was bad. He called Bradley 'Mary Jane' and told him to go snivel on home to his mama. Brad turned beet-red. His face puffed up. It would have been easier for Brad if one of the guns we'd been cleaning had gone off." I looked over at my handsome, innocent son and saw that his main concern was to be on the right side of his drill sergeant, not to incur the same insults, to fit in, to be acceptable to the only available men in his life, the ones who'd eventually invite him to pay with his life.

"That's bad, Teddy. It's wrong to humiliate people, especially in public," was all I could think of to say at my son's induction into misogyny. Now he'd learned that the worst possible insult was to be called a woman's name.

~

A year later, I had full custody of Teddy and Nell and waived any child support. When Father Conway called to ask for my help in paying the utilities bills at the church, I told him I was too busy looking after my children, my studies, my mort-gage, and teaching at three schools. I could no longer solicit local merchants. I went so far as to proffer the suggestion that the three local churches, each less than a quarter full, merge into one church. The sale of even one building would pay for years of heating bills, but that idea was quickly dismissed. Still, weeks later, when Father called to request that I pitch in for the annual church scrub-up, I heard myself consent to volunteer with church members Mabel and Marta on a rare Saturday morning off, time I wish I'd spent with my children over a delicious pan-cake breakfast. I chose to wash out two refrigerators. With a bucket of hot soapy water, a kitchen knife, and scratch pads, I set to work. At midday, I spied a dozen boxes of Kraft Dinner. Reaching for a pot, I opened one, joking that I'd make us a worthy lunch of macaroni and left-over frozen peas I'd found in the freezer.

Mabel stopped me. "Eleanor, I don't know. Don't you think you should ask Father's permission?"

"For what?" I asked.

Mabel glanced at Marta. "Don't you think you should get the go-ahead from Father to open that box?"

"Mabel, this macaroni was donated by IGA. It doesn't belong to Father. We're all in this together, aren't we?"

Marta and Mabel decided they weren't hungry and, smiling and friendly, sank to their knees and continued scrubbing. I reached for a smaller pot.

Just then, Father strolled into the kitchen and thanked us for our good work. Mabel jumped up to explain the boiling water on the stove. She fell all over herself to make it clear that only Eleanor was hungry, and that Eleanor, all on her own, had decided to cook up the Kraft Dinner for herself, though neither she nor Marta would be eating any.

"Would you care to join me, Father?" I asked, embarrassed for my co-volunteers.

"You go ahead, dear," he said. "Juanita's already roasted a bird for me in the house." I ate my lonely meal without enjoyment, and fired myself from the scrub team that day too.

Nell learned that she might fail her school year. She begged me to intercede for her.

The following morning, her principal told me that another year in Grade Five would add to Nell's math competency.

"While subtracting from her self-esteem?" I asked. "No, Nell's been through a lot this year. In fact, she's been through too much. She can't fail."

The principal settled back into his chair and shook his head. He didn't tell me that parents have the final say on whether or not a child passes or fails. He didn't disclose that Quebec schools can only make recommendations.

"Nell was molested by her father," I blurted out. "She's a brilliant little girl, so brilliant she just walked me out of my sick marriage, all by herself."

"I'm required by law to report this information to Social Services," he said, sitting up sharply. "I have to. It's law."

"Go ahead, but I don't want Nell repeating her year."

With the proviso that Nell would receive math tutoring at home and that the principal would call Social Services following my disclosure, permission was granted for Nell to pass her year. In this indirect way, our small family began to receive real help in our community. Unlike my doctor, Nell's principal did the right thing for us. He wrote down the address of Social Services for me. It was a stone's throw from the church.

The following afternoon, I slid the piece of paper with a social worker's name through a thick glass wicket in a waiting room packed with women and children. In his office on that first day, I informed Aiden, a counselor assigned to help me, that I'd told our family doctor about Stan "touching" Nell, but both Nell's physician and Stan had agreed that the abuse wouldn't happen again. Aiden asked me for the doctor's name and phone number so he could let her know that Nell had, in fact, been molested again. He wanted to tell her that her compassion had served

Stan's purpose, not Nell's. That day, Aiden gave me two books to read and so began my research. I learned that in order to come out of persistent denial, I needed to revise my vocabulary. Soon, I replaced the word "touching" with "molestation," "trouble" with "crime," and "it" with "sexual abuse."

"Everyone has his cover," Aiden said when I told him that Stan was a practicing Catholic.

He explained that pedophiles are often so afraid of authority they dominate little children, the only ones who would ever look up to them in the first place.

"Nell told me that Stan lay beside her as she recited her multiplication tables, so she could be the math whiz he was; all the while he was molesting her."

"Tragic," he said as I bent double with grief and anger. "What about Teddy?" asked Aiden.

"Stan says he never touched Teddy, but Stan lies. So I may never know unless Teddy remembers one day. Right now, he refuses to discuss anything but cadets, Dungeons and Dragons, St. Michael the Archangel brandishing his sword, war, and semi-automatic rifles."

That week a new social worker visited our rented home.

"You're what's known as a colluder," she said to me at the kitchen table. I didn't like the sound of that word. "It means either consciously or unconsciously, a part of you knew that your husband was a molester. Deep down, a part of you knew. Secretly, without realizing it, you enabled him."

"Colluder?" I said. I could feel my body tightening.

"It means that secretly, you cooperated with the molestation of your daughter, maybe your son too, and that you did nothing about it because, deep down inside, you were seeking revenge for your own childhood trauma. Or, alternatively, you were trying to trace, research if you will, what happened to you." My heart began its drum beat, a squall sounding in both ears.

"And look at your bedroom," she said, sweeping down the hall. "Your son has the master bedroom? And you, the mother, the head of this family, have the smallest room? A mattress on the floor? It looks like a prison cell in there. It shows how guilty you feel."

"I don't want her to come here again," Nell said afterward. She had listened to the conversation. "I don't like the way she talks to you."

"I'm sorry," I said to Nell. "She's untrained, I think. She's inexperienced." I too was inexperienced. I had no idea how many attacks there'd be from those who blamed me for everything.

All the relief I had felt at leaving Stan only weeks before drained away as I reconsidered the meaning of the words *enabler* and *collude.* Now I had been accused of being complicit in the abuse of my own children. I hadn't had a drink in years, but I thought of buying a bottle. I'd stopped smoking too, but now I craved a cigarette. The dark nausea that roiled within was worse agony than I'd ever felt while living in denial with Stan. I was being blamed for participating in the abuse of my children. In that moment, I understood that my new education would be one of the most painful ordeals of my life.

"Am I a colluder?" I asked Aiden. Intense nausea continued to roll from my abdomen into my throat.

"I'm sorry, Eleanor. That was someone showing off, way too much and much too soon." Aiden picked up one of the wire paper clips he liked to reshape. "It would have been far more helpful to say that that women who've never dealt with their own sexual abuse often end up with molesters."

"So paying the rent when Stan wouldn't was an act of collusion?" I asked, ready to scream.

"You believed you were helping out, Eleanor. But way before that, you accepted Stan into your life," Aiden explained. "And it wasn't because you were head over heels."

"Why did I marry him? Was I a sleepwalker in my own life?" For some reason, I found it easy to pose these questions to Aiden, a social worker I had only recently met. I felt that our conversations were real, that he would be fair. I knew there'd be help, not blame.

"Do you agree that some lights may have been off in your life?" he asked. "Some doors closed, or even locked?" I thought of the hundreds of times I had heard Mother's bedroom door click into locked position, her chronic sleep an escape that never helped.

"I thought I was different from my mother," I told Aiden. "I prided myself on never napping during the day. Now I find out I've been in a coma for years."

"Pedophiles often partner with people whose trauma they can manipulate to their own advantage. They're quite brilliant that way. Stan successfully found himself an attractive, competent, and frightened young woman who gladly supported him. Your job now, Eleanor, is to get your claws back." As he spoke, I thought about Edna's gnawed fingertips and of our inability to confront her son.

"I thought freedom from Stan would be wonderful. Right now, it feels like a conviction."

"So now you understand why your group's participation dropped by half this month," he said, lifting a sheaf of files. "Even though the reception room is forever jam-packed."

~

The instant we stepped into the meeting room each week, a door clanged and a double lock clicked behind us, as though we were prison inmates. I found it offensive and depressing. But when Greta's husband stormed in to bash the bullet-proof wall behind which his wife and all of us watched in horror, the impact of his belt buckle on treated glass turned my resentment into relief. As Greta's hands flew to her face, I saw Stan's fist slamming close to Mr. Sauvé's head and knew there had been no mistake. I did indeed belong here. Since I'd been told that I was an enabler, though, and been blamed for being so unaware, I continued to feel as ashamed on my way to the Parents of Sexually Abused Children meetings as I did afterwards. How I could have been so numb, so dazed, so tolerant, so passive, and so stupid? I'd been disturbed for a long time. If I wanted to restore my natural instincts, if I wanted to avoid repetition of a similar disaster and become the fierce, protective mother my children deserved, there was a way for me to accomplish that, but it was going to cost, not financially, but emotionally.

"Why are we the only ones to get this education?" A tall, dark-haired woman named Ruth, a lawyer, caught my attention. "And the abusers go scot-free? Why are we the clean-up crew?" Her face flushed an angry red. Ruth admitted that she was stunned to find herself a member of our group. "My older brother molested his nephew," she said. Her brow furrowed in grief as she broke it down for us. "My fifteen-year-old son."

"We're here to learn," I said. "So we won't land in this hole again."

We moved to the smaller room as attendance diminished, the same few showing up each week; and with our cups of tea to hold onto, we began to talk, one by one. Over time, I listened to each mother tell her life story and, although the details differed, there was no variance in the themes of abuse, entitlement, and ownership.

"I don't blame anyone for whatever addiction they may have. It's no one's fault how badly problems twist," Aiden said in his opening remarks one day. "What I do blame addicts for is not taking responsibility, not seeking help about their compulsions, and that's why you can be so proud of yourselves."

"Is he talking to us?" asked Marta, looking bewildered.

"What do you mean, Aiden?" I asked. "What addiction do we have?"

"That would be the addiction to rescuing, pleasing, and accommodating others at the expense of your own health and happiness. Your addiction involves avoiding looking into yourself and your own history. And all addictions hurt others," he added gently. By the soft way he pronounced "others," I sensed he meant our very own children.

Over time in that group, I stopped calling myself a liar every time the truth escaped my mouth. The first time I heard myself say that I came from a violent alcoholic family with few survivors, an inner censor accused me, "Why did you tell that lie?"

But it wasn't a lie. Most of my siblings were suffering serious depression now, with a variety of disabling features. Over time, we talked, each getting to know other, and slowly re-connecting. I recognized the wisdom of a much younger woman who advised me to let my family be, enjoy the phone calls we exchanged, make the best of them, but stop forcing my idea of closeness, which is family visits and fun outings. Instead, she suggested I build mutual relationships wherever I might be. I liked the word "mutual." I could share friendship now, rather than work so hard to earn it. It was nice having coffee with the other mothers after the meeting, or sharing a fun potluck meal with all of our kids on a Sunday. It seemed that over time, two disparate worlds, a world of denial and a world of pretense, were being replaced by a larger, more complex world that contained both happiness and sadness for me. I learned that tears and laughter could co-exist. I learned I could handle both.

Many times after the meetings, as I fell asleep at night, my whole body jolted off my bed as though shocked by unseen prods. I'd calm myself and try to sleep again, but as I entered a dozing state, one dreadful image or another alarmed me. It seemed as though I had to remain vigilant and well-defended. I often awakened violently, my fingers drumming my face. In one intrusive image, my younger siblings were carried along on a mechanical conveyor belt covered with a beautiful hand-stitched altar cloth: Joey and Danny, then Eric, Sheilagh, and Paddy, all hungry, dirty, and crying. One by one, the machine cast them into a heap on a cement floor.

One day after work, not in a dream but in reality, I went to visit a Jesuit in Montreal, an elderly gentleman who had often dined at Mother's table. He was as honest and as blunt as I had asked him to be.

"Your mother had what seemed to me a personality disorder of some kind. She displayed aberrations typical of a psychiatric diagnosis. For example, her mood swings, pleasant one day, screaming the next, that sort of thing. I understand that her own mother suffered from dementia, so it may have been genetic."

"Do you have any other idea of why my mother might have become depressed, Father?"

"No, I don't really. She had a husband supporting the family and a nice house to live in. She was a talented fundraiser, an excellent public speaker." He sat quietly for a moment and added, "It couldn't have been about having a large family either. In my profession as priest, I've met hundreds upon hundreds of women with big families who managed quite happily. And believe me, Eleanor, I knew their children, who grew up to be successful priests, lawyers, and doctors — and nuns. I saw them at church every Sunday, come hell or high water, and they functioned quite nicely, it seemed to me. Your mother had a personality disorder, Eleanor. I'm sure of it."

As Father Richard concluded his assessment of my mother and walked me to his front door, I heard a thin wail, a peal, a prolonged siren scream from above. We looked up, startled, and Father smiled. "Oh, that's just Emily's vacuum. We have to get her a new one of those contraptions."

~

It was wonderful when our group laughed together—grim amusement in strengthening solidarity. One such occasion occurred when Aiden announced that an invitation had been hand-delivered to Social Services. Our group, the Parents of Sexually Abused Children, had been warmly invited to an Evening of Forgiveness by a local Christian church. Refreshments would be served. Would we be interested?

"How thoughtful," said Marta. "How very kind."

"How ridiculous," I interrupted, surprised at the rush of feeling, the hot anger that erupted when Marta was too nice. More and more, being "nice" equaled tolerance of cruelty, which in turn twisted into a pretzel of permission to passively accept abuse.

More than anything else, I was mad at myself. "Tell them to round up the pedophiles first and invite them over. Your kindly church members will get a big fat surprise if they attempt that sorry task. Why are they so eager for us to forgive? Nell's father has never asked for forgiveness, so why the rush to reassure? " My chest on fire, my mouth working better than it had in years, I asked another question. "Why so quick to pull the blankets over a crime that needs to be examined and analyzed and prevented from happening as it still is, every day and everywhere on this patriarchal planet? Why the race to forgive? What's the motivation there? Should forgiveness come *before* investigation?"

Except for Marta, who dressed up and attended the church event, the invitation was declined by our group. With renewed motivation, we opted instead to review our own lives. On sheets of legal-sized paper, a long line down the middle, we worked together to highlight the best events of our lives in blue ink and the worst events in red. Together, the teapot always full, we worked one tolerable hour each session before we got back into our circle to share, if we wanted to. When baby Eric's name appeared, along with inexplicable dread, I talked with women who listened quietly. I wept as I counted the rapes in my twenties and was shocked at how closely my marriage followed the last assault by Grandpa. My marriage was, I could see now, a mere escape ploy. With my red pen, I listed the call from the parish priest, telling me that Stan had "touched" a little girl in the First Communion class.

"How long ago was that?" Aiden asked.

"Twelve years." I understood then, without anyone accusing me, that yes, there was a lot I knew that I hadn't connected with conscious reality. My denial had endangered two little children, my little children. Across the page from my notation of the joy of Nell's birth was her head injury, blood red ink in shaky script.

"Denial is *not* a river in Egypt, is it?" said Ruth grimly, not as a joke.

Our group successfully traced the beginnings of our passivity to our religious childhood training, our earliest invitations to tolerate the very evil our godparents renounced for us at the baptismal fonts. From the beginning, we were taught to rescue evildoers, known as sinners.

"It's like a two-pronged pitch fork." I shared this image with the group after much personal study. "One prong is our grooming for a high tolerance of suffering that God would one day reward. That's the first pointed lie. The other is that bliss begins only after we've missed out on our own lives."

∾

It was Maureen who called. "I'm sorry to say I have bad news, Norda."

"Okay," I said, waiting for it.

"It's Joey. He was on a demolition project out in Thornhill, you know, where he used to live with Mother and Stuey. The police found him early Friday morning in his van. He's dead, Norda. I went out to the new condo site right away. I saw him." While I gripped the phone and remained standing, Maureen told me that Joey had been parked by the church he'd torn down, the dust of toppled brick coating his van from front to back bumper.

"He had beer on the passenger side, but I was able to tell his kids the case was unopened. He bled from every orifice, Norda, even his hands and feet were soaked in blood."

"Would the real crucified of god please stand up?" I asked bitterly.

"There were little blue bruises, the size of fingerprints, all over his body. The doctor said that's a sign of liver disease. Joey's kids are pretty upset," Maureen said, her voice soft as we considered this next generation.

I thought about Joey's loveless childhood and about Mother's ex-priest boyfriend, who disliked children except those he pawed when he was drunk, a man my mother hoped would love her as her own groping father had not. I retraced the dark thread to a religious doorstep where it turned lily white and where holy hands reject any responsibility for our family's history.

Flying home from Joey's funeral, I looked out over the condos dotting the West Island farm my parents had once owned. As the wheels of the plane touched the ground, I felt gratitude. Somehow, I'd received enough of a sense of self to be nourished by all that had been given to me during my lifetime: the teachers who'd taught me to read, my parents who had valued education, hundreds of authors whose wisdom had both situated me and anchored me in the world, the social workers and my support group of neighbors who'd shared their own powerful insights with me. Not one of these had ever passed a collection plate.

# EPILOGUE

It's been twenty-five years since I left a marriage that wreaked so much havoc in our small family's life. Perhaps because I'm one of the lucky ones, I can carry my history well.

Long after I'd left the group, I didn't discover my teenager hanging from a rope in the basement, as Ruth did, or dead from potent drugs that failed to numb the evil that persists because of chronic passivity. My children are well. How do I express my gratitude? I do so by becoming the best human being I can possibly be. I continue to study about religiously-approved incest, the kind that traffic in human life without the soiling of hands: through dogma. Mine is only one Canadian chapter of a worldwide history of religious destructiveness.

I recall the time I was barely making ends meet while teaching part-time at three schools in Montreal. I received a phone call from Concordia University, telling me that there was a check for $700 designated for a single mother, head of a family, over 35 years old who was in the final year of a second university degree. The gift money was awarded to me – and spent in a day. Hydro and Bell paid, new running shoes for Teddy and boots for Nell, the purchase and installation of a second-hand washer and dryer, and a grand load of groceries, including two buckets of Rocky Road ice cream. What a difference good people have made in my life.

Today, Nell is studying psychology. She's interested in brain plasticity and our ability to shape our own lives. Teddy is a public speaker, like his grandparents. My children are purposeful and stable and committed to living well. Now a secular humanist, I also live well in the uncertain mystery of life. I welcome my anger. I listen to it and investigate it. On my CV are the schools in Quebec where I've loved my positive, professional life. There's nothing I like better than to encourage my fellow human beings to honor their lives, no matter what the cards they've been dealt.

Does this mean I don't have nightmares or don't wake up mumbling feeble utterances that in my dream were screams? Does it mean there are no toxic flashbacks that stun me with their ferocity? Not at all. I was born to the same patriarchal inheritance as my mother and foremothers. Our choices were few. Thanks to committed activists before me, I've learned that I too can be a change-maker. For example, I believe that if investigation about the root causes of pedophilia were preached as ardently as massive forgiveness still is, change could happen. Abusers often preach forgiveness. It works well for them.

My search for root causes has led me to understand that just as I was, Stan was under a religious gun too. I will never forgive him, nor has he asked because he cannot do that. It would crack the thick wall of denial that is his real refuge (not religion) and who knows what would happen then? As a child I'd committed "my whole mind, my whole heart and my whole soul" to an invisible male God I feared, and in living that promise, I was groomed to tolerate oppression, domination, and injustice. I disappeared from myself

Children can do little about their circumstances – until they grow up. Then they will dish out what they got, withdraw into life-long depression, or, if they can, cook up a wonderful new life recipe. It is in this way that loving teachers make a world of difference. In fact, they make the world different.

Here at my oak desk by the St. Lawrence River, two and a half decades later, I have detailed the course of my escape from marriage to a Catholic pedophile I supported and defended for fourteen years of "pathological loyalty." I made his life far more important than the one I hid from – my own – and in recovering my life, paid the price consciousness costs.

It's a sunny winter day in my cozy home. Fragrant homemade soup is simmering on the stove and the washer has finished its spin cycle. I'm excited about my purposeful life. I value my skepticism. I know what I don't believe. I am the first woman in the history of my family to get the chance to even consider her own story. And I am the first to write it.

—*Eleanor Cowan, 2013*